American Heartbeat

American Heartbeat

Some Notes from a Midwestern Journey

by

SIMON WINCHESTER

Faber & Faber
Three Queen Square
London

First published 1976
by Faber and Faber Limited
3 Queen Square
London WC1
Printed in Great Britain
by W & J Mackay Limited, Chatham

ISBN 0 571 10878 4

For Rupert, Angus and Alexander
who normally only get postcards.

Contents

Acknowledgements and Bibliography

Americans delight in being written about by foreigners, and came forward by the dozen to offer help once they had heard a stranger was in town trying to write a book. A number of members of the United States Congress were particularly helpful and enthusiastic, among them Albert Quie and Bill Frenzel of Minnesota, Jerry Litton and Richard Bolling of Missouri, Tom Harkin and Neal Smith of Iowa, Larry Winn and Garner Shriver of Kansas, Tom Steed of Oklahoma and a Texas contingent that included Alan Steelman, Jim Wright, Bill Poage, Jake Pickle, Abraham Kazen, Olin Teague and Henry Gonzalez. Senator Dick Clark, the young new Senator from Iowa, took the trouble to offer his assistance, which was gratefully received.

Governor Wendell Anderson and his staff in St. Paul, Minnesota, provided a great deal of useful information on the North Star State. Governor Alfred M. Landon of Kansas, retired but still vastly energetic, gave me a multitude of tips and hints that helped my appreciation of the Prairies. And policemen, reporters and television and radio station staffs in almost every community that could afford such luxuries provided facts, figures and impressions that tie the book together. To all these unnamed, but unforgettable Midwesterners, my most sincere thanks.

And there were, in addition, a number of individuals whose assistance was so time-consuming for them, and so invaluable for me, that it would be remiss of me not to include them by name: Bob Bulcock, of the Atomic Energy Commission in Kansas City; Dan Schoenfelder of Chillicothe, Missouri; Tom and Patricia Judge of Nevada, Iowa; Mr. A. F. Ennis, of the Boise Cascade Corporation at International Falls, Minnesota; Bill Smith, of Ames, Iowa; Ron Handburg of WCCO-Tv in Minneapolis; Susan Peterson of the CBS News Bureau in London; Lorrie Temple of the American Telephone and Telegraph Company in New York, and Mr. Bob Hinckle, at AT&T in Kansas City; Iola Hayden of Norman, Oklahoma; Joseph McNamara, the Kansas City Police chief; Kaye Northcott of the Texas Observer office in Austin; Mr. W. J. Wilkes, of the Federal Highway Administration in Washington, DC; and to Neal Peirce, author of the most readable,

definitive handbooks on political America of the 1970s, who was
cheerful on every one of the occasions I bothered him for facts.

My wife Judy, in spite of having three boisterous children tug-
ging at her skirts unceasingly, typed the manuscript in less than a
month, and was tirelessly devoted to a task that no one else could
have done as well, and which I would have been loth to entrust to
one less enthusiastic than she. My debt to her is vast, my gratitude
enormous.

Because most of my researches were inevitably done from distant
motel rooms in the middle of Nowhere, USA, the library from
which I drew most sustenance had to be limited. There were a
number of books without which I could not have managed: Neal
Peirce's *The Great Plains States of America* (Norton, 1972); John
Gunther, *Inside USA* (Harper and Row, 1947); Michael Barone,
et al, *The Almanac of American Politics* (Gambit, 1972); Bill
Moyers, *Listening to America* (Harper and Row, 1971); Irving
Stone, *They Also Ran* (Doubleday, 1966); and the two superb
analyses of the gigantic American census by Richard Scammon and
Ben Wattenberg, *This USA* (Doubleday, 1965) and *The Real
America* (Doubleday, 1974). The relevant volumes of the *Mobil
Travel Guide* and *Fodor's Guide* were also invaluable. Acknow-
ledgement is due to Bob Dylan for the extract printed on page 44
from 'My Life in a Stolen Moment' (taken from *Writings and
Drawings* published by Knopf/Random House), and for the two
lines on page 46.

Other books and papers to which I made constant reference
were: *The National Atlas of the United States*, US Department of
the Interior, Washington, DC; *Rankings of the States*, National
Education Association, Washington, DC; *Statistical Abstract of the
United States* and the relevant *Congressional District Data Books*,
Bureau of the Census, US Department of Commerce, Washington,
DC; *Social and Economic Effects of Highways*, US Department of
Transportation, Washington, DC; *Uniform Crime Reports for the
United States*, Federal Bureau of Investigation, US Department of
Justice, Washington, DC; the *Congressional Quarterly; Editor and
Publisher International Year Book*, New York.

There are scores of newspapers, some good and most downright
awful, in towns between International Falls and Laredo. The best
papers and journals, or at least those upon which I placed most
reliance, were: The Minneapolis *Tribune*; the Kansas City *Star*;

ACKNOWLEDGEMENTS AND BIBLIOGRAPHY

the Des Moines *Register*; the *Daily Oklahoman*; the Dallas *Morning News*; the Topeka *Capital*; the *Daily Ardmoreite*; the Fort Worth *Star-Telegram*; the Austin *American-Statesman*; the San Antonio *Express* and the Laredo *Times*. The *Texas Observer*, the *New York Times* and occasional pieces from the *Washington Post* were also of considerable use. And although their news columns left a little to be desired, the names of two newspapers en route stick firmly in the mind: the Waxahachie (Texas) *Light* and the Larned (Kansas) *Tiller and Toiler*. Finally Mrs. Fanning and her four-page weekly, the Fairview *Enterprise*, which summed up so much of the American heart's beating in every issue: as in that of March 13, 1975, which led its front page with an announcement that the Miss Teenage Kansas Contest would be held the very next week. No nonsense about pulchritude in this sensible part of the world: as Mrs. Fanning observed, the winner would be the teenager who displayed the most creditable 'scholastic achievement, poise, and civic contribution'. Without Mrs. Fanning's noble *Enterprise*, the Midwest would not be quite the same.

'Look up, America—see what you've got. . . .'
from a 1974 Coca-Cola jingle

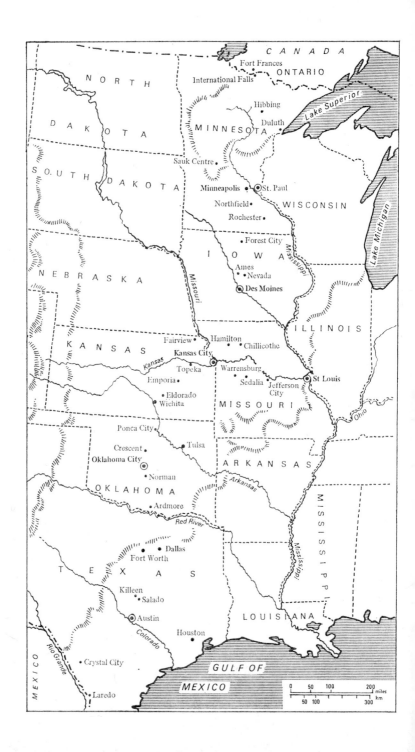

Preface

'Why do you dislike America so?' Many Americans who read the *Manchester Guardian Weekly*'s India-paper editions that one could buy in 'specialist' shops in San Francisco and New Orleans and, of course, on Manhattan Island used to write and ask me that. I was— or rather, we were; for the whole British press seemed to find itself, at one time or another, on the wrong end of similar accusations— told off repeatedly for being 'too harsh', 'unkind' or 'too critical'; and an impression formed abroad that a vestigial superciliousness still coursed in the veins of every Englishman, and that it displayed itself to advantage each time a citizen of the United States hove to on the skyline.

That supercilious quality came into its own just about the time I first arrived in Washington to write there for the *Guardian*, in the autumn of 1972. The offices in Watergate had just been broken into; the *Washington Post* was only then beginning to unravel the seamy tale; and the White House was posturing in a state of injured majesty, as if those who could think impure thoughts about the then incumbent—a man who had pledged, among other things, to 'clean up the language in the Oval Office'—deserved to be banished to some distant Purgatory to have the notions flushed from their evil minds.

But as it all started to ooze from the woodwork, and as the courts and Congress and the supportive press began the long process of giving a corrupt megalomaniac, in whose hands lay the very survival of mankind, the benefits of doubt not normally accorded many black or Puerto Rican or Chicano Americans, so reports in many British newspapers, the *Guardian* among them, began to change.

Writings started to snarl with venom; stiff upper lips began to curl; and for a while the transatlantic sobriety was ruffled. 'The Sour Stink of Success' was how the Deansgate sub-editors entitled one commentary on Mr. Nixon's election victory: a great number of Americans wrote to congratulate Peter Jenkins, its author, for having the courage to question the morality of the Nixon majesty. A lot of others wrote in to ask what was to become a regular: 'Why do you dislike America so?'

Now, happily, it is all over. Richard Nixon is out of sight and, to the extent that greedy literary agents and film barons can permit, out of mind as well. A new law of monstrous complexity is now shakily in place, seeking to prevent excesses of the type that characterised 1972; a new President, seen variously as a dullard and an honourable stalwart, is on the throne, attended by regiments of cardboard yes-men all looking and sounding remarkably similar to those who attended the villain before. A lot has changed; a good deal has improved; a great amount is still just the same.

The long journey I made in the spring of 1975—halfway in time between the disgrace of Watergate and the thrill of a two-hundredth birthday party—took me, deliberately, to a side of America that could rightly claim to have been most severely disappointed and shaken by the scandals. Middle America, a physical and topographical whole that embraces the psephological creations whose savage exploitation won the supreme powers of state for men like Richard Nixon and Spiro Agnew, is truly still the heart and soul of America, its apotheosis, and its conscience. It was to see if the disgrace of East and West had been channelled into disappointment in the mid-country that I went; to try and find if the conscience had indeed been pricked. The short account that follows attempts to explain, by illustration rather than by argument, that disappointment has come and gone, that a conscience has been felt, and that, in spite of it all, Middle America is surviving, strong, and worthy of honour and respect.

It is fairly easy to dislike America and her people. Once it was fashionable for Europeans, especially the former colonists, to come away from the Americans' shores allowing as how it was a fine place but that we would not like to live there. Such condescension! And the xenophobia that typifies the British was rarely more ugly than when directed across the Atlantic; the sanctimonious attitudes that have made Britons infamous from Travancore to Trinidad were rarely more acute than when an American president of the last few decades has stumbled during his imperial progress.

But I do not dislike America at all. At times she infuriates me, at times she sickens me, at times she frightens me. But my long trail through the middle lands proved for me—and would prove for any other Old World cynic, I feel sure—that beneath all the grubby horrors with which this society has invested herself, beneath all the glitter and schmaltz and cheap scandal, there is still a remarkable and a deeply honourable people. Examples of the breed may be hard to find up on Capitol Hill; they may be rare as hen's teeth in the swimming pools of Palm Springs; and they may not be found at all within a mile of Times Square. But they are to be found—and in great abundance, it was delightful to note, in the Middle country.

Out on those plains from Minnesota south to Texas, across fifteen hundred flat, unending miles, are arranged millions upon millions of Americans worthy of the deepest honour one can bestow.

To these people, in Iowa and Kansas, Oklahoma and Missouri, to those I met and those I was forced to speed by, a Happy, Happy Birthday! To the rest of the United States—watch these people; for they are both your future, and your hope.

Washington 1975

Along the Half-Way Highway

'. . . and the coldest place in these United States last night was, once again, International Falls, Minnesota . . .'—Frank Blair, newsreader for NBC-TV's *Today* show, on almost any morning in January, February, March, April or May this year, last year, next year, or any year.

I could well believe it. It was just a little after six in the evening, and I was in a telephone box in the village of Fort Frances, Ontario, about fifty yards from the border with the United States of America and the infamously frigid border town of International Falls. And certainly it was piercingly cold.

It had seemed a perfectly ordinary sort of phone box, for instance. The only problem was that you had to climb up and into it, thanks to the accumulation of six months' worth of unmelted snow inside the box, and its compaction by hundreds of booted feet into a three-foot-thick ice carpet. You couldn't very well stand outside in the wind to call, unless you wanted to risk freezing to the receiver and having to be cut free by a Mountie specially equipped for such emergencies: you had to climb up, like hoisting yourself on to a warhorse, and poke the dimes and nickels down into a telephone that seemed to have been placed at knee level. 'Please hurry,' I said to the operator. 'You must be freezing,' she laughed back. 'That's a great box for sobering up in.'

Eventually I got through to Maryland, where everyone seemed to be basking in subtropical heatwaves and quite unable to understand why I was in such a hurry. Never mind, Canada's a cold country, they helpfully suggested. It'll be a lot warmer when you get down into the States.

From just north of the Rainy River, which forms the border in this part of the world, America certainly did look a little warmer. One could say that from this least elegant of viewing points, America looked positively hellish. A gigantic factory, spurting smoke and steam and sooty flames, loomed just south of the river.

The words 'Boise Cascade', the name of one of the country's pre-eminent timber processors, in red on its vast grey walls suggested it was a pulp mill, and a powerful smell of burning wood and boiling glue and fish and diesel oil and sulphur confirmed the impression. Railway engines clanked and whistled along bridges and into marshalling yards. Level-crossing gates were raised and lowered unceasingly. Ice floes jostled and crashed about in the spray and foam of the river below, and the Falls roared into a black chasm a hundred yards upstream. Unseen men shouted into the gales, a siren blew mournful notes intermittently, lights flashed on and off, gobbets of fire shot out into the air, glared briefly and then faded away. A long line of snow-covered cars and trucks ground down a narrow road just south of the torrent that separated the two countries.

This was the first view of America. Most travellers would enter more grandly, through rather more distinguished members of the 455-strong clan of what the Immigration and Naturalisation Service in Washington calls the country's Ports of Entry. Some such Ports really are ports—places like New York and San Francisco and New Orleans, that sport customs sheds and wharves and lighters and the unmistakable scent of internationalism. Others are vast, ever-open border crossings from Canada and Mexico that gobble thousands of cars every day, taking millions of people a year through customs inspections and past border officials who ask stiff questions about just why one might be going from Acapulco to Omaha, or from Montreal to Phoenix, Arizona. Most ports present a grander view of America than is offered at International Falls; most are busier, better known, more devoted to the typical industries—cheap whisky, poor motels and fast women—of the frontier town. And assuredly most—excepting those few crossings between the Yukon and that vast new state of Alaska—are a great deal warmer.

But there was good reason for coming a-calling upon Columbia in her fortress via this apparently satanic northern town. A map of the continent provides one answer. From Eastport, in the state of Maine, to Cape Flattery, in the state of Washington, the continental United States stretches through some fifty-seven degrees of longitude: the middle of it all, very approximately, is represented by the ninety-fifth parallel. And the border crossing nearest to that middle line, albeit cold and satanic and irredeemably ugly (though by day, they say, it's even quite a pretty town) happens to be International Falls, Minnesota.

Arriving in America from the liners docked on the Hudson River, the visitor is confronted at once by the splendid vision of the country—the energy, the power, the gaudy spectacle that is so proudly summarised in the pinnacles of Manhattan. Presenting one's passport at the western gateway, in San Francisco, the charm and the style of the country become instantly apparent. And similarly dramatic impressions could be gained by arrivals in Chicago, or Seattle, or even in Philadelphia. But here, in a steaming industrial oasis amidst the pines and snowbanks of the wild north— what could one possibly gain from such an ignominious, back-door entry? The town could scarcely be rated as America's tradesman's entrance: more suitably it might be the nation's scullery hatch, or the manhole to the coal cellar, or the boiler room.

Beyond International Falls, though, runs a road—two roads, in fact, though one in essence—that journeys, without a single traffic light to interrupt any of its one thousand, five hundred and sixty-four miles, from this border river to another, much more famous, in the south. That river is the Rio Grande, a brown, turgid stream set in a shallow limestone valley in the extreme south of Texas, and it separates the United States from the Republic of Mexico. The same road that crosses the iron bridge across the Rainy River also crosses the concrete span across the Rio Grande at Laredo, Texas. There is an equivalent of Canada's Fort Frances there, known as Nuevo Laredo, in the flat deserts of Tamau Lipas province.

For very nearly all of its length the road between these two towns is known as the US Interstate Highway 35 or, in the patois of the truckers and salesmen who speed up and down short sections of its immense path, just I-35.

Of all the hundreds of thousands of miles of highway that criss-cross America, I-35 is the one that perhaps uniquely connects that part of the heartland appropriately known as Middle America. Between Fort Frances and Nuevo Laredo live and work millions upon millions of Americans who share something quite unknown to New Yorkers and Angelenos, Washingtonians and San Franciscans: they share a state of quarantine—imposed by the vastness of the land—from the foreign influences of fashion and sophistication that so affect those closer to the sea; they share a certain isolation, imposed upon them by the press barons of the big cities, from where they are regarded as slightly primitive and even a trifle savage and unrefined; they share an enviable state of having been

18

largely forgotten by the rest of America 'outside', of having been
overtaken in all the rush and scurry of the undefinable national
mission.

But these millions also share their common entity—the fact that
they are indisputably the heart and muscle of America—and, some
would say, the soul of the country. The highway that connects all
these men and women is truly America's backbone. A journey from
the Rainy River to the Rio Grande, I had thought one dripping hot
summer's day in Washington—what better way to see and hear a
nation ticking over, what better vantage point from which to listen
to the country's heart?

Interstate Highway 35 passes through six of the country's fifty
states. For the first 300 miles it slices across the snowy woodlands
of Minnesota, the North Star state; then, straight as a Menominee
arrow, it rolls down south through the state of Iowa, the countryside about which no better précis had been written thirty years ago
than John Gunther's simple chapter heading, which said only
'Corn and Pigs'.

After this lengthy southward progress, it bends, subtly at first,
and then more and more severely, to the west, and sneaks, almost
ashamed of its diversion, through the north-western corner of
Missouri. In Kansas its western error is corrected, and by the town
of Wichita, high on the flat grass plains and the everlasting wheatlands, it backs to the south for the remaining 900 miles of its four-
lane majesty. As in Iowa, it streaks through Oklahoma without a
waver; it crosses the Red River into Texas without ceremony, and,
after splitting in two for a few dozen miles so that its forks can en-
compass both of the mighty cities of Dallas and Fort Worth, it pro-
ceeds, as one shimmering raft of searing white concrete divided by
a hundred yards of waving grass, down to the Rio Grande and the
heat and dust of Mexico.

One could go on to Monterrey and Mexico City, as a north-
bound traveller could go on to Winnipeg and the oil town of
Calgary, Alberta; however, few of the thousands of cars and trucks
which daily and nightly thunder up and down the road do, according
to figures put out by the Government agency that studies the road
in detail. Most ply between the American cities served by the road;
and most of the people who travel on it are there essentially for
business, not pleasure. The middle of America is, for the holiday-

maker, somewhere to pass through rather than to stay in or explore—the roads that form the arteries of this part of the country have become a visible expression of the urgency and endless toil of the country—proof that the heart, whatever its condition, is working hard to keep the nation alive.

The cities that form the staging posts for travellers up I-35 are spaced more or less evenly 300 miles apart. The major, world-famous cities are Minneapolis-St. Paul, in Minnesota; Des Moines, in Iowa; Kansas City—which has the distinction of straddling the two states of Missouri and Kansas, but having its more esteemed half in Missouri; Wichita; Oklahoma City; and in Texas the new and glittering centres of Dallas-Fort Worth, Austin and, that final, most cherished, of all American shrines, San Antonio, the site of Davy Crockett's sinewy little fortress, The Alamo.

Between the major staging posts are the smaller towns where horses once were changed, and where the motorists now fill up with petrol.

In Minnesota, the towns of Duluth and Albert Lea fill the function; in Iowa, Ames and Osceola; Missouri's share of the route is so meagre that the run into Kansas City can be accomplished without stopping; in Kansas the prudent traveller will halt at Emporia, or even wander a little to the north, and to the state capital of Topeka. Oklahoma offers the wayfarer two small towns, Ponca City and Ardmore, each a hundred miles or so north and south of the sprawling mess of Oklahoma City; and finally, in Texas, where the horse-trails of the last century are still well marked and preserved in the sage brush and pampas country, there are towns like Waco and Temple, Salado and Cotulla at which the journey can be broken before the last run-in down to the shanties of what all Texans know as 'The Valley'.

One of the extraordinary aspects of all these cities and towns—and all the little villages between, like Eveleth and Mason City and Fertile and Chillicothe and El Dorado and Blackwell and Pauls Valley and Gainesville and Waxahatchie and San Marcos and New Braunfels and Dilley—is that while so few of them are on any tourist routes, and while so very few Americans will have heard tell of more than two or three of the smaller villages listed here, it is not at all difficult to find in any group of New Yorkers or Californians someone who came from one or other of the places through which our highway passes. Back east, exiles from Minneapolis or Kansas

City or San Antonio would become positively crushed with nostalgia at the thought of someone going out to their old stamping ground. It was more than simple homesickness, I always thought: those Washingtonians who would plead with me to be sure to look up old Mrs. Stevens up at the mill outside Hibbing or to go and visit the parents on the farm just north of Iowa City or send a postcard from Whitewater in Kansas were exhibiting a longing for a place—and a place alone, not a place and time—that was in so very many ways better than the power jungle of Washington to where they had migrated. There are not many Easterners who have much real affection for the national capital; unless you are a New Yorker born and bred that city has a magic that can be endured for only just so long; and out in Los Angeles, and even in San Francisco, where most of the residents come from states to the east of California, many will sigh and wish for an opportunity to go back to the heartland, to settle back and live what nowadays seems to many a more real and decent kind of life.

The people who live in the six states on the highway together adhere only very loosely. They are, in terms of geography, truly inhabitants of Middle America—though they are a long way from being a part of what was meant by Richard Nixon when he took the phrase for his own and forged his constituency from it. Middle America to Mr. Nixon was a nationwide amalgam of that vast, shadowy body known as the Silent Majority, combined with the New Middle Classes and well seasoned with a sprinkling of prosperous minorities, ethnic cliques and conservative Southerners. Many Middle Americans lived in Middle America—the neat, well-clipped suburbs of Kansas City and Dallas provide legions of affluent Republicans who would close ranks in support of the man who promised to battle neighbourhood crime and cross-town busing and high taxes and exorbitant welfare spending on their behalf. But not all Middle America, in its geographical sense, was Nixon country, in either 1968 or 1972, even though George McGovern was, in theory, such anathema to the stolid citizenry of the six central states. Politically, socially and traditionally, there is more to Middle America than twenty million of Mr. Nixon's Middle Americans.

The people are hardly Midwesterners, either. John Gunther found less difficulty in defining the American Midwest than many have done since—he gave to what was once called the 'true

America' those states and parts of states that lie in the upper basin of the Mississippi River—Minnesota, Wisconsin, Iowa, Missouri, Illinois, Indiana, Michigan and Ohio. To these eight he added fractions of the Great Plains lands of the two Dakotas, and Kansas and Nebraska, and subtracted sections of northern Minnesota and southern Missouri. He ignored Texas and Oklahoma altogether: from the Texan and Oklahoman viewpoint, which is markedly different from that of the true Midwestern citizen, that was just fine with them.

But, again, the six Middle American states are *partly* Midwestern. Iowa is, without a doubt, the apotheosis of the Middle West—'corelike and indisputable', the very pivot of the nation. Kansas, too, is very much a warmer, drier version of Iowa that is both Middle and Western, and more typically middling than Missouri, which has undoubted shades of the South about it, especially down on the farther banks of the Missouri River which churns its way turgidly west to east through the centre of the state. Minnesota, it is true, is very different: where the Iowans and Kansans are by reputation conservative, Minnesotans are by nature liberal. That state, timbered and rolling, and covered with rocks far older than those that have produced the thick black soil of the corn and wheat states, is the birthplace of Populism and Hubert Humphrey, a philosophy and a politician quite apart from the kinds of thinking liable to be created or born in Iowa or Kansas, or even in Missouri. And Oklahoma and Texas are different too: once Wichita is north of you, and the first oil wells of Oklahoma are spotted by the roadside, one is in the South-West—that still burgeoning, tough, brash, wealthy region that has more in common with some hypothetical offspring of California and Louisiana, or Arizona and Alabama, than with the four states to the north.

So the Interstate bisects and skitters through a more diverse assortment of regions—geographic, geologic, climatic and ideologic —than a brief glance at the map might suggest. Truly the states are all representative of the middle of America—but taken together, not singly. Any one state, taken aside and dissected parish by parish and acre by acre, would reveal as little about the mind of Middle America or the condition of America's heart than would the scrupulous examination of New Hampshire, Utah or Hawaii. To have any meaning, the six states have to be taken together.

Between the half-dozen men who run the immigration post on

the Rainy River Bridge to the fifty or so who man the large and eternally busy crossing point at Laredo, lies a complicated assemblage of crafts and skills and hopes and fears and accomplishments and ideas that severally, but not individually, go to make up what is the heart of the American nation—as young Americans of the 1970s would say, the people and places between the Rainy and the Rio Grande 'are what Middle America is all about'.

The factors that have shaped the character of the Middle Americans are as diverse as the countries from which their forebears came—and communities that still speak German and Norwegian abound in Minnesota, as do others in Texas where Spanish and French are the dominant tongues, and villages in Oklahoma where the strange sounds of Shawnee and Comanche are taught in the schools, all attesting dramatically to the varied roots of these people. But the factors of climate and topography were, more fundamentally, those that created both the hardships and the opportunities for the earlier settlers—and it is these two factors still that both unite, and yet divide, the six states on the route.

Basically the land is flat—hugely, tediously, endlessly flat. In the north of Minnesota the planity is disguised in part by the long stands of pine trees that roll away on either side of the road, and by the lakes, hundreds upon hundreds of lakes, large and small, round and ragged, deep and shallow, that were scooped out of the ancient shield rocks by the departing ice of the last glaciation. Once the road has dipped down into the Mississippi River valley—for this Mississippi rises in the state, at a little body of water called Lake Itasca—and has risen over the bluffs and irregularities of the alluvial plains, then the uncomplicated flatness of the land becomes vividly apparent. All through Iowa and Missouri and Kansas and through nearly all of Oklahoma the countryside stretches away from the concrete edges of the road in a seamless tablet that joins the sky in a perfectly flat surrounding circle. Nowhere is this more dramatic than in Kansas. Here, grain elevators, those mystic white castles that provide the marker posts for truckers trundling over the unyielding miles, appear above the curvature of the earth, grow larger and imperceptibly larger, then flash past. Then they appear behind in the mirror, dwindling slowly until they are snuffed out by the horizon, only to be replaced by another that appears in front, to grow as its neighbour, now thirty miles behind. The spectacle of total smoothness is an unforgettable phenomenon of the middle lands: it enables the country and its towns to be utterly dominated by the sky and the wind, to be at both the mercy and the pleasure of the weather, particularly the wind that gallops across, unhindered by any upheaval of the earth below.

There are isolated patches of hillside: in Oklahoma, for instance, a small block of Silurian and Ordovician limestones peeks through the great swath of younger and softer rocks, to form a low range of hills known locally as the Arbuckle Mountains. Rushing streams course through the canyons—the only rushing streams visible for 500 miles on every side, and the local inhabitants count themselves lucky they have such strangely behaving waters nearby, and have made a semblance of a tourist attraction from it. Elsewhere the rivers grumble sluggishly through the fields losing a foot of altitude every mile or so in their unhurried progress to the catch-all of the Mississippi or Missouri or the Gulf of Mexico.

South of the Oklahoma irruptions, the land resumes its evenness, just like a dinner plate beneath the great inverted bowl of blue cloudless sky, all the way down to Texas. Only the cities and the water towers—for in Texas water is scarce, and every little village has its hundred-foot aluminium tower with its name painted boldly around it—rise above the plain: Dallas can be seen from thirty miles away at least, its silvery slabs of office buildings towering out of the grasslands like the conning tower of some distant submarine.

This flatness is at once an advantage—it makes travel easy enough, allowing the older towns and villages to be spaced an exact twenty miles apart, a day's buggy ride from each other—and a disadvantage. The weather in the midlands is, to say the very least, extreme. There is no soothing Gulf Stream to take the sting out of winter, and no cooling lakes to relieve the awful dust-dry heat of July and August. It is in theory the perfect climate for growing corn and wheat, and raising cattle and pigs and turkeys: but then only when the weather is comparatively kind.

From just to the east of the giant Lake of the Woods—a hundred miles upstream from the International Falls Bridge—to a point close to the border city of Brownsville, in deep southern Texas, there runs an important climatic demarcation line. This line straggles about a little, running out through the Dakotas and Nebraska, western Kansas and western Oklahoma, across the Texas panhandle, down through Laredo and on to the border; but

24

it follows, more or less, the ninety-eighth parallel of longitude. It represents the crucial limit of rainfall, that divides desert from cultivable land—to the east of the line, more than twenty inches of rain will fall per year: to the west, less. On the east of the line it is possible to grow almost anything that thrives on sunshine, wind and rain, and appreciates the thick black soils of the Mississippi and Missouri River plains. To the west is brush and mesquite, gale-torn badlands that support only a few spindly cattle and stands of spiky cactus and the wire-shouded factories of the Pentagon and those other establishments who like to operate where farmers and their families do not.

To the east of the line is the land which has become the storehouse and the breadbasket of America—and, indeed, the world. Maps of the distribution of the nation's farms show thick black crowds of them running like a massive swarm of bees down from Lake Superior to the south of Texas, eastwards to the Appalachian Hills, westwards to the ninety-eighth parallel. West of the line are the ranches—incredibly large spreads of land that support few animals and even fewer men, where fences are dozens of miles long and wells are a day's march apart. The difference is as dramatic and as sudden as the difference between east and west that is so clearly apparent on crossing the Missouri River up in North Dakota: on the one side is greenness, trees and wooden gates; on the other is brown dryness, scrub and barbed wire.

Most of the area of the states served by the Interstate lie within the region watered by the all-important rains: only in south-western Kansas, and again south beyond San Antonio, does drought become a real problem: irrigation pipes, a common feature of the dry potato fields of Idaho or the hop-meadows of eastern Oregon, are rarely seen in the midlands. There is usually enough water for everyone, and a bit more besides. The dreadful prospect of another drought still hangs over the farmers in the region though, a sword of Damocles that is ugliest of all to those men and women who remember the dustbowl that so wretchedly coincided with the economic Depression, and forced so many of the corn and cattle farmers of the time to abandon the plains and flee to the cities and the car production lines. The twenty-inch rain-line is a fickle beast, shifting eastward every twenty years or so, and some climatics specialists worry that the cycle is about to repeat itself and the drought and wind that ravages the land so easily may strike again in the decade. John Borchert, a geography professor at the University of Minnesota is quoted as prophesying 'the next widespread deterioration of summer rainfall in the mid 1970s'. Farmers in the Dakotas and western Iowa whose soy-bean crops were ruined by the parching heat and dryness of 1974 wonder if that cycle has not begun already.

The uncertain rains and the wild unstoppable winds are but one aspect of the savagery the atmosphere can unleash on the plains states. Temperature is another. On the northern borders, the winters, springs and autumns are the coldest in the country; on the southern borders there are heatwaves that rank only second to the merciless blazes in Death Valley and in the townships of Needles and Barstow, California. Some of the deepest snowfalls in America occur within fifty miles of International Falls. In January the freezing line hovers in the middle of Kansas, meaning that all the land to the north—all of Iowa and Minnesota—is subject to temperatures that are *on average* below freezing. The twenty-degree line passes through central Iowa, and the ten-degree isotherm through the city of Duluth in northern Minnesota. Even the zero line—meaning an *average* temperature of thirty-two degrees of frost—sneaks south of the Canadian border into the unpeopled wastes of North Dakota, a few miles away from Minnesota and the Rainy River. Gales that whip down from the blue ice-zones of northern Canada and the North Pole bring the dreadful wind-chill factor with them, meaning that winters in the northern states can be so cold that a bucket of water tossed into the air will fall back as ice crystals, or a man's eyelids will snap shut, and stay shut, if he turns his head into the merciless wind. Winter storms—like a blockbuster that struck the states in January 1974—dump hundreds of inches of powdery, car-stopping, cow-smothering, door-blocking snow on to the land every year. Nothing grows, little moves. The livestock goes indoors, city folk put on goloshes for their rare excursions from heated cars into the slushy streets, the trucks that normally race along the freeways go gingerly, and wear thick-treaded snow tyres, a requirement both of law and common sense.

All during the long northern winter—and climatic charts show freezing days can be expected for very nearly half of any year; 180 days in most of Minnesota, three and a half months in Kansas—the southern part of Texas is summery warm. Laredo enjoys temperatures in the seventies all year round, and statistics show that along with Florida and the Louisiana bayou country and that climatically extraordinary oasis of San Francisco, the city experiences less than five days of freezing temperatures out of every 365. In March, the isotherms displaying the seventies and eighties begin to creep north, at the rate of some sixteen miles every day, bringing spring to the hard-frozen soils of the plains. By the time the sun is warming the April snows in Iowa and the Dakotas, and Laredo is experiencing its first triple-figure temperature of the season, the floods have begun. Land is too wet to plant, tractors become trapped axle-deep in mud, and corn fields stand miserable and shivering in inches of standing slush. The rivers begin to fill up, the ice broken and the mud choking their sides; they overflow, and huge acreages of alluvial land submerge. The Mississippi begins to roar and foam, and thousands of tons of rich brown soil are rushed downstream in the mess of turbulent meltwater and dumped pointlessly in the Gulf of Mexico. Mark Twain—who wrote *Tom Sawyer* in the riverside village of Hannibal, Missouri, and knew the bluffs and the twists and turns of the huge old Mississippi like his own back garden— once noted that the river carried more than one million tons of good Midwestern soil out to sea every day: in the melt months of April and May, when the upper Midwest is sloughing off the whiteness of winter, the figure must reach into the tens of millions.

The weather, the unending starkness of the scenery, the loneliness and the distance from metropolitan excitement have taken their toll—or did, until very recently—on the spirit of the Middle American people.

Only one of the six states actually experienced a net inward migration of new people during the forty years since 1930, and that was Texas. Natural increase, the excess of live births over deaths and migration east and west, kept the populations of all the states rising during the period, but their contribution to the United States as a whole fell steadily throughout the period. In 1930 the states held some 14.6 per cent of the total population of the nation; in 1970 their share had shrunk to only 13 per cent, and little evidence has come to the notice of the Bureau of Census to suggest that the trend is about to be dramatically reversed. Indeed, forecasts of the populations of the states for 1974 suggest that for their first time ever, Iowa and Kansas will actually experience a net loss of population, either through the natural effect on already depopulated states of the end of the post-Second World War baby boom, or a new migration to the more comfortable climates of the Pacific, Atlantic or Lake Michigan shores.

Texas continues to grow as industries flock into the big cities of Houston and Dallas-Fort Worth—the former now trying to call itself the 'South-Western Metroplex', the latter unquestionably destined to become the biggest city in the entire United States long before this century is out. But Texas is the odd man out of the six plains states in terms of its potential: the five states to the north are solid, reliable, by reputation a trifle dull. Texas is brash, colourful and as suitable a place as California for the needs of avarice to be quickly and painlessly satisfied.

Oklahoma, the Census Bureau reports, is also enjoying something of an unusual growth in its population these days—not because its people are unusually fecund, but, like Texas, because industry and people are being attracted to the sunshine and the low taxes and the still untrampled open spaces. Oklahoma is, however, of a kind with the northern states; it lacks the tough one-upmanship of Texas, and its success in attracting outsiders is rather harder to explain. Oklahomans will try to explain it themselves later on.

In Kansas, the figures show that men and women—and usually their grown-up children—are leaving. This is the state in which, as one writer noted in 1971 'the lights are going out . . . small towns are shrivelling and dying, farmhouses stand abandoned and stark, sun-bleached mementoes of an era lost in a sea of prairie grass'. There are reasons for the peculiarly and tragically unhappy state of Kansas, which we will explore when the highway curves through the wheat capitals from the Missouri River to the Oklahoma border.

Minnesota and Missouri are both growing slightly, but less rapidly than the national average: in Washington it is thought that both states still enjoy a net inward migration, but that the rate at which people move to cities like Minneapolis and Kansas City is less rapid than the average movement between states in this traditionally mobile society. So while the position at the very north and in the very centre of the highway's path is more encouraging than in Kansas, but less so than Texas, the net result is a continuation of the now established pattern of life in the middle of the nation: that fewer and fewer people want to live there, and steadily the people, like the prairie soil of forty years ago, is being eroded away.

The surprising exception is Iowa. Here is a state that, in many ways, seems ready to become extinct. It has one of the highest percentages of elderly residents in America—only Florida and Arkansas have more; and it has one of the lowest birth rates in the nation—it is forty-first out of the fifty states counted in the surveys carried out by the US Government. Its population was expected to decline a little in 1974, together with Kansas, and its vitality would appear, at first glance, to have been all but exhausted.

But wait. Leafing carefully through the figures one finds another morsel of the data in which America's foremost statistician, Richard Scammon, advises any student of the country to 'marinate himself in'. And that is the odd note that, very recently, there has been an inflow of people to Iowa—a flow well above the national average. One can understand the movement of Americans to Texas; less understandable, but not impossible to grasp, has been the recent shifting of people to Oklahoma. But to Iowa—to the flat, 'corn and hogs' country, where all the old people live and all the ideas are as square as the fields that grow that most prosaic of crops, soy beans? To find out why the state is sucking people in—gently, albeit, but most certainly not spitting them out—was one of the more abiding puzzles that confronted me when I began the journey. The middle of America is a land of such surprises—it is a place where nearly all of my long-standing assumptions came to be challenged as the most foreign of illusions. That Iowa is taking in Americans remains one of the more intriguingly shattered of these.

But generally, the people are leaving. Those that remain are, by and large, older than the national average; whiter than the national average; less afflicted by crime; less mobile; less adventurous, both in theory and in practice. That, at least, is the assumption. In all other ways, John Gunther found, the men and women and children of the region are best characterised by their strong involuntary adherence to the great national norms. 'The most interesting thing', he wrote about the Middle West—and remember that his definition of the region is somewhat different from the far more haphazardly chosen area around the highway—'is probably its actual Middleness, not only in geography or sense of moderation, but in its averageness and typicalness. The region is', Gunther added, 'the part of the nation that most strongly resists change.'

In matters of momentary significance, Gunther was certainly

right. A friend who lives in Missouri once told me that a close watch on local people would always tell whether a new fashion created in the racy centres of Fifth Avenue or Market Street would really catch on in America: wedge shoes for girls, for instance—they came in from Europe to the East Coast, were transported without a day's delay to the girls of the west coast, but somehow never really got past the twin bastions of Appalachia and the Rockies. A few travellers might briefly tout them in St. Louis or Kansas City: but they would never make Des Moines, Emporia or Ponca City— and if they failed to make it there, my friend would say, they'll die out in time. He was usually right—the hula hoop caught on in Kansas City, and nothing could stop it after that. Makers of new products such as soap powder and cat food prefer to test their wares out on the good citizens of Duluth and Dubuque and Dallas, rather than risk the possibly spurious results from modish and mercurial centres further from the heartland: if the Middle Americans are willing to change their habits, the makers reason, then anyone can. Missouri in particular has such a reputation for conservatism and scepticism—though less noticeably in politics than in more mundane matters like the purchase of breakfast cereals—that it has become known as the 'show-me' state. Oh yes, young man, its residents will say to the fellow who claims to have invented that legendary better mousetrap—well, show me.

American conservatism is only a relative condition. And in politics—especially now, in the wake of Watergate, and with a most extraordinary Presidential election due in 1976—the old-style conservatism that was once held to characterise the political outlook of the typical Midwesterner is gone. There has been a remarkable revolution in American politics in the past decade: there was the sudden appearance of the 'New South' (an appearance, it might well be noted by smug Midwesterners, that was essentially triggered by a court case fought over the issue of school segregation in the unlikely setting of Topeka, Kansas); then, in the early 1970s, the 'New West' was on us, with a startling rapid overturn of the once inviolable principle of 'Growth is Good for You' and its replacement by such pejorative words as 'Californication'; and then, at the same time, and partly only in response to the scandalous happenings in Washington, there has been the revolt of the Nixonian Middle Americans. The six states through which I-35 passes have changed in outlook and political expectations more rapidly, perhaps, than nearly all others in the land—and perhaps, just perhaps, that is because these of all people, were the Americans whom men like Richard Nixon so badly let down.

On only five occasions this century have the six states voted together for the same President—and as they all voted, so voted the nation. In 1928, the six went for Hoover—a choice they later would regret. In 1932, and again in 1936, the voters from Minnesota to Texas sent Franklin Roosevelt to the White House—the second time, even though a local Kansas boy, Alf Landon, the epitome of Midwestern frugality and plainsmanship, was his opponent. In 1952 they went for Eisenhower; and in 1964, for Johnson; not even they could stomach the conservatism then espoused by Barry Goldwater, the man who until George McGovern was trounced by Mr. Nixon in 1972, suffered the biggest defeat ever in a Presidential race.

The six states have only existed in totality since 1906, when the famous land-races were held to distribute Indian prairies among the new Oklahomans. Missouri is the oldest of the others; Texas and Iowa came next; then Minnesota and lastly Kansas—all created from the disorganised territories of the unexplored West in the forty years ending in 1864. For the next twenty-four years Minnesota, Iowa and Kansas voted together for the Republican candidates; only in 1892, when Kansas decided to give its electoral college votes for Mr. Weaver, the Populist candidate, did a split develop in what seemed then an unwavering picture of conservatism on the new frontier. Since then the pattern has shifted with the political winds of the day: usually, though by no means invariably, the states north of the Oklahoma line—with the exception of Minnesota—voting for the Republican contender, and those to the south, including Missouri, going for the Democrat. But there are so many exceptions that it is unwise to draw conclusions about the overall Presidential affiliations: Midwesterners are not convincedly doctrinaire men and women, and their choices often reflected their hard-headedness and rugged independence, rather than their adherence to any party line.

The men and women these states have sent to Washington to be their Senators and Representatives more accurately reflect their feelings than do their Presidential choices. The fact that Minnesota can send men like Hubert Humphrey and Walter Mondale to be their chief spokesmen in the capital tells more about the long tradition of agricultural liberalist politics than does the occasional aberrations, such as in 1956, when the country people turned their backs on Stevenson and voted instead to keep old Eisenhower in the Executive Mansion. That Iowa has sent for years and years a cantankerous old curmudgeon named H. R. Gross to represent the corn and hog farmers of the Third District speaks eloquently of the harsh frugality and uncompromising devotion to toil of most Iowans: Gross, perhaps the most grudgingly respected of all Congressmen, had a deserved reputation of being the principal Scrooge of Capitol Hill, reading and re-reading every line in every Bill presented for action, and constantly demanding to know how much money every morsel of legislation would cost, and whether his taxpayer constituents would consider the expenditure good value or no.

Missouri, a politically marginal state, nevertheless personifies for many Easterners the distillate of Middle-American big city corruption because of the efforts of one of the nation's most notorious scoundrels, Thomas J. Pendergast, the long-time absolute master of Kansas City. Pendergast was a man who gave concrete—from which he chiselled himself a fortune—a bad name; and his stain is left still in Kansas City politics, an unwelcome, but undeniable symbol of how the middle country can, in its haste to bring itself as up to date as its neighbours to the east, find itself afflicted by problems more akin to New York than to the airy pastures of the midland farms.

But Missouri also gave the world Harry Truman, who in essence too is the Middle American, just plain folksy, next-door-neighbourly type, so loved by this sentimental public. Truman shares almost every characteristic, except politics, with his lean, bespectacled neighbour from way-back Kansas politics, Alf Landon. These two, perhaps above all others who came from the Midwest, stand most aptly for the decency, the averageness and the reputed lack of imagination of the men of the heartland. Truman, a Democrat, was a great success (even though Kansas was one of the very few states that voted for his opponent, Thomas Dewey); Landon, a Republican, was a failure, who failed even to take his own state, and who naturally lost Missouri too.

Oklahoma, more famous for contributing Will Rogers to enrich American humour than any politicians to enliven American rhetoric, is the hardest of all to which to assign a typical political product. Perhaps Carl Albert, minuscule of stature, but of formidable intellect (a Rhodes Scholar, no less), who is currently the Speaker of the House of Representatives, is the personality of whom the 'Sooners' are currently most proud. For the rest, a depressing lack of inspiration, dynamism or depth tends to have kept Oklahomans away from the mainstream: most of the more energetic men from the state realise where they'll best make their fortune, and accordingly go to join the oil industry, and leave politics well alone. There is one man, Fred Harris, a former Senator and now a candidate for the Presidential nomination of the Democratic Party, who bears watching, and we will return to him later.

Lastly, Texas. Almost every other political figure from the state seems to symbolise it: there seems not to be a single one who is either physically small or soft-voiced or who fails to dominate entirely the company into which he is placed. Lyndon Johnson, the crude, compassionate, lovable, laughable and utterly tragic figure who reigned as President between the death of John Kennedy and his own miserably forced abdication in 1968, remains the most colourful standard-bearer of the Texas political scene. There are others too, at least one of whom—Lloyd Bentsen—can now be considered a definite possibility as a 1976 Presidential candidate. Texas manages to breed fine cattle and unforgettable politicians— the very opposite of Oklahoma, the very same, though for opposite reasons, as Minnesota.

Only four American Presidents were born in the heartland— Herbert Hoover, Harry Truman, Dwight Eisenhower and Lyndon Johnson—and with the exception of Johnson, what singularly ordinary men they managed to be! Hoover came from West Branch, Iowa; like Eisenhower, whose family lived in the hamlet of Dennison, Texas, he was of good immigrant stock, Swiss-German, and typical of the Midwestern immigrant nature. Truman, who came from Missouri, was of Scottish, Irish and English blood, and Johnson, whose birthplace is marked as 'near Stonewall, Texas', has an origin of which the nation's archivists are unsure. As befits a man who was just a little bit of a rogue, his pedigree is stated simply as 'English, and unknown'.

The 1976 election sees just two candidates for the Democratic nomination from the midlands—Fred Harris, who will be running on a Populist platform with the smell of his now long-gone Oklahoma Senate victory still in his nostrils; and Lloyd Bentsen, the junior Senator from Texas and, unlike Mr. Harris, a millionaire several times over. Walter Mondale had thought of contesting, but late in 1974 withdrew his name, saying that he felt he could best serve his state from his seat in the Senate, and that really he was not all that keen to have the tribulations of Presidential office thrust upon him. Many sympathised with Mondale, and liked him—a likeable man at the best of times—all the more so for having the courage to stand up and say that really the Presidency rather bored him.

And that, as I stepped into my car that freezing winter's night in Fort Frances, Ontario, was the approximate sum of the narrow, harshly delimited sector of America that lay on the other side of the bridge. It was going to be very big, very flat, very windy. The days and nights would be bitterly cold in Minnesota, Iowa and in northern Kansas; the days would be bearable in Missouri, in southern Kansas, and in Oklahoma; and in Texas, all being well, it would be positively warm. Indeed, the local Canadian radio station in Fort Frances was saying the Gulf Coast states were enjoying heat well up into the eighties at the very time I was turning the volume control up with shivering and scarcely sensitive fingers. The contrast seemed too great to be believed.

Politically the states would be less conservative than I had been told; there would be bitterness still towards Richard Nixon, and yet in many corners remarkable hostility towards the perfidy of the press and the back-sliders and bleeding-hearts in the Congress. There would be farmers who were content, and farmers who were upset. There would be a lot of wealthy people, and a few very poor people. There would be blacks—mostly in Kansas City, and again in the big Texas cities; there would be Indians—in Minnesota, Oklahoma and again in Texas; and there would be, especially in the south of Texas, thousands of Spanish-speaking 'Chicanos'. There would be scientists, philosophers and visionaries; and there would be elderly narrow-minded malcontents whose views had long ago been assumed to reflect the true thinking of this invariably ignored part of the American nation. As Gunther had said, a lot of very average, very real America stretched ahead.

Before I set off, one word about the road. Earlier I noted, not just for the confusion of the reader, that there are in fact two roads between this bridge and that across the Rio Grande. For very nearly all of the way, the four-lane Interstate would carry me: for the first 150 miles, however, I would have to travel into America on an old Federally-numbered road, US Route 53. There is a reason: the Government says it does not have any plans to extend I-35 from Duluth, where it nominally 'begins', up to the Canadian border because the volume of traffic simply would not justify the expense. Any traveller wanting to go to Winnipeg will travel up Interstate 29 through the Dakotas; anyone wanting Sault St. Marie and the industrial cities of Sudbury and North Bay would travel on Interstate 75 through the Michigan peninsula and across the immense Mackinaw Bridge. Where I-35 may some day be extended to depends, basically, on where Americans want to go in this icy border country. Perhaps the road will always start at Duluth, and have the only slightly diminished distinction of running, rather than from border to border, from America's most northerly big city right down to its most southerly.

A final note about the numbering system used in the roads that form what the Government formally calls the National System of Interstate and Defense Highways. Even-numbered roads pass eastward and westward—Interstate 10 takes drivers from Los Angeles, via Phoenix and El Paso, Houston and New Orleans, to Tallahassee and Jacksonville; I-90 goes from Boston to Chicago to Sioux Falls, South Dakota, then Billings and Butte and on to Seattle. The odd-numbered highways go north and south: I-5 from Seattle right down the Pacific coast to San Diego, I-95 from Miami up to Houlton, Maine. Interstate 35 is just one of these, bounded on the right by I-29 going north from Kansas City in to the wilds of North Dakota, and I-55, from New Orleans to Chicago. Naturally, the odd and even roads cross—sometimes at big cities, at other times, much more romantically, in the middle of some flat and unfeatured Nowhere: I-35 crosses the highway to Seattle in such a Nowhere in southern Minnesota; it crosses the route to San Francisco and New York at Des Moines; that from Washington to Denver at Kansas City; and that greatest of all east-west highways, I-40, the old Route 66, at Oklahoma City.

But all these crossings and flyovers and clover leaves and temptingly attractive signs for the Pacific and Atlantic capitals would have to wait—they were two weeks' hard driving southwards, at the very least. Ahead immediately was one grimy iron bridge, sixty feet above the ink-black, ice-chocked waters of the Rainy River: at the end of the bridge was a low white shed, on which I could just read, through the swirls of drifting steam, the words 'U S Immigration and Naturalization Service, International Falls'. There was a Stars and Stripes whipping crisply in the wind.

I nosed the car on to the iron grille of the bridgeway. A brief wait as a large diesel engine pushed beside and then in front of me, and then I was above the stream. Twenty seconds later the car was under the arc lights of the border post, and a heavily muffled guard dressed in blue-grey, and with a much-brassed cap came over to the car, his breath visible as short, steamy bursts.

'Good evening, sir,' he said. 'Welcome to the United States. Can I see your identification, please?'

2

Minnesota:
Follow the North Star

The Canadian immigration authorities at Fort Frances who were crammed into a small wooden hut at the north end of the bridge had been friendly and very nearly slap-happy. The Americans, by appropriate contrast, were brisk and mannered, polite according to regulations and recommendations made by the Tourist Board, but unaccustomed to much in the way of levity. The officer who took my passport flipped it open to see my visa—'An "I" classification— we don't see too many of these about up here,' he allowed ('I' class visas are given to 'Representatives of Foreign Media', and are valid far longer than the normal 'B-1' visas handed to tourists); he then asked me to wait a second while he went inside. He spoke to a colleague who seemed to be sitting behind a large computer console; then he came back, asked me briefly if I had any goods to declare, and waved me through.

The computer terminal is a new and very special piece of Americana, the first indication of the well-regulated society Washington would like imposed upon the country. For the terminal is, indeed, hooked up to a vast data bank down at the Treasury offices in the centre of Washington, D.C., 1,200 miles or so away to the south-east. The clerk was punching into the machine the two letters and four numbers of my car licence plate; the brief wait was to allow the circuitry to digest the information that a car of that number was wanting access to the fortress, and then flash back, in one line of glowing green, 'O.K., permit to proceed.' It was quick, impersonal, and highly efficient: clearly it had its purpose, too. But it seemed a little odd that to get from a crime-infested country into a peaceful, quietly dull old Canada, you only had to run the gauntlet of half a dozen cheerful customs men who seemed to work under the assumption that anyone wanting to come to Canada couldn't really be all that bad; while to pass from the tranquillity of Canada into the most powerful, and yet most internally tortured country on the globe, a computer had to make its scan and nod its electronic approval before the portcullis was hoisted.

The first few hundred yards of American soil seemed paved with railway tracks. Most, it appears, were operated by the Minnesota, Dakota & Western Railway Company, which, in the tradition of the incredibly cumbrous American railway network, is a company owning only four and a half miles of track (from Fort Frances to Falls Junction, Minnesota), and not really owning that, either. A note in a splendid monthly publication called *The Official Guide to the Railways* tells us that the single mile across the bridge and up to the connections with external railways is run by an outfit called the International Bridge & Terminal Company, whose President, a Mr. F. L. Sigloh, actually works from an office in Boise, Idaho, deep in the mountainous West. The paper mills in the town are all run by Boise Cascade, a pulp conglomerate with headquarters in that same Far Western city: the connection became clear in an instant. The railways belong to the paper mill; the bridge I had come across, although administered as some no-man's-land, was actually the property of the paper giant, and so was half of the town of Fort Frances itself. A classic example, of course, of how tightly poor Canada is bound to her all-powerful neighbour to the south.

International Falls itself is a dreary little spot consisting largely of the mills, and low-cost rooming houses for the fishermen who make their way through in the summer and for the fishermen who brave the winters to come up and try for bass and char under the two feet of frozen lake water. At daylight, it is said, you can see clutches of the small wooden sheds the ice fishermen build out on the lakes: some would stay in them so long, using so much of the air, that water would ooze up through the hole the fisherman had bored in the ice and freeze, making the floor just a little higher than the rest of the lake. A few weeks of this, and there would be a two-foot-thick ice layer in the bottom of the hut, firmly welding it to the lake surface. If the fisherman wanted his hut back at the end of the season, he would have to saw it off above the ice, two feet shorter than when he brought it to the lake six months before. At the end of the winter there could be dozens of these shed stumps littering the lake, all of them destined to float off and become driftwood once the ice melted.

The fame that International Falls has established for itself over the past two decades has been due entirely to the establishment there, twenty years ago, of one of the US Government's best-known weather stations. All across the world meteorologists will be familiar with the place as Station Number 72747, one more in the complicated chains of observing and relaying centres that help the giant computers in Washington—and Britain's own, in Bracknell, Berkshire—decide how the atmosphere is planning to move, and thus how much snow will fall in Winnipeg the next day, how high the waves will be in the South China Sea, or whether Manchester businessmen should take umbrellas with them to work.

The station at International Falls, where America's lowest temperatures are invariably reported each day in winter, is in a two-storey hut, warm and well insulated, at the tiny airport (served by a regular airline, North Central, which offers, incidentally, the best food of any American domestic airline). The station comes under the aegis of Washington's National Oceanic and Atmospheric Administration—a body that, so arrogantly named, performs the much milder tasks of providing weather forecasts and 'easing the human burden of hurricanes, tornadoes, floods, tsunamis and other destructive natural events'.

Tom Fairhurst, one of the men who runs the station, is a gentle scientist with red hair and a wispy moustache, not at all the kind of person you would imagine warning us of hurricanes and tsunamis. He has performed this kind of work for all of his career, and has spent four years at the International Falls reporting station. 'It's much more comfortable now we have machines. When I started you had to go out every hour and look at the thermometers and into the rain gauges and stuff. Now—', he gestured around at the chattering, whirring machinery that filled the room, 'these beasts do it.' The temperature sensors were no longer thin tubes, U-shaped for maximums and minimums, nailed inside a white vented wooden box. They were small electronic sensory devices buried into the runways, half a mile from the hut. The dewpoint reader was up on the roof, connected to the inside by wires, and the rain gauges and the sunshine recorders all fed their data from the brisk outside into this cheerfully cosy inside. 'I don't often go out there,' Tom Fairhurst said. 'It's much too cold.'

The chattering machines are mainly telexes and teletypes that automatically relay every hour on the hour, the latest 'synoptic reports' back to the Central Region headquarters in Kansas City, and from thence to Washington and the outside world. All American stations, he explained, bear the initial number of 72: the 747, nicely jet-aged, was the designation for this icy location.

And how cold was it? 'You heard the snow squeaking on your boots outside?' Tom Fairhurst asked. 'That means it's at least ten below. The snow changes then—it is so dry and brittle it sort of sings to you. Rotten for making snowballs, it just won't melt and stick together. And it blows everywhere, like dust.' It was, in fact, eighteen degrees below zero Fahrenheit—fifty degrees below the melting point of ice, and only a few hundred degrees above the temperature at which all atomic motion stops. It certainly felt that way when I opened the door to walk back to my car. A couple of technicians were just walking in from the runway—the first weather men I had seen actually braving the frigid air: they had been launching a balloon to take a routine measurement up in the night stratosphere: it would go twenty miles up into the sky, and take an hour and a half to get there, its little radio sending messages down to Mr. Fairhurst and his colleagues in their snug den, and helping them predict what America's high-level weather might be the next day. (International Falls, by the way, was not to be the coldest spot in the nation the night I was there: Helena, Montana, looked like getting it, the weathermen said, with about twenty-five below: they were absolutely right, I noted next day—out by only a single degree.)

The car swung back on to the highway, skidded briefly on the fresh blowing snow, and then settled down to a steady hum south-wards through the night. It was 160 miles to the next big city, Duluth: between here and there was a wasteland of pines, and lakes, and miles and miles of snow.

There were only a few items on the way that interrupted what would otherwise have been an unrelieved tedium. Five miles out of the town, for instance, there was one of the most familiar of all American advertising signs: a red billboard with two golden arches painted on it, and, in yellow, the word 'McDonald's'. The largest hamburger chain in the world, whose sign told you each day the accumulated total of its products sold to that very moment—a sum that was, in 1975, in the region of sixteen thousand million. Here, five miles away from the border, then, was the first true indication of American suburban culture; and I must admit my mouth watered at the thought. But the selling slogan, 'You deserve a break today', also reminded the motorist he had a longish wait until he could eat. 'The next McDonald's', the sign noted coyly, in tiny letters 'only 154 miles south on US 53'.

For most of the journey the road was flat and straight. Ninety miles gone, however, the terrain suddenly jumped upwards, and there were lights and trucks and curious steaming machines to be seen on all sides. This was the Range—Range meaning 'district' in north Minnesota, not hill—and it was the site where once the vast bulk of this country's iron was extracted from the earth. The hills that bulge up for a few hundred feet around the Range are significant in one other sense too. They form a remarkable watershed: to the north, all rivers flow either into the Great Lakes, and thus to the St. Lawrence, or to the Hudson's Bay; to the south they flow, eventually, to the Mississippi and the Gulf of Mexico. The other Continental Divide, one side of which directs its streams to the Pacific, the other to the Atlantic, is marked for all its length with signs and posters: this Divide which marks the limit of Gulf waters and the start of the Arctic and north Atlantic contributions, could happily be passed by without remark.

The mines on the Range—the Mesabi, Vermilion and Cuyuna—are still among the biggest in the world. Vast pits miles long and thousands of feet deep, like the Hull-Rust-Mahoning pit at Hibbing, have been excavated by gigantic gouging machines that strip away rock and ore for processing in mills that are springing up all about. The old high-grade ore is all but exploited now—there were only two thousand million tons of it, and eighty years of insatiable demands by the car-makers in Detroit and the shipbuilders on the Gulf soon put paid to the store. In its place there is a low-quality stuff called taconite, from which iron can be extracted, though at high cost: it is the taconite that is at the focus both of the new economic boom of the area, and of a worrisome environmental squabble that has afflicted Minnesotans for nearly the past decade.

But the taconite has brought blessings. 'Iron Range boom getting louder', proclaimed the *Duluth Herald* while I was there. 'Minnesota's Iron Range, traditionally in a boom-or-bust way of life, is facing such a boom it may bust at the seams.' The reporter who penned that introduction was clearly happy with the way the Range was going. His story recounted how Bethlehem Steel and Pickands Mather & Company had just announced they would spend $100 million on building yet another taconite reprocessing plant near Hibbing, even though the factory they started work on three years before had not opened for business at the time. Three thousand men and women would be employed—the women happily not in the capacity of twenty years ago, when a small army of them was set to work sweeping up every last ounce of high-grade ore from every hole and crack in the mine floor, 'as a child licks a chicken bone'.

The high-grade ore of old was shipped, courtesy of the Duluth Missabe & Iron Range Railway Company, to the dock and off to plants like Ford's vast River Rouge Factory at Detroit. Little was done in the way of preparation on the Range: the 'boom or bust way of life' was a reflection of the simple process that was carried out on these piney hillocks—the ore was dug and sorted, graded and tested, and then shipped. It is all very different now.

Taconite is a form of ore some long way removed from the simple oxides of iron that sparkled or glowed red and dull in the high-grade ore. Iron is there, all right, but wedded with powerful chemical intimacy to silica minerals in a hard, insoluble chert. To extract the iron was, until lately, difficult in the extreme, and very expensive. Only when the price of iron, and America's need for it became so acute, did Hibbing and the towns near by start to enjoy the prosperity that the taconite deposits owed to them. The mills, long, ugly plants that reek smoke and are shatteringly noisy places, crush the cherty rocks that the mighty electrical excavators have torn from the pits: the ancient boulders are pulverised until powerful electromagnets can steal the iron particles away from the silica and dump them as a fine powder ready for shipment. For convenience the factories then bond the iron particles with a little clay-like material and water, and bake them into small pellets: they are then quite ready for the blast furnaces, and are heaped into the Duluth Missabe & Iron Range cars and shipped down to the Lake and the waiting mouths of the retorts.

The process leaves behind a great deal of waste—ugly, grey-green rubbish that, in most cases, can be put straight back into the holes from which the ore was dug in the first place. But one of the biggest companies operating up on the Range, the Reserve Mining Company of Silver Bay, has chosen to dump its wasted rock not into the ground again, but into Lake Superior. And the volume of rock was an astonishing reflection upon the volume of Reserve Mining's business: each day a wide channel, brimful of foul-looking slurry, would carry no less than 67,000 tons of waste rock chips into the Lake—an amount that would cover an American football field half a mile thick each year.

Environmentalists first came to attack Reserve Mining in the early 1970s, when Lake-watchers noted that a faint greenish cast had crept into the hitherto sparkling clear liquid in Superior. Traces of very fine particulate matter began to be noticed in the drinking water of a few lakeshore communities: it was abundantly clear that the mining bosses' forecasts, that the waste would travel five miles or so and drop abruptly in the Lake's 900 feet Great Trough, were not being realised.

But then something even worse was noted: the taconite waste was, in part, composed of asbestos fibres. And asbestos, it was well known, causes cancer. Slowly, but very surely, it will kill you, if once it gets inside your body.

Cities in the area panicked during 1974 when this news leaked out; trucks brought in water for drinking, filters were installed that would weed out the very tiniest trace of asbestos, and everyone sank back into calm acceptance of the situation. All, that is, except the environmentalists and the three states, Minnesota, Michigan and Wisconsin, whose lands bound on to the shores of Lake Superior. They went to court to try to force Reserve to dump her tailings elsewhere, or else close down. Reserve—which is owned by two of America's wealthiest steel giants, Republic and Armco—said it would cost too much to dump its waste on the land. And it was, in consequence promptly ordered by a tough-minded federal judge in Minneapolis to close down.

For a moment there was ecstasy and panic: environmentalists rejoiced. Workers at Reserve Mining began to cry with worry for their future. The classic confrontation between progress and protection had reached, in Minnesota and beside one of the world's largest and loveliest lakes, its natural conclusion.

The judge's ruling, though, was reversed days later by a Superior Court appeals judge in St. Louis—too far away from the cleanliness of the northern woods and streams to know much about the goodness of clean air and rain; and then the Supreme Court of the United States refused, in 1975, to overrule him. So Reserve Mining stays in business; workers in the region continue to work; the boom gets louder still; and Lake Superior turns an evil shade of green.

Hibbing, the central Range town, gave the world more than iron. It also matured and educated a young Jewish boy called Robert Zimmerman, who went out with a guitar and a head full of solemn lyrics, changed his name to Bob Dylan and proceeded to enchant a world.

> *The Iron Range is a long line of mining towns that*
> *begin at Grand Rapids and end at Eveleth*
>
> *We moved up there to live with my mother's folks*
> *in Hibbing when I was young—*
>
> *Hibbing's got the biggest open pit ore mine in the world*
> *Hibbing's got schools, churches, grocery stores an' a jail*
> *It's got high school football games an' a movie house*
> *Hibbing's got souped up cars runnin' full blast on a Friday*
> *night*
> *Hibbing's got corner bars with polka bands*
> *You can stand at one end of Hibbing on the main drag*
> *an' see clear past the city limits on the other end*
> *Hibbing's a good ol' town.*

Dylan wrote a lot about the Range, but, strangely, sang about it only rarely. Perhaps he realised the romance of the poplar, birch and tamarack forests and the snow and the vastness of the Hull-Rust-Mahoning Pit and the polka dancing clubs was limited in its appeal; or perhaps he never wanted the town he grew in to become a mecca for the young and restless Americans his songs were primarily directed towards.

Between Hibbing, Virginia and Eveleth, the three principal Range cities, and the big old city of Duluth, is another fifty miles of piney wasteland. In the middle of it some courageous entrepreneur has had the nerve to build the United States Hockey Hall of Fame—a low, square structure that contains pictures and statuettes of the men who have contributed most to the rough-and-tumble game of ice hockey. Halls of Fame for various sports are dotted across America, usually in small villages well off the beaten track: the Hockey Hall of Fame must hold the record for being the most remote and, I dare say, the least often visited.

Just as you come in to the first straggles of suburban Duluth there is a large concrete blockhouse on the east side of the highway.

A shield and a blue and white sign proclaim its identity as '23 NORAD Region HQ' and from time to time a Phantom interceptor fighter sweeps into the air leaving a trail of dark smoke thickening behind it. To perennially insecure Americans, this building is vital. It is one of eight such installations spread across the United States from Alaska to Florida which, together with a series of radar towers in Canada, Greenland and Iceland, and three vast golf-ball-shaped 'radomes' in Alaska, Greenland and on the Yorkshire moors, makes up the nerve endings of the North American Aerospace Defense Command—NORAD.

From Duluth, fighters can be sent that will investigate and, if necessary, shoot down, any object that strays uninvited into North American airspace. The system is designed for the protection of Canada as well as the United States—flags of both countries fly outside this blockhouse, as they do outside the twenty-ton doors to the brains of the entire system, a thousand miles away in the industrial town of Colorado Springs, Colorado.

Deep inside Cheyenne Mountain, by Colorado Springs, there is now a small city, said to be totally invulnerable to nuclear attack and capable of surviving quite unworried even after the rest of the nation has been flattened and burned by blast and radiation. This is the NORAD headquarters, and it has two functions: its radars, spaced out across the Arctic, peering over the horizon towards Russia and China and weaving an invisible net across the skies to detect anything that flies in, high or low, towards the coastlines of North America, will flash details of all possible threats on to twenty-foot-tall glowing console maps high on the bunker walls. The commanders who sit forever gazing at these walls then have the duty to inform the President and Strategic Air Command of the invasion, if that is what it is. They can order the civil defence emergency teams into action, can direct the new wing of anti-missile missiles buried deep in the prairies of North Dakota to bring down the intruders, and they can send up the fighters at bases like the 23 Region HQ at Duluth to investigate the problem. They can warn the nation, order it underground into the myriads of shelters, and tell the occupant of the White House when and if he should retaliate with all the missiles and bombs unleashable by one brief push of his thumb. Duluth, the old tired town of the north, is one of the most important links in this chain of protection, evidence that the Arctic wastelands of the far north have their uses in protecting the frontiers as adeptly as the immigration computer at the International Falls Bridge.

A mile past the NORAD base we pass the McDonald's advertised all those miles to the north: a few young men and women are waiting, in desultory fashion, for their milkshakes which, in view of the six-foot snowbanks on every side of the building, look less than suitable refreshment. But there's no stopping American children from being American, whatever the temperature.

Then, suddenly we are in Duluth. The road heaves up and over a slight ridge, and there in front is a most marvellous sight. A steep hill falls away in front, 500 feet or more of slope, leading down to a vast, shining, white expanse of ice that stretches away as far as it is possible to see. It is Lake Superior, frozen almost solid and glistening peacefully and beautifully in the morning sun. A few puffs of steam from some factories down on the shore form shadows on the ice. A couple of ore carriers beat slowly through thin patches in the ice, or are led gingerly by Port of Duluth tugs into the only lead broken by the dock entrance, and taken up to a berth underneath the tipples from whence pour the tons of ore and wheat that have made the fortunes, and the world-wide reputation of this town.

For Duluth is the very apex of the American cornucopia. Like the Hudson-Mohawk Valley and the Pacific Cordillera and the Port of Churchill, Manitoba, the city of Duluth is one of those sites on the North American continent known by almost every European twelve-year-old. Children will draw maps of America, colouring the Great Plains for 'wheat' and 'corn', with a black smudge up in the north saying 'iron'; and from these great producing centres will flow the hatched lines of the railroads, all leading to the western tip of the westernmost of the five Great Lakes. From there, a little figurative ship will take the tens of thousands of tons of grain and ore across the Lakes, through the St. Lawrence Seaway and out to the Atlantic and the world. The tiny dot on the map, where railroad melts into shipping lane, is the city of Duluth, through which has flowed the bulk of American largesse and trade for the War years and beyond.

Duluth's an iron ore shipping town in Minnesota
It's built up on a rocky cliff that runs into Lake Superior

wrote Dylan, who was born there. A Kentucky politician, who was not born in Duluth, once made a famous sarcastic speech in Congress about the city, that began: 'Duluth! The word fell upon my ear with peculiar and indescribable charm . . . but where was Duluth? Never in my limited reading, had my vision been gladdened by seeing the celestial word in print. . . . I was confident that it existed somewhere, and that its discovery would constitute the crowning glory of the present century, if not of all modern times.' That was all of a hundred years ago, when Congress was debating whether to extend a railway into the Duluth area: the Congressman from Kentucky was taking the same silly view that Oxford students once took towards Wadham College: they would pretend to any inquirer not to know precisely where it was. As with Wadham, the joke still exists in this country—'Good God, you've been to Duluth have you . . . wher'n hell is it, now?'

In fact Duluth is one of the most dramatic and prettiest towns in North America, a Midwestern San Francisco, a place that sparkles and freshens by the lake waters, that is built on steep hills that tire both pedestrians and motor cars alike, and where the residents seem to have a springiness of step and a ruddiness of face unknown in the warmer, lazier cities of further south.

But, sadly, Duluth is a dying city—not dying from the same inner-city slum problems that have affected almost every other large urban centre, not dying from crime (there were no murders there in 1973, only one in 1974; there were fifteen cases of rape in 1974, one less than in the previous twelve months: few cities of 100,000 could display such civic restraint). It is dying simply because of a lack of money, and a lack of confidence by the rich old families who still hold sway in the region (and who live in vast old houses on the north side, off London Road) who have shown themselves reluctant to sink their fortunes in the development of what could be one of America's showplaces. The closing of US Steel's mighty plant at the south end of town hit the region badly; possibly the taconite revival may bring new life for the place, and the building in 1974 of a great recreation and convention centre, Spirit Mountain, is being quietly viewed by local people as the last chance the city has to revive its once-proud status. It would be a great shame if Duluth were permitted to become a ghost town by the lake. But it is already a lonely, isolated sort of place, where bears have a propensity for wandering in from the piney woods and raking about in the rubbish bins. Nature, it appears, is trying to get her claws back into the old town, trying to take back what was stolen from her when John Jacob Astor set up his fur trading post there at the beginning of the nineteenth century.

Duluth, being poor, has many unemployed and any number of its citizens receiving US Government Food Stamps. I spent half a day waiting with the tired-looking mothers and the pasty-faced children who had come to the St. Louis County Welfare Building to receive their monthly allotment of stamps. It was a sad education in the miseries of living at the base of the glossy American pyramid.

The Welfare Building itself, set up high on one of those slithery hills, is a dowdy red brick structure some eighty years old. The crowd that jammed the Food Stamp distribution centre in the basement was almost equally comprised of elderly widows, young mothers and the kind of children you rarely see in films and pictures about this country. In their shabby, tattered clothes and with their runny noses and thin legs, the children were the most pathetic of all. And they didn't scamper mischievously around the room, shouting and yelling with glee. They sat quietly on their mothers' laps, staring wide-eyed and worried, and old-looking, while the queue gradually shortened before them.

To qualify for Food Stamps—which are not stamps at all, but substantial-looking certificates, a fancy version of scrip or a kind of Savings Bond—you have to earn less than a certain wage every week. The clerks at the stamp centre will want to see your pay cheques if you have anyone working in the family, will want to see your bills for rent and gas and electricity, and will make the most Byzantine of calculations to make quite sure you qualify for stamps and how much you will have to pay for them. They are not free: the amount you pay for the book of stamps the Government allows you to have each month, depends on the amount you earn and the kinds of sums you are forced to pay out for the other essentials of living. A typical woman in the room, a Mrs. Gustafson, whose husband had to take a job at a city parking garage after his steel company had laid him off, would get stamps to the value of $150, which she could exchange for food in her local shop. But because her husband did earn a little, and because her rent and power bills did leave her with a little extra at the end of each month, she was asked to pay about $32 for the book of stamps—meaning, in other words, that she would be able to get $150 worth of food for a total cost to her of one cent for every five.

Although the clerks in the centre were kindhearted and as

generous as they could possibly be, the system seemed both cumbersome and a terrible affront to the dignity of the recipients. Not only did they have to clamber through the cold blizzard and up to the centre—and seeing one old, hungry woman slip over in the ice and crash pathetically into a snowdrift, her stick flailing about in a vain attempt to retrieve her balance, underlined the cruel realities of this situation—but they had to bare the most intimate details of their finances and then, once the precious stamps were in their hands, subject themselves to the harshest indignities when they presented them in the checkout line at the supermarket. 'The girls there can be really mean,' said one young woman who had been taking food stamps for the past two years. 'They look down at you like you're dirt when you take the book out of your purse. And everyone else in the line looks at you. They sort of say to themselves "she's out of money, she's down on her luck, how awful!",' and I can't say that's very pretty to go through each day. I try and shop when no one else is in the store, but you still have the checkout girls to go through.'

And the Government is not all that generous. Pamphlets given with the stamps warn they can only be spent on food. 'Freddie the Food Stamp', a cartoon character who, in an insultingly crude advertisement, explains the programme to potential recipients, warns gravely that 'I am for food . . . not for alcoholic beverages, beer, soap, detergents, cigarettes, paper towels and cosmetic items.' No one expects Government help to buy bottles of beer or the occasional packet of Lucky Strike—but no soap or detergent? 'I pay my last cents over to the Food Stamp people to get the allotment to buy food. Why can't I buy soap to wash, or powder to do the kids' clothes in? I don't have anything left to get those with, and I have to go round begging or borrowing them,' the young woman told me. The language too, is obtusely confusing: 'adverse action', 'non-assistance household', 'roomer' and 'verification' are on the long list of questions on the application forms: the same kind of harsh bureaucratic language that frightens and offends those people, here and in a thousand other American cities, who happen, invariably for reasons far removed from them, to be temporarily down on their luck.

Interstate 35 starts in the very centre of Duluth, when Superior Street, which in the town's heyday was as smart as Broadway, or

Sunset Boulevard, turns into a four-lane overpass which lifts up above the crowded, lorry-infested dockside streets beside the ore terminals. There is a brief confusion as US 53 leaves us, bound for the neighbour city of Superior, Wisconsin, and to points east and south; and then the Interstate comes into its own. Four white lanes, free from all obstruction, limited by law to cars and lorries and large motor cycles, open only for entry and exit at often irritatingly distant points. From here, the road stretches smooth and almost uninterrupted to the Mexican border, a spectacular testimony to the power and efficiency of American will and engineering.

From the city of Duluth and the Wisconsin border it was just about one hundred easy and unspectacular miles to the next staging post—the glittering, enviably successful stars of the North, the Twin Cities of Minneapolis and St. Paul. You could see them from twenty miles away—dominating everything, a single spire of a structure, black as ink with an abruptly flashing light on the very top: the IDS building, tallest structure between Chicago and San Francisco, a monument to the steady prosperity and growing importance of these Capitals of the Prairies.

More than any other city in America, with the possible exception of San Francisco itself, Minneapolis has managed to achieve a reputation as 'a city that works'. It seems that everyone who has been there loves it; everyone who has not, scorns it as cold, dull and backward. It probably is a city worth loving: it is without a doubt one of the most climatically disastrous towns in the nation; but it is never dull, and is probably as forward and revolutionary a city as any other in the world.

American cities are in a sorry state. Most now are exceedingly ugly—John Gunther reckoned Knoxville, Tennessee, the worst; while Birmingham, Alabama, is my own special hell-hole—and many are chronically unsafe. The reasons for their decline are by now well known: the increasing affluence of the middle classes allows them to live some miles away from where they work, in the suburbs, from where they commute—the word, derived from the old phrase for a season ticket, 'commutation ticket', is still very young—to their offices in 'downtown'. Those who remain in the central city then tend to be the poor and, often, the black. The frenetic activity that speculators enjoy results in the demolition of much of the central core of houses, and then replacement by massive office blocks, driving the few poor inner-city dwellers into smaller and smaller enclaves: they become virtually the sole inhabitants of echoing canyons of glass and concrete during the night, and the suburban people, accustomed to staying within their social territory, rarely stray in to rub shoulders with them. Shopping, theatre-going and the trivia of café society do not take place within the suburban rings of confidence: the inner city, except for the day-time working hours, appears to be sickly and dying. A hundred once-proud centres have followed this classical pattern of decay: St. Louis, Detroit, Toledo, Indianapolis and Nashville among them. All are problem centres, many are already urban basket cases.

But not so Minneapolis. For some reason that continues to mystify social scientists from all corners of the United States, the Twin Cities that span the narrow, cliff-edged Mississippi River work, and work well. St. Paul still has some problems; Minneapolis, in spite of having succumbed in part to the seeming inevitability of suburban flight, is still a pleasant and a peaceful landmark, where one can walk at night without particular concern, where one can shop and see the theatres and the art galleries and the concert halls, and where there are children and smiling policemen and flowers and grass and sky and all those other attributes that make Paris and London and Copenhagen the truly civilised centres they still manage to be.

How has Minneapolis managed it? One basic reason is that, unlike so many other Midwestern cities, Minneapolis is a headquarters for dozens of important, wealthy and prosperous corporations. Kansas City and Columbus, Ohio, important Midwestern cities though they may be, are still only 'branch towns', in which the corporations that inhabit their big office blocks do so only at the behest of corporate headquarters in far distant places like New York, or Los Angeles, or London. Minneapolis, though, is the all-important city of the plains—a railhead, a bridging for the Mississippi, a milling, banking and insurance city upon which an entire region—the flat, productive plains lands that stretch from the Mississippi River clear through to the Montana Rockies—depends for its market, its money and its machinery. Minneapolis is to the plains as Chicago is to the true Midwest, New York is to the East, San Francisco is to the West and Denver is to the mountain states—an essential pivotal point that has sucked the power away from all the rest of the competition.

So the buildings in the central city are those belonging to the giants of the plains: the food mastodons of Pillsbury, General Mills and Hormel; Honeywell and Univac and the Control Data Corporation, the leaders among Middle Western computer makers; and most important of all, the Ninth Federal Reserve District Headquarters, the pre-eminent money suppliers of the region. Architects of considerable talent have been brought to the city—Minoru Yamasaki, who created the World Trade Center in Manhattan (and by contrast the disastrous Pruitt-Igoe apartments in St. Louis) came in to design the superb, soaring Northwest National Life Insurance Company; the Federal Reserve Building, its exterior entirely plated with gold reflecting glass, is one of America's most spectacular office towers. The Tyrone Guthrie Theatre is the Middle American's best venue for drama; the new Concert Hall is reckoned to be the apotheosis of acoustic excellence, and in consequence attracts to Minneapolis artists of talent and achievement from all over the world: Rostropovich was playing while I was in town, the London Symphony was booked for a week or so later.

Time magazine wrote a cover story about Minnesota in 1973, to the mixed pleasure and embarrassment of the local people and their government who felt, probably justifiably, that the writer had saturated his prose with too much saccharine. The opening paragraph of the account was one of the best:

On an August Saturday afternoon, the scene is a slice of America's Norman Rockwell past. Barefoot children play one old cat and race their wagons down gently sloping sidewalks. Under the overhanging oaks, their fathers labour with hand mowers and rakes. On one lawn up the street, a rummage sale is in progress. Station wagons, laden with children, groceries, dogs and camping equipment, and trailing boats, slide out of driveways, heading north for a week or two at the lake.

It could as well be Little Rock, Ark., or Great Barrington, Mass., or Portland, Ore., for the nation is in its easier summer rhythms. But the setting is in the north side of Minneapolis, in Minnesota, where the Rockwell image pertains with a special consistency. If the American good life has anywhere survived in some intelligent equilibrium, it may be in Minnesota.

Charles Krusell, the Director of the Greater Minneapolis Chamber of Commerce, and one of the city's most prominent professional 'boosters' agreed that one basic reason for this town's uncanny success where so many failures litter the routes to and from it, is its siting as a headquarters centre. 'It's gratifying that we don't have to rely here on decisions made in New York all the time, that's certainly part of it. But there's more. There is the extraordinary philanthropy of the businessmen here—the big department store owners, for instance, have contributed huge sums to building things here like the Guthrie Theatre—they look on it not so much as an investment, but as part of their civic duty, and that's both unusual and encouraging. The politicians are rather progressive too [in Gunther's time he was able to dismiss Minneapolis as 'milling, Scandinavian, Republican by-and-large'] and with a city government structure that denies power to the elected mayor and gives it instead to a city council chairman who is elected by the council. He is the man who holds the power—a European concept, I guess, and one that's worked pretty well here. The taxation is very high—that keeps a lot of people who might want an easier life out—and the way the government is arranged there are enough checks and balances to make sure that every proposal is given a thorough airing before it becomes a fact. The civil service is hard-working and dedicated too. Altogether, the money, the Democratic government, the excellent professionalism and the dedication, and we have a really good mix. It's almost a certain formula for success.'

There are minorities in Minneapolis—blacks and Indians—but their neighbourhoods are so organised that there are majorities of white people in both, and integration has become a fact that prohibits the creation of ghettos. Crime is extremely low, in part, Krusell says, 'because of the character of these Scandinavians—very gentle, very honest'. The citizenry is unusually well informed, and unusually active and concerned. Unemployment in the recession of 1975 was mercifully lower than elsewhere. The air is pure, the transport system is excellent, there are streets given over entirely to bicycles, and there are so many parks that every eighty of the city's 434,000 people can expand in one acre of city parkland, even if they never bothered to explore the millions of acres of unspoiled Minnesota that begin twenty minutes from the city centre. There are twenty-two lakes inside the city limits too, and waterfalls that enchanted Longfellow, among others.

But however enthusiastic one might be about it, Minneapolis is not another London or another Dublin. It is attractive, but not spectacularly so; it is civilised, but only just (thirty-nine of its citizens were murdered there in 1974); and after dark its central area is only slightly less unfriendly a wasteland than in the neighbouring cities of the midlands. It is about the best America has to offer, and yet it is very far indeed from the ideal. Charles Krusell agrees it is not, in the real sense, a Great City. 'For the middle classes it is a fine place. They all have their boats and their lake cottages, and they can all work here pleasantly enough during the week and then take off north in the summer each weekend and get away to some peace and quiet. The highways are packed end to end with cars and boats. While they're up there they can hunt for grouse and pheasant and deer; they can fish and sleep and drink and forget. But that's not really saying Minneapolis is a successful city, is it? It's just saying the country's great and so it's quite a good place to be based. The Guthrie Theatre and the Concert Hall are grand— but they are fine for just a few of the middle classes only. They give us a name—but they don't do much about the problems we are bound to have, and that worries me a bit. In the Twin Cities' metropolitan area we have two million people just now. That seems to be the break-even number—the taxes pay for just the right amount of service, the crowding is just about bearable.'

'But we are growing, both of us, and in a while we'll be pushing two and a half million, and then three, and then four million. At that point I am pretty darned concerned things are going to start to go wrong. I can't in all honesty see a great future in the long term: England seems to have this power to make big cities work. We don't, and I'm not sure we can with this place either, no matter how nice it seems now.'

And on Watergate, Mr. Krusell said just: 'I think it helped the country. Nixon was showing us how powerful the Presidency can become, and how too much power can be bad for one man. I think it has helped us all that Watergate happened, and this post was cut down to size a bit.' Mr. Krusell is a Democrat. His father came from Scandinavia and worked on the Duluth railroad, shipping timber from across the Canadian line. He would have felt the same about Nixon, his son believes.

It would be unfair to leave with a bad impression of the city of

54

Minneapolis: the predominant feeling of students of the American urban condition is one of concern that this proud experiment above all, does not fail.

One outstandingly successful feature of the city that should proceed from success to success is the best of the six excellent local broadcasting stations, WCCO, which Neal Pierce describes as 'one of the most influential local stations in the country'.

WCCO-TV, the affiliate in the Twin Cities of the CBS network, is, unwittingly and perhaps unrecognisably, the most famous television station in America—perhaps in the world. It was used as the model for that distillate of middle-class situation comedies, *The Mary Tyler Moore Show*. Miss Moore, an actress who has become the electronic *alter ego* of the suburban housewife, plays herself, a producer of a medium-time evening news programme beamed out from studios in the centre of Minneapolis—chosen, one assumes, because the city is so decidedly typical of all that is best about the middle-class situation. WCCO-TV still has to endure the monthly arrival of a film crew from Burbank who come to find and film some newsroom atmosphere to inject into the show; and Minneapolitans—for that is what they call themselves these days—see Miss Moore occasionally acting in the most peculiar manner in front of cameras parked on their city streets. The city is probably grateful to have the exposure and WCCO is amused, though perhaps a trifle embarrassed, with having itself parodied as a not entirely successful news station from coast to coast.

Because WCCO really is successful. Ron Handberg, the news director, controls a newsgathering staff of fifty, and has 'no budget —that's what makes it so great'. The station sells so much advertising he can spend money with something approaching impunity, 'though I do call the boss and tell him—just out of courtesy, you know—if I'm hiring a new reporter.' For the three news programmes each day—one at lunchtime, one at teatime and a final late-night half-hour show just at the end of prime time—he has thirty reporters and cameramen. An eight-man documentary team produces a single film a week for a half-hour show on Sundays. The high-rollers on the team get sent to such news centres as Belfast and Bangladesh, to rub shoulders with the televisual news giants from CBS and NBC, and with the reputed lords of the airwaves, the BBC.

He has hired an Indian—Tom Beaver is apparently his real name—and one black reporter to reflect the racial make-up of the city; he is concerned, though, that the 'tokenism' that extends to some television and radio stations will lead to a lowering of standards of news reading, reporting and presenting. He is concerned that his station's reputation for providing the national networks with men and women is maintained. At the time I saw him, WCCO alumni were holding down jobs as the CBS White House Correspondent, Bonn Correspondent, London Correspondent, and ABC's Hong Kong Bureau Chief; the redoubtable Eric Severeid, who editorialises on CBS Evening News and Harry Reasoner of the ABC equivalent, both came to early fame on the station.

Minneapolis has shown what we can give to the outside world in terms of politicians and academics (seven of the University of Minnesota staff are Nobel prize-winners). Handberg says 'Our job is to show what a great town this is for newsmen. It's a reputation I intend to keep up.'

As I drove south on the Interstate again, away from the Twin Cities and the Mississippi River, which had by now turned east, bound for St. Louis and its junction with the mighty Missouri, I could hardly avoid seeing that tallest skyscraper in the rear-view mirror—a giant, lozenge-sectioned dark tower, fifty-seven storeys tall, looming high above the other office blocks of Minneapolis and the older, more genteel hotels and Capitol structures in St. Paul. It seemed something of an omen for the town that has done so very well on the big money and big ideas of the plains states. For the big skyscraper belongs to a massive, multi-million-dollar mutual fund conglomerate named Investors Diversified Services, Incorporated. And IDS, as the owner is known throughout Minneapolis, is not a Great Plains concern at all. Its headquarters are in the city of New York.

Within fifty miles of I-35, across to the east, is the city of Rochester—not strictly within the terms of this account, so no place to dwell. But Rochester is the home of the Mayo Clinic—a remarkable medical centre that is, for all its excellence, no more than one of the world's largest group practices, inhabited by hundreds of doctors on thirteen floors of the biggest country skyscraper in the state, and holding a medical records system of a complexity unparalleled anywhere. The Mayo is not just for the wealthy of the world, though: the Mayo brothers founded their clinic for the people of the plains, and it is these Middle Americans, when they fall very ill, who make most use of its remarkable facilities. While I was on this journey I met two ordinary country people, far from wealthy, who had been, or were about to go to the Mayo. One was a girl who took her mother there from Burlington, Iowa, after doctors in her home town had said there was little more they could do to help with her chronic heart condition, and the other was a store owner from a tiny village in northern Kansas who had had a mild stroke. The lady from Burlington was fully cured; the wife of the Kansas man had total faith in the ability of the 900 doctors in Rochester. 'They are wonderful people up there,' she said. 'We folks out here are lucky to have such a place. We've the best hospital in the world right in our own backyard.'

Her 'backyard' was bigger than most. She had to put her husband on a plane in Kansas City and fly him, via Ozark Airlines and North Central Airlines and a change at Minneapolis International, to the little airfield at Rochester. 'But it's worth it—the plane fare, the hotel bill, his doctors' bills. It's worth it to know he'll be quite all right when he comes home.' (He did come home, I heard later on. And he was entirely better.)

Speeding tickets, thanks to America's long tradition of 'states rights', must be considered an unavoidable expense of the journey for almost every long-distance drive. Since President Nixon introduced the federal speed limit of 55 miles an hour in an effort—and a successful effort, it should be added—to conserve petrol, there has been, for the first time ever, a nationwide ceiling on the speed a motorist can drive. Before 1973 there were wild variations: in the crowded highway lanes of New Jersey and California the police would insist that you did no more than 55; in the vast deserts of Utah and Arizona, you could quite happily cruise at 70 m.p.h., and speeding tickets rarely came your way if you stayed below about 85. But since the oil embargo of the 1973–4 winter, things have changed, and motorists are faced with the new phenomenon of extremely tough state highway patrols and fierce adherence to the speeding laws.

Officer Farrington of the Minnesota Highway Patrol really was a very pleasant gentleman, even though the big, black boyscout hat, fringed with gold braid, that topped out his six feet four inches, made him look just a mite intimidating. He had been parked about a quarter of a mile below the summit of a low hill, he said, for about half an hour, enjoying the sunshine in Rice County, Minnesota. Beside him was a device that flashed electronic numbers on to a screen: it was connected to a long, black horn-shaped instrument, the size and shape of an old ear-trumpet, that was mounted beside him, pointing backwards and out of his rear window.

As my car crested the summit, the black, horn-shaped instrument picked up the reflections that a radar beam, emitted by a small transponder above it, created when it collided with my front bumper. The reflection was travelling faster than the outward beam, of course, because my car was travelling fast along the road: the difference between the speed of the outward beam and its reflection was calculated instantaneously by the device that flashed numbers beside Officer Farrington's right hand. The figures that flashed up in my case read '68', and their being in excess of the stipulated 55, set off an alarm whistle in the Highway Patrol cruiser. Officer Farrington looked up at the figure, cursed under his breath, folded away his paper and opened his driver's door.

I was gunning along down I-35, minding my own business, looking out for patches of ice on the freeway, hurrying down to my next stop fifty miles away before darkness closed down. Ahead, on my side of the road, was a parked car. The door was opening I noticed—was someone in trouble? Could I lend a hand, I wondered? Ah yes, he seemed to want something, he was waving me down— pretty fiercely, too; big chap, I thought, and wearing a funny sort of hat. . . .

Officer Farrington asked me to bring my driving licence and come up and join him in his cab. I did *know* I had been doing 68, didn't I? And I did *know* the federal speed limit was 55, didn't I? And I did *realise* that the Minnesota Highway Patrol took speeding seriously, didn't I?

Up in his car it was warm and cosy. The Sunday paper was folded to one side, the car radio burbled unintelligible messages from time to time, probably telling Officer Farrington where his colleagues were. He had radioed in that he had a blue Volvo station wagon, Tag Number MS 6698, in front of him for what is known as a 'moving violation'. He assumed nothing was known; the suspect seemed an ordinary sort of person.

He chatted amiably enough as he filled in the buff form. What was I doing here, so far from home. Writing a book, eh? You'll put this in, won't you—and be kind, I'm only doing my duty, you know. And anyway, I'm sure you agree people shouldn't speed: it's not patriotic, and it's not safe either. The whistle sounded: a big, red Buick coming up behind at 59—let him go, Officer Farrington said, you're much worse than he is. Did I know the Governor of Minnesota, Mr. Andersen, he asked: I was his personal bodyguard for two years, you know, really grand guy, one of the best. His orders, you know—stop everyone going over 60 and give them a ticket. I think he's right, too. Now what's the colour of your eyes?

And down all the data went—weight (in pounds—always very difficult to work out), address, licence number, colour of hair, date of birth, type of road, type of pavement (by this they mean 'road surface', not to be confused with 'sidewalk', which means pavement), was the accident fatal, did the alleged offence take place in a manner or under circumstances so as to endanger or be likely to endanger any person or property—the patrolman circled NO. And that was that: would I sign a declaration that I would be in touch with the court at Faribault, Minnesota, on or before April 16th ('I'll give you plenty of time, seeing as you're from so far away'), and please drive safely in future.

I read the ticket in detail later: it alleged that I had violated Statute Number 169.141. 'In such case made and provided, and against the peace and dignity of the State of Minnesota.' Reading that was far worse than the $20 the judge eventually fined me: the 'peace and dignity' of such a splendid state should not be disturbed, and I was a low fellow for doing so.

Minnesota, then, is a state where speeding laws are invoked more or less to the letter. And yet I had driven to Minneapolis, earlier in the year, direct from Washington, D.C. at speeds well in excess of 80: no one in Indiana or West Virginia had bothered— and patrol cars elsewhere were so brightly coloured and in such obvious positions it was not difficult to avoid capture. The application of federally defined laws is very much up to the states themselves: woe betide a speeding motorist in Minnesota, and a few other states besides. Elsewhere, live free.

Minnesota is one of the few states where a motorist's word is accepted that he will turn up in court to take his medicine. Some states require the speeder to pay—in a sealed envelope—a 'bond' of as much as $100 to guarantee their attendance. In Washington state one time, I was asked for $120 cash, or else 'your car will be impounded—and we don't take cheques'. Luckily in that case the policeman relented. In other states, like Arkansas, local officials may subject the motorist to the mercies of a hastily summoned kangaroo court. One driver told me how he had been stopped in a remote Arkansas county by two patrolmen: he was arrested and taken to the local judge's house where the sleepy-looking official heard the evidence from the policemen, turned to the motorist and said simply 'Fifty dollars or a night in goal.' The driver spluttered a protest—whereupon the judge retorted: 'Make that sixty—ten extra for contempt, and I don't want to hear another word!' The motorist paid up in full, and left: he vows he will never drive through Arkansas again.

A few miles south of the spot Officer Farrington had chosen to entrap anyone assaulting the peace and dignity of his state was the turnoff for the small town of Northfield, one of Minnesota's most appealing little country communities made famous by events both good and bad.

The bad event was the infamous raid, by the Jesse James Gang, on the town's principal bank. It took place one hundred years ago, in September 1876; and it was the raid that, while sparing the life of Jesse and his brother Frank, put an effective end to the rule of terror he and his colleague desperadoes of the Bob Younger gang had imposed upon Missouri and all points north for very nearly two decades. Every summer the people of Northfield hold the 'Defeat of Jesse James Days', during which the romantic recollections of the raid on the First National Bank of Northfield are played to their rose-tinted hilt. James and his boys had killed the cashier, the story goes, after he had politely declined to open the safe. A shopkeeper next door, hearing the commotion, called out the good citizens of the town, and a furious battle ensued down on Main Street. Contemporary accounts make the fight sound more like a riot, with sticks and chunks of rock used as weapons as well as shotguns and Colt pistols. But the end was, for the Northfielders, satisfactory: one of the gang was killed there and then, and a village posse found most of the rest in a muddy creek nearby, and killed another and arrested the remainder. The final score was three gangsters dead, three sent to prison for life, and Bob Younger and the James boys forced into a hiding from which they never really emerged again.

Postcards of the dead men can be bought at the drugstores in town, and guides will show you bullet holes in the walls of the First National Bank. The faded brown daguerreotypes show the men with their eyes wide open: they were held there with pins, it is said, to increase the drama of their appearance.

The famous Northfield Raid is not the only contribution the neat country town has made to the good order of American life. There are also two universities (or colleges as they are known in America, since neither has a school for graduates) both of which are very good, and one of which is nationally outstanding.

The good college of the two is St. Olaf's—one of a chain of Lutheran institutions that dot the Midwest and provide a sound Christian education for the sons and daughters of the devout Scandinavians of the prairies. It seeks quite unashamedly to give 'quality higher education from the viewpoint of the Christian faith', and all of its 2,700 undergraduates are required to take three courses in religion ('of which not more than one may be a non-Christian religion') during their stay. Churchgoing is encouraged, and Jewish students, while not the subject of any discrimination, are politely informed that the nearest synagogue is forty miles away. St. Olaf's has one of the Midwest's best touring choirs; it had on its teaching staff for many years one O. E. Rolvaag who, a guide says, 'wrote *Giants in the Earth* in Norwegian which became an American best-seller after its translation into English.'

The excellent institution in Northfield is Carleton College—one of a dozen or fewer private, expensive, small and very exclusive four-year colleges in the country, and of those perhaps the second or third-ranking across the nation.

The tradition of the small, liberal arts college is a long one in America, and their contribution to society has been considerable. They form a bridge between the ruthlessly high-powered centres of excellence like Harvard and Yale and Stanford, and the massive publicly funded establishments like the University of Michigan and the nine campuses of the University of California, where the pejorative term 'degree factory' seems most appropriate and students have become, inevitably, numbers rather than names. The small colleges have been a part of this tradition for more than a century, offering educational excellence at medium expense and with as great a degree of personal tuition and care as possible.

Americans can easily grade their hundreds of higher educational institutions in a number of degrees of selectivity: the highest grade of all, 'Most Selective' encompasses nearly all the colleges that are the sister establishments to Carleton: there is Bryn Mawr, in Pennsylvania; Oberlin, in Ohio; Pomona, in California; Amherst and Smith in Massachusetts; Beloit, in Wisconsin; and Antioch, in Ohio. If you are bright and middle-class, but perhaps not rich enough or bright enough to make the Ivy League, or perhaps not inclined to join the ranks of the Eastern liberal establishment by 'going Ivy'; and if you feel you can buy yourself a better passport to the good life with an investment now rather than a cheap education at a big state school, then the small liberal arts college is for you. That is what the middle classes have been saying for the past fifty years; and that has enabled the private college to become one of the most lucrative of business possibilities around.

At least, that was true—until about the beginning of the 1970s. Now the small private college is in decline. Students—whose numbers have diminished, thanks to the safe passage of the post-war 'baby boom'—are increasingly difficult to snare. Classrooms are emptying, costs are rising, fees, inevitably, are having to go up to astronomical levels. At Carleton, for example, parents in 1974 had to find $4,200 a year for each son or daughter who enrols. 'Students are held responsible for the payment of their college fees,' the *Carleton College Bulletin* notes on page 140. 'The first term bill is mailed before school opens to the student and the parent, and second and third term bills are sent to the student. However, in cases of postponed account settlement . . .' and so the explanation sets in—a distinctly non-academic reminder that Carleton and Haverford and Oberlin and all the rest, no matter how lofty their aims and ideals, are businesses; and as the man said 'There ain't no such thing as a free lunch.' Fees at Carleton were expected to rise 10 per cent in 1975, and there was little prospect that the inflationary spiral in education would end during the decade.

The combined effects of the declining numbers of students and the increasing costs have driven a number of private colleges out of business already. High-school students, particularly the brighter ones, are now deluged with offers they can hardly refuse from all manner of private establishments from Maine to Hawaii. College publicity is a field now handled by the most adept of advertising agencies, with the result that Carleton, for example, offers prospective high-school leavers such perfume-dressed invitations as 'The Carleton Experience' which, among a heady diet of hazy photographs of beautiful young co-eds strolling hip-deep through long meadow grass, books in hand, Great Thoughts in head and Prospects before them, sets such gems as: 'Just as you might find a professor leading an early morning bird-watching group, so you might find a student teaching a professor a new wrinkle in computer programming, the intricacies of using a video camera or the proper waxing technique for cross country skis.' Or again, in the appended letter from Mr. Howard Swearer, the President of the College, 'The liberal arts have never been more "relevant". An age of specialised professionalisation and technotronics needs the infusion of liberal learning stressing synthesis, individual development and humane values'—all of which can be assimilated in the 'total learning environment' and amidst that 'hard to define intangible campus spirit which combines restless criticism and inquiry with concern and community'.

Publicists set themselves up as sitting targets for ridicule, and their efforts in attempting to sell Carleton to that dwindling crowd of students should deserve more scorn than the college itself which is, in truth, both a beautiful and rewarding place in which to seek a higher education. There is opportunity to pick from a well-stocked orchard of topics. During the 1974 session a student could go to lectures on The Crafts of Writing, Functions of a Complex Variable, The Viola, Markov Chains and their Uses, The Socratic Turn and Figure Skating. An undergraduate could spend a year of his four at Lancaster University, the University of Leningrad or in Kyoto or Costa Rica. There is not, so far as I could find, a single course offered in agriculture, in spite of Carleton nestling agreeably in some of the finest, richest farmland in the entire United States. That topic, it was explained, is the territory of the state schools in the farming regions—the 'cow colleges', as they are called derisively.

Yet it is the 'cow colleges' and the Ivy League schools that are now prospering, while institutions like Carleton are fast becoming a moribund breed. States like to devote large shares of their tax revenues to the financing of educational establishments, and to a state like Minnesota the campuses of the state university, one of the best and biggest in the nation, is a continuing source of regional pride. Likewise the Federal Government feels more than happy to divert millions of dollars each year for research programmes performed at the well-known, highly regarded private universities— Yale and Harvard and the Massachusetts Institute of Technology each year reap billions in federal research funding that in effect endows their effort, builds them buildings, and attracts to them staff of a quality unbeatable in the less well-endowed centres. There is, in a sense, public funding at the two ends of the higher educational spectrum—but none at all in the centre. Carleton received $530,000 in highly restricted Government grants in 1974, from a total income of $10 million. The remainder has to come from either student fees, or, increasingly, from begging—though it would never be put so crudely—from wealthy graduates. In that same year the student body paid $6 million for the privilege of being educated at Carleton, and high-pressure cadging, coupled with unprompted largess from some alumni who felt an obligation to the alma mater, brought in over $1 million. It is not difficult to see that such financing is a knife-edge way of running an institution of such demanding costs: the precision of the 1974 calculation was such that the total profit of Carleton was a mere $20,000—precious little to plough back into the investment funds with which to weather the recession and the accelerating decline in probable applications.

But happily the very best—and Carleton is one such—will almost certainly survive. Although the only notable graduate of the college is Melvin Laird, who progressed from an undistinguished Vietnam-era Defense Secretary and confidant of Richard Nixon, to a senior executive for *Reader's Digest*—a staple read, incidentally, on Midwestern bedroom tables—the reputation of the college is built on providing a solid and competent middle level in the country's society. Like the other small colleges it produces few of America's movers and shakers; it does produce, however, vast legions of stabilisers and organisers, the pump-primers without which this country would fail with alarming speed. That being so, it is probably as well that small islands of middle-class privilege continue to exist, and that the students fortunate enough to populate them continue to be permitted the luxury of comfortable scenery, cosy old red-brick buildings and wood-smelling libraries like those offered at Carleton.

There was one other old man I met in Northfield who I find impossible to erase from my memory, though he had nothing to do with either St. Olaf, or Carleton, or the Jesse James Raid. He was, in fact a railwayman—retired after fifty years or so on the Minneapolis, Northfield & Southern Railway, where he had worked as a plateman and stationmaster. (The town, incidentally, is a small but nonetheless important railway centre. Driving in from the West, and from I-35, you must rumble over no fewer than seven not-quite-parallel sets of tracks; some belong to the MNS, others to the Chicago & Northwestern, the Chicago, Milwaukee, St. Paul & Pacific, and the rest to the famous, but bankrupt, Rock Island Line. With that number of rails serving a single farm town of 10,000 souls, small wonder some people lost their fortunes on the iron road.)

The old railwayman—he must have been seventy, at the very least, and was white-haired and grizzly faced—was, when I met him, tinkering with his motor cycle. And it was far from being an ordinary cloth-cap-and-sidecar motor cycle: it was a 'fully dressed' Harley Davidson Electra-Glide 1200, finished in white and silver and blue, with panniers and chrome sissy bars and some 5,000 miles on the clock. There were rubber-treaded foot pedals, a reverse gear and, of all things, running boards. It seemed a most unlikely motor cycle and, if the grizzly old man was its owner, a most unusual man.

He completed his tinkering after a moment or two, and then hoisted himself on top of the glittering monster. He moved his right hand over to what seemed to be the dashboard of the machine and pressed a small red button. After a second or so of deep-throated coughing, a rumbling roar began to scud slowly from within the bowels of the engine, and blue smoke from the cylinders fumed from the three-inch-wide exhaust pipes. The man flexed his left foot down on the pedal, kicked away a monstrously large foot-stand, and throbbed off down the road. He made a slow turn after a hundred yards or less, drove slowly back to the oily patch where he had been working, and killed the engine. Utter silence reigned again; the old man said 'Seems O.K. now—I'll just tighten it up,' and then knelt down to tinker some more.

His name was Cyril, he said. He was seventy-two and he had lived in Minnesota all his life. His passion, aside from railways, was motor cycles. He had two bikes now, the dressed Harley and the Honda 550 Four, which he showed me, parked in his garage amidst a forest of spanners and screwdrivers and cans of oil and grease and touch-up paint. He had been everywhere, he said, International Falls and Laredo, both ends of I-35, and just about every place in between. He was a big fan of motor-cycle fairings—both bikes had great white plastic mouldings bolted to the front, designed to keep rain and wind off, and all the speed on. 'I tell you,' he said, pointing over at the Honda, 'I've been at 65 on that down the freeway in a rainstorm so bad that the big rigs—the trucks—were having to pull off the highway. But I could ride just perfect—it's so good I didn't get wet at all—just two tiny patches up here on my shoulder, where a bit of the water drains upwards off the windshield.' The Honda, he said, had cost him $1,800; the Harley, which was two years old, had been $3,500—the price today was $4,400, he complained. He had one white seat already on the Harley, but another one—a soft leather seat with chrome guard rails around it— was hung up on the garage wall, a little dusty in places. Who was that for? I asked.

'Oh, that was for Jessie, my wife, you know. She died last Christmas.' I said how sorry I was. 'Yes, old Jessie and me used to ride just about everywhere, right from when we were courting. Our first bike was a big Triumph—the British made good bikes then— but all the years I dreamed of having a big Harley like the state police have. It took me until the middle sixties until I got my first, and I've not looked back since.'

'We never owned a car, you know—always bikes. At least, that was until Jessie persuaded me to buy her a little car for going up to the store. That was last summer, just after her sixty-eighth birthday. I got her a Pinto wagon, a Ford station wagon, but I complained about it quite a bit.

'Anyway, she was killed in the car, just before Christmas. It was only about four months old. Some fool was passing on a bend and ran right into her. They took her up to Minneapolis, but she was gone. He was all right. I guess that's the way it goes. If she'd been on the bike she would have avoided his car, you know. That's the thing about bikes—you can handle them so easy, turn them anyway you want real fast. She was killed because she was talked into getting a car. I really believe that's true.'

Cyril then told me the reason he had the two bikes. He still rode the Honda every day as a work-bike—he did all the shopping and went for occasional spins out to the freeway and back, if the weather was good enough. But the Harley was reserved solely for going up to the graveyard on a bluff outside town. 'I go up there every day. I guess it must seem kind of silly to an outsider, but we were very close and she loved that bike of ours. It's the best way I have of being good to her memory.' There was not much fun riding alone any more, he said—part of the fun is having a girl up on the back. He thought he'd sell the bikes later in the year.

To many who read *Main Street*, which Sinclair Lewis modelled unashamedly on his western Minnesota home town, Sauk Centre (which once thought it should rename itself Gopher Prairie, but then demurred for reasons its citizens will quickly explain), Minnesota is the archetype of Middle American stolidity and sullen, turgid agricultural ennui—weary, flat, stale and unprofitable, or, as Lewis himself put it, filled with 'the contentment of the quiet dead . . . dullness made God'.

Sauk Centre has changed a lot from the town Lewis painted, though its people rankle still at the insults hurled so gratuitously at them thirty years ago. The cinema has an inscription above it, written by Lewis on a later visit to the town: 'These are the portals of imagination. Recover hope, all ye who enter here.' And evidently a great number of Sauk Centre's people have been inside: for far from being the porcine and unimaginative little hamlet it was when Gopher Prairie was born, it is an entirely up-to-date agricultural and marketing town, the population unchanged numerically but, by virtue of such things as television, the Interstate freeway and the fast car, altered drastically from the ways Lewis so cruelly observed. The passenger trains no longer call at the town, so Carol Kennicott would have to drive there; and the airport merely serves to handle the crop-spraying aircraft. There is no local doctor so willing to make house-calls as Dr. Kennicott, but the people are as hard-working and neighbourly as they were thirty years back, and the town is a wholesome place to live. All that has really altered, it seemed, was the narrow-mindedness and the dull contentment. And the politics: in 1974 Sauk Centre, long thought a bastion of Republican ruralism, elected a Democrat to the Congress.

The reason for mentioning Sauk Centre, a long way west of the Interstate is to illustrate the way in which Minnesota has, perhaps uniquely in America, managed to hold on to what is good and worthy about its character, discard most of what was insufferable and contemptible, attract little of the new that is detrimental to good society and create a lot of what is enviable in a civilisation. The success of Minnesota as a state should not be exaggerated—there has been a tendency for Americans, during the immediate pre- and post-Watergate months, to look longingly towards the North Star state and see in it a fount of qualities that the rest individually or severally, appear to lack. It is a tendency that is understandable: a lot of things about Minnesota are unusually good, and a lot of features about the seamier states—like Maryland and New Jersey— are unquestionably bad. But Minnesota has, as Charles Krusell pointed out for the Twin Cities, its problems on the horizon; and the state too has its share of inequities and inadequacies, just like the other forty-nine.

One would never guess that, from reading the kind of literature being pushed out by the state's legions of promoters. A document put out by the state Department of Economic Development indicated that, after surveying all fifty state governments, the Midwest Research Institute had come to the conclusion that Minnesota was the second-best place in all America to live. The Institute's selection of the various criteria was not explained; but it felt able to say, after what was said to be 'extensive study', that Minnesota rated Number One in such fields as Equality and Health and Welfare; Number Three in Economic Growth; Number Four in its use of the Democratic Process; Number Nine in Education; Number Ten in the Status of the Individual and Living Conditions; Number 11.5 (the same as Wisconsin) in a topic entitled Technology Change and Number Nineteen in Agriculture. The complex arithmetic behind this and all the other respective ratings led Minnesota to be named Number Two nationwide, with only California rated above it. Number Fifty, it might be expected, was Mississippi.

Considering the state's population—at 3,805,000 it represents only 1.9 per cent of the American total—Minnesota has given a disproportionately massive amount of talent to the country. Hubert Humphrey—although his image has been a little tarnished in the wake of Watergate by veiled references to his cosy relations with those most unlikely-sounding villains, the milk producers— Walter Mondale and Eugene McCarthy all come from Minnesota. Two of the leading lights of the US Supreme Court, Warren Burger and Harry Blackmun, made their homes there, and William O. Douglas, the giant of the Court and one of the most irrepressibly radical old men left in America, was born in the hamlet of Maine, in the south of the state. Harold Stassen, perhaps the most able of all men who dearly wanted to be President, was, for three terms, one of the best governors any state has ever had. He was perhaps the best President America never had. There are many more—academics, men of letters and science, artists and writers and poets and newsmen among them—who have made Minnesota's mark upon the nation more indelibly than the nation has made its mark upon Minnesota. There is something about the place, one is constantly finding oneself saying; it is difficult to know precisely what that something is.

Probably the people, and the Scandinavian origins, contribute most of all. The weather, too, has an effect of binding all of the state's inhabitants into a solidly united brotherhood well versed in climatic adversity. The countryside's beauty, its stillness, its room, is a treasure that unites the people too, in appreciation for what good fortune they have, despite the problems of the 'outside' country. The closest parallel I could find in Britain is with the north-east of England: there, geography, climate, ethnic origin and economic hardship have welded a people, the Geordies, into one of the most likeable and independently minded tribes in the country, each intensely fond of his birthplace, but willing and able to contribute such talents as he can to the national good. Minnesotans are in many ways the Geordies of America—I'm sure they'd not object to the comparison. They even talk with a distinctive accent.

It is twenty miles back on to the freeway from Northfield—a short enough ride if you have a car, but far enough to make the four-lane to the Twin Cities quite out of reach of the students at Carleton who, car-less, are forced to the ruthless regimen of reading, talking and thinking. It seemed as fine a place as any for a college, I thought, as the car purred down the snowy road westwards to the freeway—a credit to Minnesota which, in turn, is a credit to the college.

From the Northfield exit it was just sixty miles to the state line. We passed line upon line of fir trees, acre upon unploughed acre of snowy fields, lake after frozen lake. (The state has issued all car-owners with number plates that say 'Land of 10,000 Lakes', although there are, according to the State Survey, 15,291 of ten acres or more.) Along the route was a series of small towns with names evocative of the proud eastern Yankees, or the first-generation immigrants from the north of Europe who settled here a century ago and less—Nerstrand, Faribault, Bixby, Blooming Prairie, Geneva, Twin Lakes, Hollandale, Albert Lea and Gordonsville. And there was the radio from the tall tower in Minneapolis, constantly booming out the news, the weather and the farm price reports. The *Time* correspondent who wrote so lyrically of the state in 1973 was struck, as I was during the journey, by the refreshing normalcy—a very Minnesota sort of word, it seemed—of the reported happenings. He had listened to the news report 'of snowmobile accidents, city council resolutions and a pronouncement by the Governor. It was intensely local'; and then he had gone back to where his magazine had its nearest bureau, in Chicago, and he listened to the news there. 'This version was also intensely local; it featured a series of scandals, murders, police corruption and so forth. I sat there astounded. After the short trip to the Twin Cities I suddenly realised that things did not have to be this way.'

Sadly, they still are. . . . Although the last sixty miles of Minnesota were dominated by news reports that offered little other than the parish-pump happenings that are so characteristic of a peaceful community, the nights I had been in the cities were filled with shrieking sirens and the news that a policeman had been shot and a young man and woman wanted. Desperadoes still come to Minnesota—these were said to be from Montana—and they were not inhibited in their misbehaviour.

One final note on snowmobiles. These fiendish devices, half motor cycle, half sledge, are rapidly becoming the bane of the Northerner's existence. There were well over 120,000 of them in Minnesota in 1974; and to be fair, they provide, with their speed and mobility and liking for travel across the deepest drifts and on the widest lakes, an entirely new answer to the travelling problems during the harshest months. But they are excessively noisy, frightening things that roar and snarl and rush through the once-peaceful forests and drench the pure snows of the countryside with oil and fumes and ear-splitting din. Most are made in the tiny north Minnesota town of Thief River Falls, whose townsfolk are happily rich in the wake of the snowmobile boom. The products of the village now go to the nineteen states that fall within the Northern Snow Belt, and have, without a doubt, provided fun and freedom in almost equal amounts.

The National Wildlife Federation is now trying to have them banned, however—contending, among other things, that the eighty-five decibels of the unsilenced engine can easily break a human eardrum, and will do much more damage to the innocent animals of the Minnesota woods. In winter, the Federation says animals are at a low physical ebb: snowmobiles could easily shock them and kill them by frightening them to death. The earthy pragmatists of Minnesota are seeing their way to dealing with the device that is at once a menace and a miraculous invention: they are having them banned at night and at certain times of day, and restrict them to running on only certain of the snow slopes around the state's communities. Thief River Falls, needless to say, will neither ban nor restrict the creatures, except from the city centre at the very busiest times of day.

But, snowmobiles aside, and worries for the future forgotten for the moment, I came away from Minnesota glad to have seen it and stayed in it, enchanted by its people, its stillness and its countryside, impressed by its government, by its cities and by its politicians. It is a fine example of how America should have, or could have developed, over the last twenty years: from America the state must learn, before it is too late, the type and size of the pitfalls into which it may so easily drop. Otherwise it will not be too long before Minnesota is just like everywhere else, and that would be a sad loss to all concerned.

3

Iowa:
Vegetables, with Mineral Connections

'Control corn rootworm: With Dyfonate 20-G insecticide. Ideal for the big corn grower!' The words, a foot high and painted red, were emblazoned on the first billboard I saw once the flat snowy plains of southern Minnesota had given way to the flat snowy plains of northern Iowa, and they left no doubt at all about what really fascinates and obsesses the people of this ostensibly unremarkable state. 'Iowa spells agriculture,' wrote John Gunther, 'and agriculture in this part of the world spells corn.'

America's celebrated Corn Belt, like its Bible Belt away to the south and east, is a great deal larger than one might expect. The precise combinations of sun, wind and soil required to give the tall, leafy plants their best chance to thrive occur in a vast swathe that cuts across the plains and the prairies and the hills of western Appalachia, from South Dakota, by way of Nebraska, northern Kansas, Missouri, Iowa, Illinois, Indiana and through to central Ohio. Within ten miles of the smoky and almost eastern industrial town of Cleveland are fields of corn, looking for all the world like the fields that lie within ten miles of that quintessentially western town of Omaha, Nebraska. Corn is a great leveller, so far as national identities of the midlands are concerned.

In Britain, the word 'corn' is used generically, to indicate the major cash crop of the region—so that in England, corn is wheat; in Scotland it is barley; and in Ireland it is oats. In the Corn Belt, the word is used specifically, and the tall plant that stands stiffly in endless rows for mile upon regimented mile is true corn—though Englishmen will call it maize—that sports the small, hard kernels of white, or orange, or yellow hue.

No other agricultural product—except, perhaps, the humble pig—has ever managed to become so deeply associated with the unkinder views of the men and women who grow it. Thus Iowa, which grows more of the stuff—900 million bushels a year, creating an industry worth nearly $3,000 million a year—is said to be corny, its people are noted for being cornballs, or else they are rudely referred to as corn-crackers. Corn-cob pipes, corn-pone, corn-shucking are Iowa terms that immediately tell the haughty Easterner that his prejudices about the region were quite correct—that Iowa is dull, tedious, limited in excitement as its people are limited in imagination and outlook. 'Aw, shucks!' a New Yorker will mimic the angry Iowa farmer, and raise a laugh in any bar in town.

But of course the Easterner's stereotype is wrong, and sadly so. True, the precise mix of Grade A topsoil—and Iowa's fortunes with glaciers and limestone have given it 26 per cent of the country's very best soil; some of it is so good Robert Frost once said 'It looks good enough to eat without putting it through vegetables'—and sun, quick summer rainstorms and long, lazy drying and growing days have given the state a massively satisfying abundance of grain. The satisfaction permits the state the kind of stability that breeds political conservatism and, a New Yorker might think, a tendency to dullness. But my tours of the region turned up, aside from the very kindest and most fascinating of all American farmers, men whose financial wizardry and typically Midwestern mechanical bent had made them vast fortunes overnight; men who produced neutron streams with the facility and enthusiasm they are produced in scientific laboratories at Berkeley and Oak Ridge; university students who read the London and Paris papers every day for journalism courses and were better equipped to talk about the Official Secrets Act and the 'D' Notice system than I; and one of America's only two factories where atom bombs are bolted together and stockpiled for the armed services to place inside their arsenals. There is a great deal more to Iowa than corn; there is a great deal more, and a great deal better, than plain country-boy conservatism; and there has been enormous and imaginative advantage taken of the benefits that agricultural prosperity has given to this remarkable little state.

Ten miles south of the Minnesota state line the Interstate runs out into a field and, for forty miles, the trucks and cars are shuffled a couple of miles westward and on to US Route 69, which the Interstate was designed in this part of the world to replace. The diversion takes you past a dozen little towns and villages so typical of the plains, delightful, with their red-washed mills, their small, brown churches, the clapboard houses and the ring of sturdy farms, with barns and byres and tall metal corn-driers looming over the low trees, a few hundred yards out from the dusty main street. These small towns, though, are a dying breed; the buildings are becoming dilapidated, the streets a litter of rusty cars, the shops dusty and rat-ridden, with grimy windows and little in the way of stock. The fresh-painted, tidy, clean-cut appearance of the farm villages in Vermont contrasts sharply with the rather pathetic un-kemptness of so many small Iowa villages, and the reason is simple. In Vermont, family ties are strong enough and farms efficient enough for the small communities to continue to survive: in Iowa, as more and more people leave farming to the businessmen—for nowadays the term increasingly in use is 'agribusiness', and farms increasingly are run by corporations, not single families—so the very smallest towns are on the verge of extinction, rather like the small towns in County Durham in the aftermath of the coal boom. County seats in Iowa are doing well enough, and some towns, like Ames and Waterloo (which, strange for Iowa, had race troubles in the late 1960s. It is about the only country town with any Negroes—the remainder of the state is traditionally a WASP stronghold still) have grown rapidly in the past decade, sucking people in from the villages for miles around and consolidating them under the shadows of the supermarkets and the petrol stations where they would be forced to drive to from wherever they live. The supermarket and the car have forged as dramatic a revolution in the movement of population in rural mid-America as any decline in numbers on the old family farm.

The first town of any consequence that Route 69 passes through in northern Iowa is Forest City (although Mason City is only just bypassed: it is where the jolly song of the 1960s, 'Seventy-Six Trombones', was written, and where marching bands are so much a way of life all Main Street appears to walk in time). Forest City is a town that, until ten years ago displayed every single symptom of rural decay, but which has since, for an unusual reason and thanks to the efforts of a very unusual man, turned into one of the most interesting success stories of mid-America for years. There are concerns about the success, though, as we shall see.

Back in the late 1950s, when the increasing mechanisation of America's farms triggered the drift from the land that we see so widely today, Forest City, a town of 1,200 or so people, older and less vital than many of its neighbours, was on the verge of succumbing to a possibly terminal disease. The economy was wasting away, men were without jobs, the welfare system pervaded the shabby streets and the peeling houses. In one final effort, a gaggle of remaining businessmen formed a group which would try to sell the benefits of Forest City—its clean, fresh, somewhat staid and old-fashioned styles of life, and its worthy and willing labour force—to the outside world. In 1958 came the group's first, and only success —one that very rapidly stumbled into what seemed destined to be a doubly unkind failure.

At that time, caravans—or travel trailers, as Americans call them—were still popular, especially in the West, and the summer roads would be choked with lines of cars towing in their wake outlandish, space-age vehicles in which the comforts of home life could be safely carried around and transplanted to the prettier and less-crowded sections of the continent. A small California caravan company with the ungainly title of Modernistic Industries was wanting to hawk its product in the Midwest, and in 1968 accepted Forest City's generous offer of a site, a tax break and the readily available work-force. A small plant was built, a few hundred of the townsfolk were hired and then, for a few short months, prospects for Forest City appeared to have taken a turn for the better.

It was, however, a cruel mistake. Modernistic Industries found that they could not make money in Iowa with the ease and speed it could be made out in California; they were not willing to invest the time and effort needed to succeed in a region less obviously suited to them than the sunny Pacific shores. And so, instead of persevering, they left—a departure about which Iowans still feel both bitter and cynical: a commentary, many saw it, on the fickleness and greed of Far Westerners.

But Forest City was able to prove the California directors wrong in their suppositions. Within a few weeks the local undertaker and owner of the town's principal furniture shop, John Hanson, asked to buy the empty plant. He cadged a few thousand dollars from friends and store-owning colleagues on the main street, set a few of the newly unemployed men to work building caravans again, and changed the name of his factory to an unusual Indian tribal title: Winnebago. He had seventeen employees, and, after he had bought the plant, $100 in the bank.

John Hanson is the perfect example of what Gunther described as the 'gadget mind'—a feature, purportedly unique to Midwesterners and New Englanders, that sprang from every farm boy's absolute necessity to learn just how to bang and bend metal to make his father's tractors and ploughs and elderly family car keep on running. It seems that every Midwestern child—at least those born in the country—knows how to tinker effectively with everything mechanical, from the bedroom clock to the Chevrolet carburettor. Out in the isolation of the plains farm, tinkering was the only way of getting recalcitrant machinery to work again: you couldn't exactly ring up and ask the service man to pop over—it might take him a day's hard driving to get to you. John Hanson, then, was of this school: and it was appropriate that, by banging and bending metal, and meshing them together with an idea he had that towing a caravan behind a car was an ugly and impractical way of doing things, he was led to invent one of the boom vehicles of the 1960s, the 'motor home'. All across America, the name Winnebago, and the Flying W motif, is synonymous with motor homes—caravans with engines and a driving seat, basically—and the roads in summer time now present a never-ending stream of the craft, and those of the three hundred or so firms who joined battle with Hanson after realising the success of his invention. It was an important step: the creation of the motor home presaged another sharp diversion of the habits and tastes of America's astonishingly fast-changing society. All of a sudden it became possible for a family in Seattle, say, to drive off from home with all their comforts crammed into Mr. Hanson's invention, and tour 10,000 miles of America, eating, sleeping and playing cards without a single halt in the driving, except for petrol and water.

Petrol, unhappily, was to become the Achilles' heel of the operation.

By the late 1960s Winnebago had transformed the town of Forest City: from seventeen employees, Mr. Hanson and his son, John Jr., were running a plant with nearly 4,000 employees and a net worth of some $1 million. Those few Forest City storekeepers who had trusted John Hanson's judgement in 1959 were, by 1970, millionaires many times over. The peeling board houses of the town had been torn down, and gleaming new bungalows had gone up in their place. A country club had opened. The town had a brand new hospital and two new churches. In the early 1970s they were due to get a sports stadium—all courtesy of Winnebago, and Mr. Hanson.

But then came two problems—one foreseeable, the other quite unexpected. Firstly, like the man who tried to make a fortune selling the potato-peeler, John Hanson soon found that the market for his motor homes had a saturation point. By 1972 that point had been reached, and the production lines in the vast ('fifty-three football fields') factories began to slow. Men were laid off, a few at a time, but in a steady stream by 1973.

And while that was going on, the Arabian and other oil-producing nations imposed their oil boycott, and the bottom suddenly—literally overnight—fell out of the motor-home market. 'We were making 600 motor homes a day in early 1972. The day after the oil embargo was announced, the production lines stopped dead,' John Hanson says. 'We had to lay off the entire plant: there was virtually no work at all in Forest City. People just were not going to buy a vehicle from us, no matter how good it was, if it only did six or seven miles to every gallon of gas. We were sunk without trace, thanks to the Arabs.' Mr. Hanson, a bearded and extremely large man, banged his fist on his oak table when he talked of the Middle East. He had no doubt at all that the United States should invade the oil fields. 'If there was a situation where our industry had to make big cutbacks because of the Middle East we would simply have to go in. There's no two ways about it.' Hanson was optimistic about the future for his business, though he is now producing farm truck-bodies and small caravans to keep his production lines ticking over during the shortages. As people win more and more free time from work he believes they will want to explore the country, and get away from the cities and just relax—motor homes being 'ideal' for that kind of thing. But he was well aware that the kind of leisure now so abundant in Forest City—unemployment leisure—was not likely to lead to any rise in his sales; there had to be an economic recovery, and for that he was sorry Richard Nixon was not still in office.

'I would still vote for the guy if he ran again. I had confidence in him. What he did during his administration more or less coincided with my success here, and I figure he helped businessmen like me get going. I helped this town, didn't I? So Nixon helped this town, in a manner of speaking. The press, the Congress—they were all so wrapped up in this Watergate thing they couldn't spend any time looking after the economy, so look where we are now? This town is down in the dumps again, this business is doing pretty badly, the shares are down and a lot of people have lost money. But for the *Washington Post*, maybe I'd still be a happy man. No sir, I say bring Nixon back. He was tough and he was pretty good, and Watergate was just irrelevant. Everyone did that sort of thing—so why pick on Dick Nixon?'

It is a strange irony that Forest City's fortunes have changed so very radically in the past twenty years. From a prosperous little market centre it, like so many of its neighbours, fell victim to the combine harvester and the other mechanical energies of 'agri-business'. Then a local genius transformed the place, and over-night turned it into an oasis of wealth among the corn stalks. Now it seems well on the way to reverting to the status of its neighbours —an unkind blow if ever there was one. Little wonder Midwestern-ers are well aware of the externals of life—well aware of America's Middle East policy and of the politics in Washington, in this case— in stark contradiction to the traditional assumption back east or out on the west coast that the average Middle American is blind and deaf to everything that happens outside the confines of his own state, his own county, or his own town.

Time was when most immigrants to a state like Iowa were given, as part of the incentive to populate the windswept wastelands, a 'quarter section' of land to till. Cartographers and surveyors divided the flat land into mile-wide squares, with a six-mile-wide square for the townships each a day's buggy-ride or so apart. The rural mile-wide sections were then simply apportioned so that each potential farmer was given a quarter of it—160 acres of the best soil America has to offer—and was told, more or less plainly, to get on with it. Until about twenty years ago, the 'quarter-section farmers' proved the backbone of the Corn Belt's economy: there were hundreds upon hundreds of small, cosy, family farms, each ten miles or less from the market town where the farm implements were bought and the corn and soy beans were sold, and each run with little eye on big profits or expectations of big riches.

But then came inventions like the tractor and the combine and the mechanical tiller and the rotary bailer and nitrogen fertiliser, and as they prospered, so went the horse, and the quarter-section farm began to die out. Between 1930 and 1945 Middle America lost 25 million horses, that, until the John Deere and Massey-Ferguson and International Harvester behemoths came along, performed every task of dragging and hauling and journeying on the 160-acre spread. The yield of crops on every acre also went up dramatically, thanks to the prodigious use of chemical fertilisers: in 1930, an average farmer could reap twenty-six bushels of corn from each acre: today he can take nearly eighty. And whereas forty years ago it took him half an hour of his time to produce every bushel of the rich yellow and white grains, it now takes him three minutes, or even a little less.

Pressures of efficiency have already claimed the horse, and they are well on the way to claiming the quarter-section farmer: in fact, while I was in Iowa, the only people I met who were farming less than a hundred acres were schoolteachers and university employees around the tidy little town of Ames, who reared a few pigs and turkeys and grew a little corn and soy beans on the side. Such small acreages would hardly bring in a profit, they all said, but they brought a spiritual satisfaction that went some way towards lightening the rather urban roles they played by day; and it brought them a lot of good, tasty and fresh food.

The typical Iowa farmer of today will own lands of around 600 acres, perhaps a little more. Tom and Pat Judge, whose truly Norman Rockwell farm lies a couple of miles north-west of the central state town of Nevada (pronounced with a long middle 'a', not at all like the reprobate state to the west) has an entire section of 640 acres, on which, in the spring of 1975, he was planning to sow half corn, and half soy beans. Thanks to the plunging prices of livestock, he was keeping out of hogs and cattle this year, but would return when things were a little better on the markets in Kansas City, Dubuque and Chicago.

The farm radiated the warm homeliness of kindly and cheerful prosperity. It was March when I first called: a brilliantly sunny day, about ten below freezing, and with a foot or so of fairly old snow covering the fields. There was not a great deal the Judges could do until the spring melt got properly under way, and so things were quiet and comfortably lazy. Pat Judge, pretty, shy—'We don't get too many visitors from outside the area,' she explained by way of excuse—was making cakes for tea: the cosy warm smell of baking filled the kitchen, and a pot of coffee was bubbling on the stove— all, I discovered, for their visitor. Tom Judge was downstairs, mending a runner on one of the children's sleds. The children

79

themselves were just coming back from school: a long yellow school bus had come gently up the driveway and dropped Jeff, Cathy and Khristine by the kitchen doorstep, and then reversed, the children waving and smiling back at the driver, and he tooting his horn in the daily routine of friendly farewells. The children were sturdy and red-cheeked and every bit as handsome as their parents: they rushed in, grabbed a cake each—'Hey, that's for our guest!' Pat yelled cheerily—and dashed out to the barn nearby. A moment later three black and red snowmobiles roared out on to the fields and away towards a creek half a mile off. We didn't see them again for an hour, but the snarl of the little engines and the distant yells of childish delight filtered in through the double-glazed windows as we sat in the sunshiny kitchen eating fresh cakes and drinking new coffee, and talked about farming in Iowa today.

It was, Tom Judge said, just about the best life imaginable. He was thirty now: his father had farmed nearby, and he had helped his two sons buy a few hundred acres for a small property between them. Things went well for five years or so, then Tom made enough money to branch out on his own, as did his brother, and the two of them live some miles apart, each with his own section and his own life. The land in that part of Iowa—where the topsoil is as much as three feet thick, and good and rich dark brown like coffee—was selling for about $1,000 an acre, and so the purchase price for the farm was into the half-million-dollar range. But federal and state grants and loans were easily available to help anyone wanting to get into the craft of farming the land, and so raising the money, so long as reputation and credit rating were all right, was no real problem.

The investment an American farmer is called upon to make is truly staggering. Tom Judge has three tractors, one large, the others very large. The large one is a simple four-wheeled Massey-Ferguson he has had for the past six years. It is painted red, and it cost about $3,000. It has no cab, and little protection against rolling over: in the Judge family it is very much the fine weather runabout, rarely used seriously any more. The two big ones, which cost around $10,000 apiece, are marvellous inventions. As tall, almost, as a London bus, they have vast air-conditioned and heated cabs equipped with radios and stereo systems so that a farmer can drive and plough huge fields for hour after hour without getting unduly tired or unduly bored. One farmer I met liked to tell how he had once shown a trumpet player from the Boston Symphony Orchestra around his farm, after some Bostonians were flown out to get the feel of the corn country. 'I told this feller I had heard him only the day before when I was running the disc through up on field number four,' the farmer told the startled musician. 'It was a recording you did of the "New World" Symphony a couple of years ago—I remember the trumpet part very well.' The idea that an Iowa farmer would have either the taste or the ability to listen to Dvořák while tilling his soy bean fields was the most stunning thing the Bostonian had ever heard, he said later.

As well as his tractors, of which he is every bit as proud as a suburbanite with a brand new, sparkling Oldsmobile, Tom Judge owns a disc, which cost $3,000; a plough, which was $3,000; a rotary hoe, $1,000 (second-hand: everything aside from the plough, the disc and the tractors had been bought at the second-hand store in Nevada); a planter, $2,000; two cultivators, $1,500 the pair; and an assortment of other gadgetry that cost around $3,000.

The one item missing from the list, of course, is the combine harvester, without which the Tom Judges of this world would simply not be able to manage to reap more than a hundred acres. Farmers in this part of Iowa, he explained, club together to form a combine co-operative, and either buy one machine and split the cost between themselves, or else rent one from a sort of agricultural Avis office, and each pay about $3,500 for the fortnight or so it is needed. Tom paid $3,500 in 1974, but thought that his 1975 costs would be in the region of $5,000. Tractor costs, he said soberly, had gone up 100 per cent in two years.

The total cost, then—leaving aside the mortgage costs on the land—is in the region of $40,000 for equipment alone—equipment that has an irritating habit of wearing out all too fast and having to be replaced. On top of the material with which to attack the land, there is the cost of fertiliser and seed which, for a farm of 640 acres, is even more astonishing: Tom reckons on about $12 an acre—an investment each spring of more than $7,500—money which, should there be a dismally wet spring, or a wet August harvest-time, would be lost forever.

For the Judges the year has an unrelenting, secure routine, which is geared more to the vagaries of wind and rain and sun than to the artificially contrived months that form the basis of other families' years. Sometime in the spring, when the snow has just gone and the first warming suns have burned the surface moisture away, the fertiliser goes on—plain nitrogen fertiliser, with none of the aldrin and dieldrin chemicals that were so damaging to the environment and thus banned from production and use by the Federal Government. Herbicides of less noxious kinds are poured into the warming earth a week later, and the discs and the cultivators are brought in to turn the soil over to dig in the air and dig out the staleness of six months under snow.

Planting usually takes place in the last week of April for corn, and the middle of May for the soy beans. The 'keyhole' for planting is extremely small—two weeks at the maximum, 'and if you don't make it, you're screwed up for the season'.

Then, said Tom Judge, 'I take four or five days' holiday. We're not like some folks look on corn farmers—we don't take the entire summer off and go to Florida. We don't take the winter off, either. During the summer I'm selling real estate on the side—just farm properties for about fifty miles round here. There's a lot changing hands and so it keeps me busy. It's possible to get pretty bored just watching the corn grow. Selling stuff makes it that much better.'

The warm weather of May, June and July, with the addition of the inch of rain each month usually brings with it, draws the corn stalks up and out of the ground, so that by midsummer the Judge fields are huge patchwork quilts of green and darker green and brown. There is not much to do in the latter few weeks of the summer: Tom will drive his small tractor through the fields looking for and getting rid of any weeds he spies—Smartweed, Cocklebur, Jimsonweed and the Giant Foxtail are the bane of a farmer's life in Iowa; and Pat, for the only occasion she is truly employed as a farmer rather than a farmer's wife, goes 'walking the beans'— wandering along the beanrows, pulling out any foreign plants that will foul the harvester and spoil the crops later in the year. The critical time comes late in the summer, when Tom and all his colleagues up and down the Iowa sections have to decide to order the combine and begin the harvest. The vital factor is the dryness of the corn: you can usually tell if the crop is ready to be harvested in the way the heads of corn, by now bright yellow in colour, hang downwards to the earth, instead of pointing upwards to the sun. The longer the corn is left, the better. Wet corn costs money to dry: corn that is too dry is designated Number Two corn, and will bring in a poor price at the market.

'The big thing is the water content. The next big thing is the weather. It's always a rush to get the harvest in before the first rains come and the first frosts snap down. Usually we've been getting it pretty right: if you get caught you can do what that guy did'—and he pointed to a field on the next door property (the farm buildings were two miles away) where stalks of unharvested corn reared coldly over the snow. 'He'll be able to get a bit back for swine feed if he harvests it first thing this spring. But really he's lost out on that—a hundred acres at least—that's a thousand bucks down the drain for a start, and no return at all.'

From his 300 acres of corn he will expect to get 40,000 bushels (a bushel of corn weighs fifty pounds), from his soy bean fields he will take perhaps 12,000 bushels. These truckloads of grain Tom will take, in two or three expeditions during later summer or early autumn, to the nearby elevator—the focal point of all farming activity in the Midwest.

'Cathedrals of the prairies', the elevators have been called; and for a journeyman across the limitless wastes of Iowa and Kansas— and even more so in the wheatlands of Manitoba and Saskatchewan —the grain elevators are landmarks that, if not indicating scale, at least serve as distance markers on the flatlands. They loom up, a hundred feet above the land, like windowless skyscrapers, a cluster of attendant outhouses snuggling close to them, and a long line of railway wagons on a rusty siding stretching away from them. The elevator is where the farmer sells his grain, and where he buys his feeds, and where he buys his seeds and his additives and fertilisers and boots and caps and medicines for his cattle, his hogs and the farm cat. When a man like Tom Judge arrives with a massive 40,000 bushels to sell, the merchants at the elevator—men who work in a small office perhaps fifty yards from the base of the grey monolith—will look at the telex from Chicago or New Orleans or Minneapolis and quote a price. If Tom accepts it, his corn will be taken and with the use of an immense augur, screwed upwards from his truck and up into the elevator. If it is not dry enough it goes into a propane-gas drier first. Drying costs money, of course, hence the need to have the grain as dry as possible before the sale; and the moment when the merchants test the grain by driving great moisture-detecting instruments into the trucks, is a moment of unbearable tension for all concerned. 'When Tom has harvesting to do, that's bad enough,' says Pat. 'He's as nervous as a cat. But when the elevator men check his grain to see how dry it is—that's a moment too.'

The price varies, of course, from day to day and hour to hour. Generally corn prices have held up well in the last few years, and Tom Judge—who can expect to bring home about $40,000 a year from his hard work—is a financially secure and cheerful man. Only the weather is his constant worry: he's a good enough farmer to know that he will do all he can—'but you never know if you're going to get enough rain, and that's worrisome all the time'. He makes as much as his Congressman, though—fitting reward for what is now having to make do with a title like 'agri-business'.

Farmers in general out in Iowa were sick of Richard Nixon in the weeks of agony before he left. Their Republican sentiments did not, though, mean an automatic extension of goodwill towards Gerald Ford; and by the spring of 1975, when *Wallace's Farmer*, a local Iowa journal, completed a survey of farming attitudes towards Mr. Ford, the figures for approval indicated rather less than unlimited enthusiasm for the new man. Only six out of a hundred strongly approved of the way Ford was running America; not four out of ten felt they could 'mildly approve' what he was doing—and a depressing 36 per cent had no opinions, no feelings one way or the other. A farmer's wife in the western Iowa region named Pottawattamie County summed up a lot of the feeling of these prairie people when she said: 'What has President Ford done of value? Since he's been President he's only travelled and pardoned Nixon —neither of much value to us.' And her neighbour concurred. 'He really hasn't done much yet except to use a lot of fuel.'

Agriculture in America is now unashamedly big business—so big that even the Japanese have bought a number of farms in the state of Iowa, and rumours suggest the Iranian Government may be about to do the same. There is considerable hostility in the state legislature in Des Moines, and among the farmers themselves, that this might happen. A Family Farm Act was under discussion in the state senate in 1975 that would prohibit foreign investment in state farms: the Act, which was intended to curb the vast growth of corporate farms as well, looked like having every chance of success. In Iowa alone, the sponsors of the Bill noted, the average size of a farm had risen from 200 acres in 1950 to very nearly 400 acres in 1972—and the increase in size—which matched an exactly parallel decrease in family ownership—was accelerating.

Small wonder, then, that farms were as tempting for business-men as gold mines or camera factories might be. In Iowa, farms make money. They are set up to do so. They may be attractive places to live and work, and the men and women, like the Judges, who become farmers, may be hard-working and thoroughly attractive people. Those facts would not weaken the basic idea that you farm to get rich, in Iowa as in the rest of the Corn Belt. It seems, in that case, that farmers are fair game for avaricious businessmen from New York or from the new Iran: every bit as much fair game, at least, as Pan American Airways, which the Shah of Iran nearly bailed out to polite American applause in 1974.

The attitudes of Midwesterners are often assumed by arrogant Easterners to be stiff and narrow—a sort of mental 'American Gothic' that is somehow enchanting in its *naïveté*, but somehow unsettling in its antiquity. Early in the spring of 1975, some 12,000 farmers from Kansas and Iowa and Nebraska returned a completed survey form to the publishers of *Successful Farmer*, a Des Moines magazine that circulates to nearly every farming household in the heartland. The survey—a series of some fifty questions that had been carefully selected to weed out the prejudices and predilections of the farming community—painted a profile of rural mid-America that was in some ways surprisingly at variance from the assumptions of the arrogant.

But the basal assumption—that the Midwestern farmer like Tom Judge is conservative—is probably still correct. Of those who replied—and the typical respondent was an active farmer, not in partnership, about fifty years old, with a high-school diploma and perhaps a year or two at college and a gross income now of $40,000 a year—a goodly number still clung tenaciously to the values that make Middle America the governor of the wild machine that is the rest of this turbulent country.

Seven out of ten concluded for instance that religion was losing its influence on the family. Nearly the same number opined that family life was in trouble. Nearly half replied that in their view mass communication was exposing the family to 'undesirable influences'. Three out of ten farmers say that divorce is morally wrong, even if no children are involved; one out of every five says he will 'think rather less' of a person who uses moderate amounts of tobacco—one out of every three has the same disapproval of anyone who makes moderate use of alcohol. Every other farmer resents advertising for cigarettes and whisky—one reason why, perhaps, the roadside billboards are for substances that prevent pigs from eating each others' tails, or for a new hybrid corn type that yields 10 per cent more per acre, rather than, as in New York or the suburbs of New Orleans, for Winston and Salem and Canadian Club.

A social scientist explained the reasons for the staunchly conservative nature of these, perhaps rather narrowly chosen, views. 'Many rural people now find themselves caught in the precarious position of holding to a system of beliefs and values that does not correspond to the realities of the socio-economic order in which they live; and they know it. To be competitive they know they must constantly adapt their way of life to the technological changes that now come more frequently. They know that in doing so, they are moving away from realisation of many of their ideals.'

Here is a selection of some of the more revealing results of the poll:

Is the dominant role of the husband in rural American family life declining?   No, 53%.

Among the couples you know best, would the wife's unfaithfulness cause a divorce?   Yes, 60%.

Should family planning include legal abortion as an alternative?   No, 73%.

Do farm children have more, or fewer advantages than children raised in town?   More, 75%.

Have your children ever experimented with drugs?   No, 80%.

What are the greatest threats to American family life? Divorce, 10.7%; War, 1.1%; Drugs, 6.5%; Permissive Parents, 37%; Overpopulation, 5.7%; Crime, 4.6%; Pollution, 0.8%; Materialism, 19.1%; Permissive attitudes towards sex, 6.5%; Communism, 6.1%.

Should sex education be taught in school?   No, 40%.

Are farmers more or less patriotic than five years ago? More, 6.8%; Less, 29.3%; The Same, 63.9%.

How often do you take a vacation?   Never, 13%.

How many meals a month do you eat out?   None, 12%.

And 16 per cent of the farmers admitted they had no hobbies at all.

It is conservatism, all right, but a softer, more realistic brand of conservatism than the popular caricature allows. The answer to the question about the reasons for the weakening of the American family was one of the more interesting—a decade ago, one would expect that the view of Communism as the greatest threat would have been held by twice as many farmers as now, and the view that materialism was the greatest threat would scarcely have figured at all. The values and ideals of the farmer, as suggested by the poll, and exampled by the Judges—kind, hard-working, ruthlessly honest and scrupulous people with enormous concern for their fellow man and an intimate, though not especially active interest in the world outside—would seem thus to be the values and ideal that America needs sorely to enable some degree of internal faith and self-confidence to be re-established. Political change in the heartland is halting the laughter one would once hear on Capitol Hill when one of the rock-ribbed Corn Belt preachers would rise to speak. Social stability and continuing standing of the more reliable ethics would seem to prompt America, before too long, to realise that Mid-westerners deserve more respect than scorn, and can teach more than others from more mercurial regions.

Des Moines, the capital of Iowa, and a city some fifty miles south of the Judge's farm, is a miserable and uninspiring city—devoted almost entirely, surprisingly for corn country, to the industry of insurance. Its sister to the east is Hartford, Connecticut: between that grim city and the west coast skyscrapers, no other centre has such a concentration of men and money devoted to the business of taking risks for return.

The name of the city—although by its pronunciation these days you would never know it—comes naturally enough from the French, and from the early Gallic settlers of the Louisiana Terri-tory. 'The Middle' referred not, however, to the middle of the country—there was no way for those Frenchmen to know if they were half-way across America, or only a tenth of the way across, or fifty miles from the west coast. The middle was the location of the river half-way between the Missouri and the Mississippi, which forms the western and eastern borders of the state respectively. The city of Des Moines was built at the junction of the Des Moines and the Raccoon Rivers, and while some distance from the geographical centre of the forty-eight continental United States (which is in Kansas), the geographical centre of the entire North American United States (which, weighted by Alaska to the north, and Hawaii to the west, is on the Montana–Wyoming–South Dakota border) and the population centre (a steadily westward-moving phenomenon which at last sighting was just south of St. Louis and on the Illinois side of the Mississippi River), it seems just about the most central of all American cities to one breed of travellers, the bus riders.

For more than a few thousand of America's young and poor and adventurous, Des Moines will be little more than a bleary memory of a half-hour wait in the middle of the night in the city bus station, as the Greyhound or the Continental Trailways bus refuelled and changed crews: they will recall it, no doubt as unspeakably uncomfortable, cold and cheerless. Des Moines deserves rather nobler memories than those; but the fact is, thanks to the bus schedules and the middleness of its location, those are probably the predominant memories of the place held in homes thousands of miles east and west of the river junction.

To waste a couple of night-time hours in the bus station there is to share some of the weary romancing of the transcontinental traveller—to see why his memories of the place will be so awful, and to see why his recollections of his journey will still spur younger colleagues to try the same back-breaking run themselves during one school or university holiday.

The bus station building is small—proportionately smaller than the Port of New York Authority Terminal in New York by the approximate ratio of the cities' populations—and fairly ugly: the walls are sludge-brown, the cafeteria has plastic moulded chairs bolted to the floor and a singular absence of tables, the neon lights glare white, or flickeringly white if they need replacing; and the timetables tacked up on the walls tell the story of the place. Short-trip coaches from Iowa cities like Ottumwa and Fort Dodge and Osceola trundle in and out all day-time long—many of them carrying shoppers and farm boys down to the big city for the day, and in consequence cheery and bustling transports that smack of corn-husks and denim and have racks for the cowboy hats most of the men wear for their more important journeys. Greyhound and Trailways buses rarely ply these small rural routes, unless they happen to pass along them on stopping journeys from one side of the state to the other. Instead all manner of little bus companies do the day-time hauling: the prominent one in this part of Iowa is the Sedalia, Marshall & Boonville Stage Line, Incorporated, which plies a healthy trade in a fleet of somewhat rusty-looking buses based at the terminal.

The timetables also show the arrival and departure times of the big buses from the east and west coasts: there are a large number of them, and they all seem to come and go between eight in the evening and four in the morning: the westward bound coaches are thirty-hours' continuous driving from their starting points, and the eastbound machines two days or so away. The travellers who spill out of the great silver coaches and into the Iowa night are, as a result, pale-faced and wretched with the lack of real sleep, and their eyes tell the misery of being bumped awake when the first few hundred miles of prairie flatness had just allowed them their first real chance to settle down, stretch out and doze.

Only the drivers, immaculate in grey uncreased uniforms, their hair slick with grease and their sunglasses reflecting back so as to obscure their eyes totally, appear rested and alert. They will jump cheerily from the door, slap the back of some other outbound driver who is just taking a rig across to Omaha or down to New Orleans, and whom he hasn't seen since, let me see, was it Council Bluffs last April, or was it Amarillo in June? The travellers—mostly young girls, it seemed the night I was there, drift red-eyed to the magazine rack and see if there is a *True Confessions* or a *Great Romance* they've not yet read, or wander to the machines and punch in a quarter for another can of cold Tab or Fresca or Dr. Pepper. Sometimes eastbounders will have a few minutes to spend with westbounders, and the conversation will be a somewhat perfunctory 'What's it like over there?', 'How's the weather this time of year?' and 'This goddam riding can get pretty rough, can't it?' There was a time when they called these gas-and-chow stops 'staging posts', and the restaurants were the best all-night spots in town. Now, though, aside from the clink of coins in machines and the ads for the United Negro College Fund and recruiting drives for the US Army, the bus depot is a soulless island of weariness.

The conversation that echoes round the building has a carpet-like sameness, once the pattern has been established. 'Make that a person-to-person call, operator,' a tearful youth sounds into one of three telephones built into shiny metal slabs on the wall. 'Miss, I lost my money in that ice-cream machine,' from a young black woman with a baby fast asleep across her shoulder. 'How much for a one-way ticket to Sioux City?' from a chubby farmhand in squashy

89

Tony Lama boots and Oshkosh B'Gosh overalls. The glass doors to the bus platforms keep on opening, letting in blasts of icy air and the steady threnody of the waiting engines outside.

The clock snaps around, minute by minute. Now it is ten forty-five and a stentorian voice wakes the sleeping, and startles the wakeful. 'Greyhound, Through-service for San Francisco from New York is about to depart. Passengers please leave through Gate Number Two, for stops in Omaha, Grand Island, Cheyenne, Salt Lake City, Reno, Sacramento and San Francisco.' A line of men and women forms instantly at the doors, each one handing the envelope with the ticket to the new and smiling driver. 'Hi, how are you tonight?' he asks as he takes the ticket and peers in perfunctory fashion down at it. And then he helps each passenger up the steps and into the dark and warm interior of his monstrous bus.

On the next platform the stopping bus to Omaha is filling up, for travellers who want their homes or sweethearts in unknown and unheard-of townlets like Reffield, Dexter, Adair and Atlantic. The passengers here are not so tired—unless they had come from the New York bus, and were going on home—but they were shabbier, and wore exhibits of the fact that they at least were going by bus out of need, and not entirely of choice. The few servicemen in army fatigues climbed in too, showing special passes, and getting special help and thanks from the drivers. An Army man stands tall in Iowa: each would have been some favourite son of the farm in some small village of the prairies, and one could guess the welcome being readied for him, and picture the farm dog, and his small sister waiting in the living room for the big rumbling engine sound to break the quiet of the grasslands night, and how they would all rush out into the still, icy air to wrap arms and paws around him and be glad he was back from that Asian posting he had so luckily survived.

Both of the buses pulled out at the same hour—eleven o' clock, westbound. The local bus thrums away first, and then, majestic and at long last truly romantic, Greyhound Americruiser 754 B, with its black and yellow nameplate glowing simply 'San Francisco': and about to delight a thousand children who would see it rushing past their Nebraska farm next morning or their Wyoming drugstores next afternoon. The front of the silver, red and blue cruiser is a maze of licence plates—big ones from New York and Pennsylvania, Nevada and Utah and California, and one even larger catch-all plate for the remainder. I am reminded of those crazy Appalachian country quilts, and think how much the front of this bus, efficient in all other possible respects, looks rather like one, and how homely that is.

But then the quilt hisses, and the image shatters. The airbrakes are let off and the lights snap out inside, leaving the weary travellers to sit back and become once more sleepy silhouettes. Massive head-lights blaze alive, the gears scrunch hungrily home, and Ameri-cruiser 754 B roars grandly out on to the freeway approach and, its tail-lights bouncing with the unevenness of the ramp, and its body glowing gold in the sodium vapour flares, it vanishes fast down the concrete spillway towards the distant waves of the west coast. By this time tomorrow it'll be gunning up the Santa Rosa Range in northern Nevada, and by breakfast on the day after it'll be on Market Street, just by the Oakland Bay Bridge, and three miles or less from the Golden Gate.

Des Moines is not a city where visions of the Golden Gate come especially easily: watching the tail-lamps of that disappearing behemoth proved the only real time I wished I could have left the Midwest and headed for the ocean. The rollers of the sea, I just then realised, were what I was really missing in the heartland, and missing most of all.

I turned back into the by-now deserted bus station. Fred MacMurray, the fatherly star of Hollywood and of day-time tele-vision serials, advertises Greyhounds these days, and his face was grinning broadly out from one wall, though it was partly obscured by a white-faced prostitute in a very short suede skirt and down-at-heel scuffed boots who looked ready to call it a day—at least if the next inbound Chicago bus brought her nothing in the way of custom. Mr MacMurray is a plausible enough fellow—an ideal person to suggest the economy and efficiency of travelling across the country by bus. His appeal for Americans to 'leave the driving to us' is tempting: and the pictures that go with the appeal doubly so: Mount Rushmore and the French Quarter and Chinatown and Upstate New York all look delicious, and the skies are always blue and the cornfields brilliant yellow and the highways blinding white and almost free of traffic. The ash-ridden, gum-sticky places like the Des Moines bus station are notably missing from the advertise-ments. And come to think of it, MacMurray played the chief villain of that classic of late-night TV, *The Caine Mutiny*—you couldn't trust him then, and looking at the Des Moines bus station, I wasn't sure you could trust him now.

Des Moines is in many ways a precise antithesis of Minneapolis, 300 miles by now back up north. Where the Twin Cities have had the foresight and the local money to expand from the inside out, Des Moines is dying still from the inside out. There was some local excitement when, after intensive lobbying from the Chamber of Commerce, the local manager of J. C. Penney, the world's largest store chain, was persuaded to construct his new main shop in the middle of town and not out in the suburbs where he had wanted. Not that the placing of an unfashionable fashion store would do much for the revitalisation of the city, but there was excitement nonetheless. For the rest, downtown is just a maze of monuments to banking and casualty risk, as well as being home to the publishers of *Better Homes and Gardens* and the radio station WHO, one of the few 'clear-channel' stations that can be heard 1,000 miles away at night-time, and provides long-distance truckers with music and news that doesn't fade infuriatingly every fifty miles or so because the range of the station has been outdistanced.

The *Des Moines Register*, whose Washington Correspondent, Clark Mollenhoff, made such a name for himself during the Watergate affair (he was a former Nixon aide who left in disgust and disgrace, to evolve, as gamekeeper turned poacher, into one of the President's sternest and loudest critics) is quite an unusual paper. It is remarkable both for its editorial content and for its distribution. Two out of every three households in Iowa get the *Register* on Sundays; and it is one of the very few newspapers in America that enjoys a state-wide, rather than a city-wide readership. It reflects in many ways the conservatism of the state, and yet in other ways reflects the thesis that any long-staying visitor in Iowa will readily develop—that conservatism is not to be equated with narrowmindedness or ignorance or anti-liberalism or lack of concern for fellow man. Rather it is to be equated with caution, care and common sense: and that, essentially, is the quality that papers like the *Des Moines Register* and the *Evening Tribune*, in their greater years, extolled. The *Register*, for example, came out for American entry into the League of Nations in 1920, and for the United Nations in 1945—and this in spite of the rednecks' advertisements beside the highways in Iowa and Kansas and Oklahoma that scream 'Get US out of UN', along side 'If you don't love it, leave it' and 'Guns don't kill people, people do'. The *Register* can happily ignore those rantings because its editors have been reasonable enough men to realise that the Tom Judges of the state do not feel too isolationist about America, so jingoist as to demean all criticism, and so insecure as to demand weaponry on hand at all moments. For these reasons, while the newspapers are not especially inspiring to read, they are worth having to redress the ill-conceived image of the Iowans from outside.

One final word about an Iowan's springtime obsession. In Iowa, basketball means girls, and for virtually all of February and March the state cuts itself off from the saner neighbours all around and concentrates to the exclusion of all other more normal pursuits on the fortunes of dozens upon dozens of teams of ungainly adolescent fifth-formers doing their best to produce a Corn Belt version of the Harlem Globetrotters.

No one, whether from Iowa or whether a writer from some fancy New York newspaper or psychosports analysis journal, has managed to explain just why people here have, for the past five decades, swarmed into Des Moines a few days before St. Patrick's Day to see the finals of the schools' competitions. No one can explain the fervour of the high school in the tiny hamlet of Wilton, Iowa, where the local girls baked cakes and buns to sell on street corners and around the farms in the county to raise funds for the bus ride to Des Moines and the final games. No one can explain why Des Moines florists are deluged with orders during the competition, as boyfriends and parents lavish the gangly girls with presents and corsages and wreaths to help them win, or lose without blubbering, during the frenetic few days of the great event.

The teams have names like the Trojanettes and the Dyn-O-Mites, and the uniforms—shorts and baggy tee-shirts and long socks—are not designed with the glamorous appearance of the players much in mind. The importance of the game can best be judged by the *Register*'s front page of March 12, the Wednesday after the first few games had been played: there were three front-page stories, a front-page cartoon and a front-page photograph devoted to the contest, and the headline 'Reds Widen Control in Viet' looked both tiny and tedious by comparison. A report noted that 'there is an old saying that the Iowa Girls High School Basketball Tournament always coincides with snow', and that it proved true this year; and there was another noting that 7,700 people had been watching in the main stadium on Tuesday afternoon—a record for the time, apparently, but nothing compared to the 50,000 that would come to town over the weekend.

The sports pages were full of the proceeding, of course—and managed to focus, as did all the colour writers, on the fact that in this game, the girls actually burst into tears when things didn't go right. One picture seemed to say it all. A fifteen-year-old sat sobbing into her hand, her face an etching of dejection. The caption read simply: 'Adel guard Colleen Carroll sobs on bench after fouling out in late stages of Tuesday's Girls State Tournament Game. The ninth-ranked Tigerettes were upset 79–66 by Audubon.' Small wonder, in that case, that poor Colleen was weeping.

This year a reporter from Kansas City was up at the stadium, trying in the best newspaper tradition to discover what it was that made Iowans engage in such an extraordinary type of sport. The account, by a girl, was as interesting as any, but like all the others did not manage to find the required Grail. Back in Kansas City a sub-editor decided to make her report more locally relevant by adding a couple of paragraphs of wire copy from the Kansas City area. This addition read: 'The National Junior College Athletic Association held its first women's basketball tournament last week at the Johnson County, Kansas, Community College. Attendance was disappointing. A spokesman said that fewer than 100 attended. "It will take time to sell the public on this," the spokesman added. "They don't think women can play basketball—but really they can. I've seen them." '

And with that I left Des Moines and turned back on to the Interstate, heading southwards again for the state of Missouri. I left the car radio on WHO for a while, and the whole time, as the car sped over the thinning snow and into the warmer plains in the far south of Iowa, the car was alive with sounds of bouncing basket-balls, raucous cheering from thousands of schoolgirls—and, every hour on the hour, a reading of the last news, and the prices of corn. It might get dull, I thought, but it was good honest fare and not really to be scoffed at all the while.

4

Missouri:
Faint Breaths of Magnolia

The map will indicate more quickly than any other source why Missouri—the 'show me' state, as it is called, because of the reputed scepticism of its inhabitants—is so very varied in its products, its prejudices and its people. The states that border Missouri are, in clockwise order from the north, Iowa, Illinois, Kentucky, Tennessee, Arkansas, Kansas and Nebraska—and any state that can sit comfortably between such politically and prejudicially and personally differing entities as Iowa and Tennessee, or Arkansas and Nebraska, must have an extraordinary mix of characters and characteristics within its borders.

Not surprisingly, its capital is tactfully located in almost the geographical dead-centre—Jefferson City, the place is called, a town that joins with Pierre, South Dakota, and Salem, Oregon, as one of the most difficult to remember in those perennial Christmas-time quizzes of America's fifty state capitals. From Jefferson City, the state is pulled and squeezed by the influences of its neighbours, and the pressures and tensions of geography. Towards the north, Missouri is pulled by cornland and by cold weather; towards the south, by peach orchards and old-time Arkansas bigotry. To the east, the rustic antiquities of the Appalachian southern states, to the west, the Great Plains, and to the Nebraska side, the vast emptiness of the prairies. The state was the home of what John Gunther once called 'The Poor White Trash Citadel' of America; it also provided Winston Churchill with the forum at which to make his 'Iron Curtain' address; and of course it gave the world Harry S Truman, the little man's President. There is cotton in Missouri, and there is corn; there are cattle by the millions, and there are men and women who, like Truman himself, are 'earthy, plain, of sturdy soil and tempered true'.

It was of more than a little regret, then, to discover that the efficient and economically minded federal highway planners had not managed to allow the Interstate to meander more than a hundred or so miles through this fascinatingly variegated state. In terms of both geography and of politics, the area of Missouri traversed by the road from its entry at the town of Eagleville to its exit at the point where Kansas City, Missouri, becomes Kansas City, Kansas, is not especially different from that part of Iowa south of Des Moines. The land is generally flat, the weather is generally cold in winter and searingly hot in summer, and the people are generally conservative and Republican in outlook. The primary products are as in Iowa, still pigs, corn and soy beans; and the television pictures come from both Kansas City and Des Moines masts, meaning that the girls' basketball *aficionados* can exist happily in northern Missouri, and any southern Iowa 'show me' sceptics can hear the television news more in tune with their disbeliefs.

Sticking fairly close to I-35 was the rule, though, and so I was going to have to accept a picture of Missouri that would be somewhat at variance from the sketches drawn by those who visit it in its entirety from St. Joseph in the north-west, to Hannibal in the north-east—the town incidentally, where Mark Twain grew up—to Cape Girardeau and the Bootheel in the south-east, and to Joplin (where the world's highest radio tower was for some long time, beaming the Biblical Truth of some extremist evangelist to the plains) in the south-west. In the end I chose to visit just two places: a cattle farm north of the Missouri River, and an Air Force base to the south. Neither was as representative of Missouri as of Middle America in general—but then in Missouri, nothing is typical of Missouri, while a great deal is typical of Middle America.

Towards the end of 1974, the Sub-committee on Arms Control, International Law and Organisation, of the Senate Foreign Relations Committee, had a most extraordinary session with the then American Secretary of Defense, Mr. James Schlesinger—a man who smokes a pipe, watches birds, and says things that, once his tortuously jargon-filled language has been deciphered, are truly frightening, about America's military will, intentions and ability.

On this particular occasion Mr. Schlesinger was more scary than ever. He was briefing the eight Senators on the Sub-committee—and they included two Midwesterners, Humphrey of Minnesota and James Pearson of Kansas—on the somewhat arcane mysteries of a new defence philosophy known as the 'counterforce strike possibility'. Until 1974 it was generally assumed by global atom strategists that both Russia and the United States were deterred from firing their nuclear weapons at each other because there was mutual realisation that an attack upon one country's cities would invite, and would not prevent, an attack upon the other country's cities—and that, in consequence, nothing would be left of the world. That, it was reasoned, was sufficiently horrible a thought to prevent anyone from ever attacking in the first place.

But then in 1974 Mr. Schlesinger, worried about the growing accuracy of missiles and the increasing vulnerability of the sup-posedly ultimate weapons platforms, the submarines, began to talk of another possibility: what if the Soviets mounted an attack upon America's weapons armoury and knocked out all her land-based missiles and her sea-based missiles too? Such an attack would be highly effective and crippling; yet it would hardly either justify or enable a response in kind—one submarine for another, say, or one set of missile silos in Texas for another near Lake Baikal. The mere existence of the postulated threat—by then more real because of the increasing accuracy and cleanliness of new and future Russian weapons—was regarded by Mr. Schlesinger, despite his Old Holborn-wreathed sang-froid, as distinctly unsettling.

If Russia had the ability, he reasoned, then America had to have it too; and he promptly sent his technicians scurrying around America's land- and sea-based missiles, changing the targets of some of them from cities to missile sites, and then claiming to feel more secure for having accomplished what was known as the 1974 're-targeting doctrine'.

Some others, however, saw his changed mind as evidence that nuclear war was once more an unpleasant reality, rather than the unrealisable nightmare it had been during the appropriately acrony-mic heyday of MAD, when the philosophy of Mutual Assured Destruction held sway.

If this all seems a long way from Middle America, it is only because of the unjust assumption that the Midwest would be un-likely either to understand or care about such recondite topics. But Missouri, in fact, has a far more practical reason for wanting to know precise details of the re-targeting doctrines than have the think-tanks in New York or California. For unlike the thickly peopled lands on the east and west, Missouri—supposedly thinly peopled and a long way from the vulnerable cliffs and beaches of the Atlantic and Pacific, and just about as far as a missile can fly from the Soviet Union—is one of the very few places in America chosen as the site for a nuclear missile base. As such Missouri, which has two giant population centres—Kansas City and St. Louis—and about 3 per cent of America's population, is exceptionally concerned these days that she is already on the wrong end of several hundred Russian missiles, either buried deep in the ground or cruising, forever waiting and ready, hundreds of feet down in the grey oceans.

Whiteman Air Force Base is where the missiles are nominally kept; and within fifty miles of the suburbs of Kansas City a traveller can stumble on the first of a great swarm of Minuteman 'fields', each containing ten weapons, each poised, fully armed and ready to go. They are so close to town that a curious commuter might easily take a Sunday spin over to look at them, and see for himself the sharp end of America's strategic armoury.

Frankly, they scarcely appear spectacular. In a half-day's drive around the flat, wooded countryside near the villages of Knobnoster and Houstonia, the towns of Sedalia and Warrensburg, and the hamlets of Emma and Shawnee Mound, I must have counted two dozen of the silos. After a while they become easy enough to spot: there is a small, cordoned-off area of farmland, perhaps a hundred feet square, with an electricity power pole inside and transformer perched on top if it, from which a black cable snakes down to ground-level. On the ground is a thick concrete slab, hexagonal in section; a small circular concrete and brass object, which from the fence looks to be the size of a pressure cooker; and three grey horn-shaped devices perched on top of six-foot-tall grey posts and looking inwards over the concrete objects. A small blue notice outside sports a letter-and-number code—H-4 or L-7, for instance; and there is a faded red and white notice, indicating that what is inside the fence is the property of the United States Air Force and the Secretary of Defense, and should on no account be tampered with, entered or photographed. Once every two hours a jeep with armed Air Force men aboard will cruise by and check on the locks. If they catch you taking pictures they will take your camera away. One old farmer whom I asked for permission to walk over his land to have a look at the collection of objects simply asked me if 'you are another of those Russian spies' before sending me on my way with a wave.

The barbed-wire fence is easy enough to climb over; but after that you get into real trouble. The three grey horns are intruder-detecting radars; the pressure-cooker-sized object is the lock for the door into the space under the concrete slab, which is the missile silo hatch-cover—and it is equipped with enough combination locks and alarms to prevent even some Houdini of the Plains from having more than a couple of minutes in which to try to open it up. If he got inside—which would involve the somewhat tricky feat of lifting an eighty-ton door by hand before the guards, alerted by the detectors came rushing up from wherever their dispatcher had sent them—he would see an astonishing sight.

Below him would yawn a cavernous hole, a hundred feet deep and lined with smooth concrete and steel. Right in the centre of the shaft would be standing, bathed in light and tended by humming equipment and softly winking lights, a huge white missile: a Minuteman Mark Two, belonging to the 351st Strategic Missile Wing, United States Air Force Strategic Air Command. He would notice that the top of the missile would be sharp pointed and painted a light green: he might know that the green part would contain a nuclear warhead of perhaps twenty million tons of TNT equivalent, with a computer tape inside telling it the precise location of as many as eight possible targets that specialists in Washington have decided are the best available for this particular weapon. He might notice too the theodolite and the complicated arrays of mirrors that are used to align the missile when it is last moved into the shaft: he might draw some sense of power from the knowledge that, were he to touch the missile with his hand and push it hard, so that it rocked through a fraction of a millimetre inside its silo, it would be sufficiently moved from its proper aim that it would miss its target completely, and instead of hitting some distant Soviet shipyard or nuclear weapons laboratory, or city, it might crash harmlessly on some unpopulated steppe, killing no one at all.

But it would be highly unlikely he would ever have time to see either the missile, the warhead or the mirrors, and fairly improbable he would ever have time to open the lid to the pressure-cooker. For five or six miles away from the silo, a hundred feet under ground and surrounded by a hundred tons of the most complicated and costly equipment, that will detect any tampering with the locks or any intrusion beyond the perimeter fence at the silo, sit two men—always two, never less—who, for twelve hours at a time, endure the bearable agonies of watching over their precious, deadly missiles. The men are sitting by the triggers of ten exactly similar weapons, ready at a moment's notice to unleash one of them or all of them, and by so doing help destroy the world.

The 'capsules' from which the individual flights of missiles are controlled are as secure as the jewel-safes at the Vatican, and just as invisible to most outsiders. All the visitor sees above ground is a large, low concrete hut, with another smaller one nearby, two air-pipes poking up out of the ground, and a great deal of barbed wire and searchlighting equipment. The gates are all electronically controlled, and when my escort and I arrived at the outer fence it seemed exactly like arriving at a block of flats in Washington or New York, where television scanners wave up and down as some person deep in the bowels of the place looks over your face and your identification or your day pass, and where a tinny loudspeaker barks out orders like: 'Cleared for entry—stand clear of the gates', before the heavy steel wires part and trundle to one side to allow us to walk through. In this case the gates snapped tightly shut the moment we were inside.

The hut itself was cheerfully nondescript. A sergeant, armed with a rifle, demanded name, rank and serial number of the escort guard, and then spoke on an intercom with the officers below. They asked him, in tones of alert precision, the code of the moment: the sergeant looked at his sheet, snapped out 'Alpha-Gamma-November', following which there was a grunt of approval from below and a dozen locks snapped open to reveal a big lift, big enough to take a car inside, with steel mesh wire at each end. The sergeant read a short official note of warning that I must neither touch nor peer into anything marked Secret, instructed me to leave the capsule on any direct order of the two men below, and then told me to 'Have a nice day'. One of his armed colleagues stepped into the lift with us and pressed the button. We slipped, extremely slowly, down through the rich Missouri soil and into another timeless world, of secrets, atoms and mutual fear.

The capsule itself, protected by cast concrete and steel doors that take a minute to swing open or shut and can seal the inhabitants off from all manner of radiation, blast or germ, is about one hundred feet long. One half of the capsule—it is shaped something like an egg-timer on its side—is filled with the necessary backup equipment of generators and air-conditioners and radio batteries:

one can spend a day inside this half and find nothing of interest to enemy or friend, and consequently there are no particular restrictions on entry to it, once having cleared the security above ground.

But the other half is different. There is another blast door for a start; it is painted in harsh black and yellow stripes, and on top of the door, in huge red letters, are the words: NO-LONE ZONE—IT HAS BEEN ORDERED THAT A MINIMUM OF TWO PERSONNEL ARE INSIDE THIS AREA AT ALL TIMES. Beyond this door are the keys, and the locks, that fire the missiles. In this sanctum sanctorum, without undue melodrama, is the potential for abruptly bringing to an end the progress of mankind.

The two officers inside were young, tired-looking and ruthlessly professional in their manner—a manner which they insisted was not put on at the behest of the USAF's extremely proficient public relations staff, which had organised this visit to this nerve centre of November Flight, after a telephone call to the Pentagon a fortnight before. The officers' names were Billy Langford and Mike Kelty: Langford, from Grand Prairie, Texas, was thirty-five and the major in charge of the wing for his twelve-hour duty shift. Kelty, thirty years old, came from San Francisco, and was a lieutenant, which of course he pronounced 'lootenant'. It seemed pointless to ask them how they felt about holding the triggers of such awesome power; but I did anyway, and it was pointless, because they returned the expected programmed answer that while they hoped they never had to turn the triggers they felt they had to be there to protect the interests of the Free World and to do the bidding of the man elected to be Commander-in-Chief and President of the United States.

Both men wore guns—.38 service revolvers, in canvas holsters. They wore dark blue shirts and trousers, and white stocks, which made them look ever so slightly out of place—rather like officers of the Brigade of Guards doing their shopping in cuirasses and white kid thigh-boots. The senior officer sat at a console with ten panels in front of him, each panel sporting an array of lights belonging to one of the ten weapons in November Flight (which would have blue plates outside, reading N-2, N-3 and so on, to N-11, the control capsule being officially designated N-1). The words on the top light of each weapon panel read the same, in amber: 'Strategic Alert'. That meant the missile involved was primed and ready to go, and all equipment on board, according to the constantly monitoring computers aboard, was working flawlessly. As I sat beside him a red lamp suddenly flashed on one of the panels: 'Perimeter Intrusion', it read. 'Oh, damn—those bloody pigeons again,' Major Langford yelled. It seemed there was a flock of pigeons in the area of Weapon N-5 that had the confusing habit of landing inside the silo fence, triggering the alarm systems; the major told Kelty to get on the phone once more and tell the security team to drive over to N-5 and make sure it was the birds, and try to scare them off well and truly. 'Worst thing was a turkey shoot last week. Some goddam hunters shot a bird and it fell right slap bang on top of the silo door. That set off the radars and brought the guards rushing over— but then the hunters climbed over the fence to retrieve their bird, and the guards found them. There was quite a scene—but the poor hunters hadn't the faintest idea what was underneath their feet, and couldn't figure out why all the excitement. The guards thought these guys were the real thing, with their shotguns and everything.'

There is a camp bed in the silo. At the foot of it, just beside the pile of grey military blankets, is a red metal post with a red metal box welded on top of it. On the top surface of the box is a flange with two sets of holes, each secured by a big brass padlock, each with a combination that faces to a different end of the silo.

If the President orders the weapons to be fired; and if the commanding generals at Strategic Air Command's vast subterranean headquarters in Nebraska received all the necessary authenticating 'go codes', then Major Langford and Lieutenant Kelty will get a single message. They will each undo their own combination lock— each man only knows one combination, and both are needed to open the red box. Inside the box are two yale keys. Kelty will take one, Langford the other, and they will insert them, after lifting hinged perspex flaps, into two locks, one on each console, and the two twenty feet apart at least, so that one man would be physically incapable of inserting and turning both keys simultaneously.

Then Major Langford will call up Oscar flight on the radio—the other missile flight with which he is permanently paired as a further preventative to an accidental, or malicious firing. The same procedure should have been followed across at Oscar-1, fifty miles away to the north; and across the hardened telephone cables Langford will ask if all the keys are in, and if he is told they are will count down from ten. At zero he and Kelty and the two officers in Oscar-1 will simultaneously turn their keys a quarter turn to the right, to the position marked 'Away'.

In the two silos, the officers will hear and see nothing save for ten lights that will each change, if all works well, from 'Strategic Alert' to 'Weapon Away'. Up above, in the flat and wooded countryside, twenty of the concrete silos' doors, each weighing eighty tons, will be blasted open by huge explosive charges and hurled fifty feet into the nearby fields. A second later, vast columns of smoke and fire will erupt from the silo mouths; and three seconds later precisely twenty giant Minuteman Mark Two missiles will thrust, slowly at first and then faster and faster out of the soy bean fields and into the Missouri sky. Oscar and November flights will be on their way to Russia, ready to kill and maim millions, and primed to wipe out a whole city or a whole valley full of industry or a whole coastline of docks. And if that same intruder who might have once glimpsed the white and green-tipped weapons were to see them as they shot from their silo, he would notice one very jarring aesthetic aberration: once the missiles had been fired and were on their way they would not be pristine white and green-tipped, but every inch of them would be charred jet black.

Most of America's 1,000 Minuteman missiles are up on the people-less wastes of the Dakotas or Wyoming. Those in Missouri, however, are within fifty miles of Kansas City, and within three hours' hard driving of St. Louis. In a briefing in 1974 Mr. Schlesinger, the Secretary of Defense, pointed out to the Senators that if the Russians were to fire a missile to burst over each one of the Whiteman silos, in a deliberate effort to destroy the base in an exhibition of counter-force striking skill, then, depending on the direction of the wind on that day, three quarters of a million people would be killed in St. Louis, and 225,000 in Kansas City. A strike on the silos, therefore, would be, *de facto*, a strike on two of the mightiest of America's cities—a fact which has prompted more than a few Americans to wonder if perhaps some awful blunder had not been made in the middle 1960s, when it was decided to place these mighty pieces of the nation's strategic armoury amidst the corn and the peach orchards of the well-populated state of Missouri. It may yet be a decision that Missourians, and Americans as a whole, will regret.

Between Whiteman AFB, and Chillicothe, my next destination, I stopped for a while in a roadside park. It was a pleasant, cold day:

the air was clean and crisp, and everything was sparkling. Before leaving home I had packed a small picnic basket with the kinds of luxuries I would not expect to find in the innumerable Holiday Inns, Ramada Inns and Best Western motels in which I was forced to stay: and so I sat in the sunshine, eating Cadbury's chocolate, a Carr's digestive biscuit, and drinking from a bottle of Guinness— 75 cents a bottle in Washington, brought direct from Dublin. God was in his heaven and all seemed very right with the world.

After a few moments a Missouri State Highway Patrol car pulled into the park: the driver, a youngish corporal in the troop, stopped his engine, reported in to his headquarters by radio, and then settled back to enjoy a cigarette. Blue smoke coiled idly up and out of his window: perfect peace and contentment, a million miles from the worries that normally afflict this straining nation.

The driver came across. His name was Dickson, a plate on his tunic said—he added that his first name was Pete. He had seen I was from out of state—would I like some maps and guides of the area, he asked. He pulled out a sheaf of papers and photographs: on the back of his cruiser were the words 'Stop Me For Tourist Information'. He mentioned there was a Mennonite colony a few miles down the road, and said that the deer were just starting to become frisky again after the winter—he had just seen one cross the road ahead of him, a few minutes before he had stopped for lunch.

Just then there was a scuffling noise from the snowbank off to the left of the cars. A small, white animal, about the size of a large guinea pig, scurried down the slope, slipping and sliding and rolling over before it reached the bottom. 'Goll-y,' said Officer Dickson, 'a white possum. Never did see one of them before.' He beckoned, and the two of us—me, armed with a long lens on the camera— crept down after it. After five minutes or so we cornered the beast as it sat in an old tyre by a tree stump. I took a dozen or so pictures of it before it took fright and bounded off into the woods. 'Guess we'll never see one of those critturs again,' the policeman said, and we walked back up to the cars. His radio was crackling with urgent-sounding din, but he reached in and turned it off. We talked for a while more about eastern perceptions of the middle lands—'Some of these guys I get for speeding on the Interstate expect me to heave up to them in a horse 'n' buggy. Some of the New Yorkers get a bigger ticket than they expect once they start to talk like that'—and then it was time for me to go. He said he thought he ought to do a little work as well; so we waved good-bye and started the engines—he going south to his next village, I going north to Chillicothe. He was a long, long way from the archetype of the American cop; yet there are probably more like him than there are archetypal cops, thank heaven.

Chillicothe is a real Wild West town, except that it is in Missouri, and should more properly be called a real frontier town. The main street is wide and long, with an assortment of banks and drugstores and hardware shops and western-clothing dealers and seed merchants and tractor salesmen spaced on either side. There are only two traffic lights, and cars race through the town in little more than a minute, for want of any more exciting way to spend an evening. The outskirts are unutterably dull: used car lots, with ancient Chevrolets and Dodges polished to gleam under the hundreds of coloured light bulbs, seem to be on every street corner. There are agricultural machinery dealers and cheap motels—including the Shamrock, a plywood-and-cardboard kind of place that, at $15 a night was neither cheap nor good. There is dust everywhere—not good western desert dust, but the kind you get after the snow melts and the muddy meltwater streams dry out. Everything in town seems covered in a fine layer of light ochre, and it gets on your boots and into your teeth in half an hour of strolling through the place.

But a hundred yards or so up from the northernmost petrol station in town is a cluster of buildings that present a dramatic, and pleasing contrast to the run-down dreariness of all the others. There are neat, white-painted, four-rail wooden fences gleaming against neatly clipped grass meadows. Inside the rails are an assortment of extremely large cattle, also pure white, that move gracefully, but very slowly, across the meadowlands like gigantic puffs of cottonwool. There are buildings—a large, pillar-fronted main house, perhaps a quarter-mile back from the main road, and an assortment of farm buildings of the same, split-roof style, with each barn building sporting two or three shiny metallic chimneys, and a lot of fresh green and white paint. The assembly looks like a show-farm, right out of some American version of Smithfield: and that is exactly what it is—the Litton Charolais Ranch, one of the prime sources of the most extraordinary, and extraordinarily successful breed of cattle in the world.

The Charollais—Americans drop one of the 'l's—is now one of the major beef-cattle types in this country. Before the late 1950s it was scarcely known in America, save in the savviest Texas circles after some of the local farmers had been down to Charolles on holiday and, with true Texan flamboyance, had brought back a couple of the remarkable white beasts as pets for their ranches. In the early 1960s the US Department of Agriculture recognised only some 2,000 head on farms and small ranches throughout the southern and western states. But by 1971 the boom, which started in the mid-1960s, had reached its peak, with total registration of 158,000 Charolais cattle. Since then matters have not gone so well: vets have discovered a disturbing rate of problem births in the breed—problems due in part to the breeding of the cattle in an effort to make the beef content of the pelvic region inordinately high, and thus a peculiar shape for the unborn calf to struggle through. Technology has now taken over in writing about cattle: and one researcher, commenting critically on the state of the Charolais breed, mentioned in what seemed to be an idle aside that 'deleterious heredity, culard and arthrogryposis will definitely be a serious deterrent to Charolais success'. It is entirely possible that white-painted monuments to the success of the breed, like the Litton Ranch, may shortly begin to disappear. While it is still here, though, the Ranch is a superb citadel in which the best of this still young prairie science can be practised.

So far as Charley Litton and his son Jerry were concerned, success started with their purchase in 1965 of a Charolais bull named Sam 951—one of the few bulls whose name appears in the *Encyclopaedia Britannica* and probably the most photographed and distinguished individual of the bovine world. 'One could write a book on the records set and the many accomplishments of Sam 951,' says a publicity leaflet given to anyone caring to stop by at the Litton Ranch. 'His greatness spanned the world, and though dead, his frozen semen and the close line-breeding at Litton Ranch permit the bull to live on. . . . What made the bull so great as to cause people to drive half-way across the country just to touch and see him, and now just to view his grave?'

One simple reason why people do come to peer at Sam, and do still come to look at his grave—a huge hump of earth with a marble headstone—is that he was a truly incredible-looking beast. He weighed more than a ton; his coat was pure white, with short tufts and curls of hair on his head, and sleek, shiny velvet on his flanks. He had a dewlap that would take two strong hands to move, and four short, stumpy legs that propped him from the ground, rather than enabling him to stand. His magnificent head, with its sleepy red eyes and its dinner-plate sized ears melted necklessly into his vast trunk; his tail, always brushed to blond perfection, draped down across a rump that, if ever he had been permitted the indignity of appearing on dinner plates, could have fed a village many times over. His passing, after he had produced more sperm than the average whole herd of Angus or Hereford cattle in the small ranches nearby, was recorded with the reverence normally accorded a great statesman:

At approximately 8.oo a.m. on April 4th, 1972, Sam 951 died peacefully in his sleep. He was going on 13 years of age. He was buried in a grassy area in front of his air-conditioned, red-carpeted barn where thousands from every state in the Union and from almost every country in the world have visited what was unquestionably the most famous bull in the world.

Even now, villagers in Chillicothe seem to display somewhat rheumy eyes at mention of the superb animal.

So Sam 951, and his equally illustrious colleague, Alfalfa John, were brought up from Texas and, housed in an ever-increasing complex of barns and byres and outhouses, began the process of mating with specially selected cows and producing sperm to order on the rubber-tyre-lined contraption cattle breeders have for such purposes. The semen from Sam and from hundreds of other Litton bulls was stored in liquid nitrogen bottles to be flown anywhere in the world for up to $400 a phial. Advertisements for Litton's 'packaged genetics' can be read in any Midwestern farm journal. How about a phial or two, for instance, of Royal President A176: 'He is a great grandson of Alfalfa John, a grandson of Sam 951, a grandson of Royal Sam M4, and a son of Sir Royal Sam 790. This bull was named President because we felt he was destined to be of that caliber'—a remark that, considering some recent American Presidents, might not be entirely complimentary to the animals, one of the ranch workers commented dourly. Purchasers of semen from Royal President have to promise not to breed any cattle that have any more than three-quarters Charolais in their chromosomes

—in other words, the cow to be inseminated by the Litton bull's product must be no more than half Charolais herself—and the buyer must pay $15 for a matchstick-sized vial, with a minimum order of ten vials a time. If you send the money and the promise, you will get a silver container, about the size of a large saucepan, filled with liquid nitrogen and the vials of frozen egg-white and Royal President. It is, farmers say, well worth having.

Aside from the sperm, the other products bred and sold at the Litton Ranch are the bulls themselves. Strict regulations have to be placed on anyone buying a Litton bull, to prevent rival ranches springing up all over the country; and huge sums of money have to be paid. The best bull of the herd recently was a small, young animal named Shane P37; for that, the ranch wanted $100,000 for just a half-share. 'We keep him here, but let the half-owner have half the semen and the title to any calves born out of that semen. So far we haven't sold him—actually we refused one offer of $100,000 only the other day—but when we do decide to let him go, there'll be no problem.'

The Littons—Jerry married a one-time Miss Chillicothe, who was the runner-up in the Miss Missouri contest—made rather more than money out of their success. Jerry Litton was able to use his not inconsiderable power as a cattle baron to win the Congressional seat in Washington for north-west Missouri, and is now one of the brightest young representatives of the farmlands around in Washington. He is enormously ambitious; he is a gifted speaker; and he is probably honest. Added to the fact that he is a Democrat, those factors, it is being said, might make him a formidable contender for some more nationally obvious office in, perhaps, the middle 1980s.

In 1974, ambition in Washington, and constituency duties in Kansas City were taking Jerry Litton increasingly far away from the technical devotion that is modern American cattle rearing. He sold the farm—for $3,800,000—to an Arizona rancher named Schoenfelder. His twenty-six year-old son, Dan, now lives in the mansion at Chillicothe with a wife who, in the spring of 1975 was heavily pregnant. 'Calving, I call it,' he said. 'It may sound rude, but I can't really look on it as anything other than breeding. But it didn't take the fun out of it at all,' he added quickly.

One thing that might detract just a little from the 'fun of it all' is the television monitor the Littons had installed in their bedroom. There are in fact five monitors—the one in the bedroom, and four in the downstairs study (from where the inside of some critical farm buildings can be seen, as well as the outer office. Jerry Litton liked the last view, he said: he could watch who was coming in to see him, and thus know how hard to be smiling when the visitor came through the study door). The bedroom TV is constantly showing the straw-covered barn floor where pregnant cows are settled down. Dan's wife said, clenching her teeth a bit, "So often Dan gets up in the middle of the night when he hears the cow grunt or something. I wish the darn thing could be switched off at nights—but then Dan wouldn't sleep at all. You just try sleeping in a room with the TV on all night, and a pregnant cow heaving and grunting just down by your feet. It's pretty off-putting, especially when you're pregnant yourself.'

Dan Schoenfelder, who has a degree in Business Administration from Carleton College, appeared happy to be running the ranch, night-time television or no. He was happy editing the magazine Jerry Litton left as a legacy—the monthly *Bull-O-Gram*; and said he was confident that Charolais is the best beef breed around just now, and likely to go on from strength to strength. He admitted that the reason for breeding Charolais, rather than any other breed was because the Charolais manages to put on so much weight so very quickly for so little cost. It was not a matter, he said, of quality of taste or the production of a texture which the beef-eater might especially like. 'Fact is, I can't really tell one kind of beef from another,' he said over a two-pound New York strip steak at the nearby grill bar. 'This is a good piece of steak, I'll admit—but for all I know it might be Hereford, and it's more than likely it is. We don't know where the Charolais beef goes—it just ends up at the supermarket, same as every other kind.'

There is no great urge on the part of Midwestern beef farmers to experiment with such exotic animals as the Beefalo, which a California rancher was breeding after successfully mating a humpless buffalo with a Hereford cow. Middle American farmers are scarcely satisfied with the price of beef—many in Iowa and Minnesota were dumping calves in trenches in 1974 rather than rearing them, because of the high cost of feeds and the low price of meat. They are ready to embark on new ventures. In Chillicothe, though, where the men are dealing in vials of frozen semen and in the future father-figures of the pastures, there is both enormous prosperity and enormous wealth. Dan Schoenfelder drives a

Chevrolet truck most days, but a big buff and gold Cadillac Eldorado on Sundays. Nearly all of his ranching colleagues from this cattle country do the same, and one Sunday we drove together to Kansas City to hear Jerry Litton deliver a speech about the woes of the cattle industry: the car-park was filled with Cadillacs and Mercedes and Lincolns: whatever woes the industry might have, it was far from evident among the beef baronies of Chillicothe.

On the way back to Kansas City I started briefly through the Whiteman missile field once more, eager to find a farmer with a weapon on his property, to ask how he felt living cheek-by-jowl with Doomsday. What I found instead was a huge, mock-English castle, built a mile or so from the town of Sedalia, and inhabited by a blue-eyed, blond-bearded young man whose father and he had made a fortune from selling bodies for farm lorries.

David Parkhurst said he had been building the house for the past four years, it wasn't a model of anything particular in England, but when he had last been there he had noticed Windsor Castle, and Stratford-on-Avon and Woburn, and had decided it would be 'neat' to wrap them all up in one building. No architect in Missouri could come up with a design close enough to his own fantasies, so he designed it himself and handed the plans over to a local builder. In 1975 it was very nearly complete—a vast structure of turrets *and* Tudor half-timbering, with Norman doors and Perpendicular windows, with enough stained glass to make an archbishop feel at home and ten fireplaces. A lift whooshed silently from basement to fourth floor, to save anyone lacking energy the long climb up a staircase plundered from a ruined Kansas City church. The master bedroom was fifty feet long; the youngest son was having his room made into a replica of Nelson's stateroom on the *Victory*; and the baby's room—conceived long before the baby—had a bath set upon an onyx mount three feet high so that Mrs. Parkhurst would not have to stoop down to bathe the infant.

Mr. Parkhurst—whose latest acquisition was a marble copy of the head of Michelangelo's David, six feet tall, which he had mounted in the billiard-room fireplace—said he felt his house was a tasteful addition to the Missouri countryside. He was just planning a new drainage system, he said: it would carry all rain water from the tennis courts down and into a pool, through the cast-iron heads of one hundred small lions—specially cast by a local foundry from a model he had found in a London antique shop. The water poured out through their mouths, he explained helpfully. He had three Saint Bernard dogs, one of which was called Winston, and bit people very badly. Mr. Parkhurst thought that was very bad of a dog called Winston to do. So far the house had cost him $400,000 and it would probably end up a great deal more. All sorts of weirdos, he said, stopped by to look at it. 'I guess they never saw a real castle in the middle of Missouri.' Few students of the castellate school of architecture will have ever seen a castle quite like this one, whether in Missouri or not. And they might not altogether appreciate the lighting behind the walnut stair screens, which can be controlled to bring up red, or gold, or blue at will; nor the eagles and griffins, made of cast concrete, which sit upon some of the smaller turrets. The thick pile nylon carpet, mostly in purple, might also spoil a little the baronial image of Mr. Parkhurst's immense Missouri folly.

And of the missile silo at the bottom of the garden, rather like some latter-day folly itself, peeking out of the climbing rose trellises? 'Is that what it is?' said one of the Parkhurst family. 'I really had no idea. To think our castle is on top of an atomic bomb. That's pretty neat. I bet the Normans never thought of that.'

On the way back to the freeway I passed through the village of Hamilton which, a notice said, was the birthplace and boyhood home of J. C. Penney—whose cheap clothing stores are as commonplace in Midwestern towns as Walgreens and Skaggs Drugs, Woolworth stores and Dairy Queens. It seemed rather appropriate that Mr. Penney, who above all had ensured that farmers and their wives could dress up well for the hoe-down on Saturday and again for church on Sunday, should come from such an insignificantly mundane village as Hamilton, Missouri. It would have been a dent in the image if he had been raised in the Bronx.

And then the road signs, blue and white and red shields, proclaimed 'Interstate 35 South, Missouri', and the familiar four-lane highway was under the wheels again. The trucks roared airily down the road, motor cycles—for it was starting to warm up now, down here at latitude 39° 05' 00" north (International Falls, by contrast, was way up at latitude 48° 36' 00", and in the middle of this giant continent nine degrees of latitude can mean thirty degrees of temperature)—went zooming past, and cars replaced the farm pick-ups that littered the muddier back roads in this part of the world.

An hour's drive, and just like Des Moines and Minneapolis had loomed before, so to the south another city loomed ahead through the haze. This one was a great deal larger than either previous centre; here there were railway marshalling yards, vastly long Ralston Purina feed elevators, truck warehouses and smoking factories, through which the concrete ribbon of the Interstate tactfully snaked; and then ahead was a confused conglomerate of tall plains-scale skyscrapers, some old and curlicued, others—the Holiday Inn was typical—slab-sided and glass-walled, and with revolving restaurants on top. This was Kansas City, the first giant metropolis of the true West: between here and the mountains there was only one more true city, and that was Denver, Colorado.

This might be 400 miles west of St. Louis, which, with its Gateway Arch and Mississippi River bridges affected a position of being the Beginning of the West: but in truth St. Louis is only the End of the East. Kansas City is without a doubt what St. Louis would like to be.

(A word about the St. Louis arch—a vast structure of shiny steel, in the shape of an inverted catenary curve, and designed by Eero Saarinen. From the air it looks very much like a croquet hoop—which, it is said, once prompted the city council in Columbus, Ohio, to vote to build a 3,000-foot-tall model mallet, and the council in Indianapolis to propose constructing a 300-foot-diameter ball. The idea was to amuse trans-continental airline passengers: sad to say, mallet and ball have not yet arisen, but hoop stands there lonely and forlorn beside the muddy Mississippi, waiting for the game that will never be played.)

In one of the best scenes of a well-remembered W. C. Fields's film, the dour old man is fired up in a rocket while in the mistaken belief that he is bound for Kansas City. The craft lands on the moon, and a bemused Fields ambles around the craggy, cratered green mountains for a few seconds until he sees a strange creature heave to on the horizon. He removes his top hat, and, with his characteristic, elaborate courtesy, asks the moonman: 'Pray tell me sir, is this Kansas City, Missouri, or Kansas City, Kansas?'

Americans have been asking questions like that for years. The assumption that Kansas City is in Kansas is generally a wrong one: the city was first developed as a railhead on the north and east of the Missouri River, and thus is in the state of Missouri, once it was realised that the Pony Express, which ran out of the town of St. Joseph, fifty miles north, was about to be outdated by the iron horses. (St. Joseph, incidentally, is a city that has suffered severely because of the incredibly rapid development of Kansas City: it is a starved, rundown little place that has only one distinction known across the country—it was the boyhood home of Walter Cronkite, the television news announcer who became such an institution that George McGovern considered asking him to run as Vice President in the 1972 campaign. Cronkite was never asked, though—one of the few distinguished Americans who was not, unkind men might say.)

So far as this account is concerned, Kansas City is being placed, for geographical, rather than political convenience, in the state of Kansas. It was more than clear to me, once the Missouri countryside was behind me and the brick walls and iron rails of the city were ahead, that this city was more a monument to wheat—the principal product of Kansas—than it was a monument to hogs, or corn, or Charolais cattle. This was almost as Western a town as Topeka or Wichita and Amarillo off into the sunset: and though many a Kansas City dweller who feels himself a resident of the 'show me' state may object, I am craving indulgence and am mentally erasing the line that apportions this city between two very different Middle American states. Kansas City, Missouri, and Kansas City, Kansas like to consider themselves almost a unit these days anyway—the two come under a metropolitan police force and a sewer authority, and indeed, almost every other important organisation save the governments of the cities themselves, which are separate. For the purpose of this account, they will be considered a unit here. It would have taken away one of W. C. Fields' greatest lines, though.

5

Kansas:
Crossroads on the Prairie

Everything still is up-to-date in Kansas City. The place has a remarkable air of modernity, in spite of the predominantly Mid-western Gothic buildings, like the marvellous old brass and marble Hotel Muehlebach, that fill the downtown section. Hallmark, the firm that makes greetings cards, has its headquarters here, and has constructed a glittering array of shops and hotels a couple of miles away from the city centre, just by the mouldering pile of Union Station, where one of Middle America's most bloody gang murders took place in the thirties. The station is now a dreary wreck, like most big city stations across the country: the Crown Center, as the Hallmark production is known, is a fabulous megalith for that most profitable of industries, that of getting people to pay money purely for wishing each other well.

There is a remarkably beautiful shopping centre in the south of the city, too—perhaps one of the more impressive collections of shops in a country where, too often, shopping is a pastime entirely subordinated to the motor car, and shopping centres are vast, warehouse-style monsters that surround three sides of some gigantic suburban car-park. The Country Club Plaza in Kansas City, all decked out in Italianate marbles and red sandstones, and with sculptured marbles of designs more akin to Rome and Florence—where many of them were made—than to the plains states, is delightfully unique. It was the first purpose-built shopping centre in America—built in 1923, some thirty years before the first suburban monstrosity was heaved up overnight in a forgettable Rhode Island traffic nightmare. It is just one of the features of the pleasantly informal, easily designed city that prompted François Mauriac to call it 'the most beautiful city in the world'. Few would in fact go so far—but Kansas City does have a refreshing quality about it, once the first brash image has been dissipated, few visitors to the Midwest leave it without a feeling of affection.

Kansas City also believes itself to have some of the best plain food restaurants in the country (though Fort Wayne, Indiana, of all places, is said to have the very best one of all—a breezeblock and clapboard place totally surrounded by sleazy car-parks, that charges as much as $30 a meal but, in the view of the *Wall Street Journal*, is more than worth the price). The restaurant that attracts the most attention in Kansas City is called Arthur Bryant's Bar-b-Que; it attracts the attention of Easterners mainly because a food journalist on the *New Yorker*, Calvin Trillin, comes from Kansas City and calls Arthur Bryant's 'the best restaurant in the world'. It is not; it has no atmosphere to speak of; it is quite expensive; and it is only reasonably good.

But a few miles south of the town is a small shack called Jess and Jim's, where you eat on shiny plastic tablecloths, and choose from a menu that sports less than a dozen items—nearly all of them having something to do with cattle. The Kansas City Steak originates in the city, of course—a 'KC' being a strip of sirloin, much favoured by cowboys and especially liked if it hangs over all edges of a one-foot-diameter dinner plate. Jess and Jim's specialises in cooking such behemoths and takes my vote, together with a supper club in Chillicothe, Missouri, and a little place in Seneca, Kansas, as the best steak restaurant in America. Calvin Trillin liked Jess and Jim's too, it should perhaps be added. The steaks cannot be described; they can only be eaten.

In more ways than its architecture and its havens for the greedy is Kansas City an up-to-date kind of city. There is also one of America's most remarkable factories there: an enormous place, hundreds of acres with well over 5,000 men and women working inside, and yet with a total volume of production each year that would probably fit quite comfortably inside a pair of large trucks, and no more. The largest producer in America of some of the smallest products in America—and some of the most secret products in America: the Bendix Corporation, Kansas City Division.

What the plant actually produces is, not to put too fine a point on it, atom bombs. Or, more accurately, the 'timing, firing and fusing mechanisms' for atom bombs. It is one of seven of the most clandestine factories in the western world, and one of the least visited by anyone from 'outside'. The six hours I spent there one day were primarily occupied with my being informed, with supreme courtesy, that I could not be told anything of substance that went on behind the wire fences and electrified walls that surround the place. And might I have a look at the plant, I inquired. 'Well, we can show you the canteen,' they said, but then told me I would not be allowed to speak to anyone there, even about the coffee.

Bendix—the washing machine makers, only that division is somewhere in Michigan—is one of seven plants that come under the direct control of what was the Atomic Energy Commission and is now, following a cosmetic name change in early 1975, the Energy Research and Development Administration (ERDA). The plants are collectively known as the Weapons Fabrication Complex; and their function is, quite simply, to make the atom bombs America and her nuclear allies—and that, generally, means the United Kingdom—so badly need.

The United States Government spends in the region of $435 million a year keeping the factories going: Bendix, which received $120 million in 1973, is the biggest and most expensive of the plants—though it is possibly not quite the most important, or the most sinister. In rough chronological order—the chronology that is, of the making of an atom bomb—the seven plants of the Weapons Fabrication Complex are as follows:

Uranium and plutonium are enriched to the proper degree for weapon use at the 'Y-12' factory operated by Union Carbide at Oak Ridge, Tennessee—the town where the Manhattan Engineering District's first uranium enrichment plant was built to supply the fissile material used in the three first bombs fired at Trinity Site, New Mexico, at Hiroshima and Nagasaki.

Detonators are made by the Monsanto Corporation, at their plants in Dayton, Ohio.

Neutron generators—nuclear triggers for the bombs—are fashioned by General Electric, in the factory near St. Petersburg, Florida.

The Dow Chemical Corporation's Rocky Flats plant near Denver machines the plutonium into the precise shapes—with tolerances of only a few millionths of an inch—that highly efficient weapons demand.

Bendix, here in Kansas City, makes the devices that time and fire the bombs; and it makes the casings for all the weapons, and such luxuries as fins, hooks and missile mountings.

And then two remote plants belonging to an outlandish-sounding organisation named Mason & Hanger-Silas Mason, Incorporated— one in Amarillo, in the Texas panhandle, the other in Burlington,

Iowa, put the components all together. Technicians working in conditions of utter Q-clearance secrecy screw detonators and neutron generators into the formed plutonium semi-critical masses, encase them in specially pressed high-explosive charges, add the timing and firing devices and load the whole, multi-million-dollar weapon into the casings provided, and finally bolt on the fins, the hooks and the missile mountings. Then the Mason & Hanger men put the finished bombs into commercial lorries and ship them to such places as Manzana Mountain, New Mexico, or to rural Illinois, where the Air Force and the Army keep stockpiles of weapons for possible future use. Or they may go further afield: nuclear howitzers shells to Europe, Polaris and Poseidon warheads to Johnson Island, the fabulously secret man-made atoll to the west and south of Hawaii.

Perhaps the one aspect of the nuclear weapons industry that strikes the stranger even more than the horror of the production is the vast distances that have to be covered by each component, and each finished bomb, before the uranium and plutonium actually become warheads, ready to be fired for the purposes of deterrence, and peace. Somewhere, one might worry, is there a weak link in the chain?

At Bendix there are some seventy civil servants who work for ERDA and, at the last count, some 5,000 who work and are paid by Bendix itself. The ERDA men farm out the work: they receive the bomb designs from laboratories in California and New Mexico— Lawrence Livermore and Sandia Labs—and put the basic plans across to the engineers at Bendix who will say whether or not the design can be translated into a working weapon. If the answer is no, the ERDA men send the designs back, and ask for something more practicable—finally receiving something that the Bendix men believe they can do.

Donald Nigg, a middle-aged Kansan whose major hobby is building hydrofoil boats and whose job is Director of Engineering for Bendix, Kansas City, is a little less reticent than the ERDA employees. He is very proud of what he calls 'our little job shop— that's what it is really—five thousand people making things painstakingly and slowly, one at a time, just like craftsmen. There's no such thing as an assembly line here—there might have been something akin for a while, while we were building all those 1,000 Minuteman warheads—but now, things are all so different, everything is built to order, just like Rolls-Royce.'

The smallest and lightest devices made in the plant, Mr. Nigg says, are the timing devices and the G-switches that tell a falling bomb when to set itself off. The tail feathers and fins are fairly large—totally secret, of course, but a lot more obvious if anyone did happen to see one. The timers and the triggering devices are manufactured from the most microscopic wafers of material. One device I was allowed to see—though I was forbidden from knowing what it was or did—was made up of 10,000 separate parts, each assembled by hand. Despite its complexity, the whole was only three inches high, and weighed four ounces. One hated to think what fiendish function it performed.

Bendix also carries out a great deal of the testing for the nuclear weapons already in store. Atom bombs, Mr. Nigg explained, have a shelf life of only a few years, after which they have to be dismantled (at Burlington or Amarillo) and the non-nuclear parts examined and tested to see if the electronics stood up to the weather, the flying, and the steady bombardment of nuclear particles inside the shielding. The testing equipment is especially precise and expensive: one piece of test-bench gear cost Bendix $750,000 to build, Mr. Nigg said proudly.

The design laboratories, he explained, are already working five or ten years ahead, producing schemes for weapons of which 'only one in five finalists will ever be weaponised'. The engineering, tool-making and other functions that Bendix must perform, comes two to three years before a weapon is deployed on the field—and then, a Bendix official said a trifle sadly, 'along comes SALT'.

There was no doubt, he said, that the Strategic Arms Limitation Agreements had had a bad effect on employment in the weapons industry. Not until 1973 had the number on the Bendix workforce ever once declined: in that year there were 6,110 employees. Now the plant is down to 5,000, and one of the two final assembly plants, the Mason & Hanger Factory in Burlington, Iowa, was due to close in the summer of 1975. Amarillo's production lines had been made rather more efficient: and there were plenty of warheads still to be built for the Trident I and Trident II programmes, and there were gravity bombs to construct, to put inside the new B-1 bombers. 'But things are getting slacker round here—détente and so on does everyone a lot of good except us. We tend to be forgotten in the rush for peace. Still, I guess I'm all for it. I'd rather be out of a job than out of a life.' Bendix, as a direct consequence of the swelling peace, was diversifying—it was 'getting into energy' as Don Nigg said. Even so, 750 men and women (and the workforce is mainly composed of women in the timing and triggering device shops; and primarily men in the case and fin plants) were laid off during 1974, and a further 196 in the first three months of 1975. The 1975 depression could hardly be blamed for that.

The security at Bendix is far more strict than at any other plant, outside Detroit during new model testing time. Arrangements for the trip had to be made in Washington. Security clearance came from Albuquerque, New Mexico, and ERDA's Weapons Fabrication Complex headquarters. Verification of my identity had to come from the State Department and the Pentagon. At the gate I was given a large one-day badge which read 'Alien' in big red letters. I had to pass through three electronic barriers to get to the reception desk. Once inside the plant, which has all its windows barred with fine grilles and metal baffles to stop spies with lasers from 'hearing' conversations from behind the glass, I had to be escorted everywhere. And I was only allowed in four offices—the manager's office (which, tantalisingly, had a big buff file on the desk, covered all over with red and white hatching, with SECRET, NOFORN, stamped across it like so much Christmas decoration), the security manager's, the boardroom and the cafeteria. Everywhere else in the building required Q-clearance, which I did not have and would never get, and thus it all remained strictly off limits.

'You're about the first reporter we've ever had down here,' marvelled Bob Bulcock, the ERDA manager. 'I'm afraid you're not going to learn one helluva lot.' But, from men like Don Nigg, there had been quite a lot to learn. He worked at Bendix because, he said, he no longer liked the East and the Far West had lost the allure it once had. The Middle country, he said, was where the best people live; the countryside was unpeopled and unspoiled; and the weather was fairly predictable. Others in the plant talked incessantly about the joys of central Kansas – they talked about it, quite possibly, because they were so tightly bounded by the strictures of the Atomic Energy Act, from talking about anything else. It seemed oddly out of place that we should be singing the praises of Middle America in a factory which constructed devices that—depending on your point of view—place Middle America, and the rest of America, in the direst of perils. But that was another Midwestern illusion shattered: the place is not all farms and isolationists. There are bomb-makers and hydrofoil racers too, and they love the Midwest every bit as much.

As I left, and the heavily armed gate-guard retrieved my pass and asked me to sign the register, he leaned into the car and grabbed my arm. 'I hope those guys in there gave you a good time,' he smiled. 'I saw you were from England, and I'd like to think they made a good impression on you.' When I assured him they had, he asked if I had learned anything of interest. I told him nothing secret and sensational, but a lot that satisfied my curiosity. 'That's more than most people learn in there,' he replied. 'Most other people like me just learn not to be curious.'

Kansas City, perhaps more than any other central city except Chicago, is a true hub around which the spokes of road and railway radiate to all the centres of importance in the country. Three interstate highways track their convoluted way high above the houses of the central city: Interstate 29, which comes down from the Dakotas and Winnipeg, and terminates at the Missouri River bridge; Interstate 70 which comes in from St. Louis and the east, and, straight as a furrow in a spring field, shoots west to Denver and the Pacific Coast—this, above all perhaps, is the great east-west road of America. And then Interstate 35, by now very nearly half-way between the Canadian and the Mexican border bridges, slices diagonally north-east to south-west across a maze of twisting prestressed concrete bridges and buttresses, from the railyards in the north to the stockyards in the south. I-435, which an *aficionado* of road numbering can instantly tell is a circular bypass road, rings the city about six miles out. It has ten lanes and more, and is one of the busiest trucking bypasses in the country, tossing the huge vehicles by the seeming pressures of their own centrifugal force, from Jefferson City to Wichita, or from Chicago to Tulsa, or from Winston-Salem to Seattle.

Getting out of Kansas City can thus be more than a little tiresome, especially if you are fighting to move into the right-hand lane for your quick exit on to I-35, and some vast Pacific Inter-Mountain Express truck rushes into the space you were looking for, and denies you any possibility of exit for twenty miles or more. Any circumnavigator of a big Midwestern city like this can tell tales of being thrown off route at some crucial turning—and most salesmen, if they get stuck with you at a coffee table in some wilderness Howard Johnson's, will tell you stories of this brand from every city in the country.

Eventually, after much cursing and double-shuffling between monster rigs and souped-up motor cycles and homebound commuters I found myself, as planned, westbound and on to the wheat plains, on Route 70—the Kansas Turnpike, no less. I was taking another brief leave from the concrete ribbon of I-35—about one hundred miles, the diversion would be—so I could spend a day, following an invitation, with one of the grand old men of Middle American politics, Alf Landon.

Thirty years ago John Gunther was in Denver, with Topeka, Kansas, as his next stop. He, too, like every reporter who strays past Topeka, wanted to see Mr. Landon, and so dispatched a wire by Western Union, explaining what he wanted. 'A reply came back so fast that it seemed to bounce: "CALL ME ON ARRIVAL UNNECESSARY FOR YOU TO IDENTIFY YOURSELF." '

I telephoned, rather than wired Mr. Landon with some trepidation. I was in Ames, Iowa, at the local Holiday Inn; and from there a Presidential candidate—even a failed one, like Landon—radiates a slightly intimidating mystique; I was certain he would have neither the time nor inclination to spend an hour, let alone a day, with a reporter from a newspaper he had probably never read and quite possibly—said I, my eastern condescension clearly visible—never heard of.

But there was no need to worry. Alf Landon has two numbers listed in the phone book in Topeka, the information operator told me. (Incidentally, information operators in America are little short of superb. There is no nonsense of there having to be information operators in every city with a vast block of directories for everywhere else. In America you simply dial the information operator in the area you want to call—the number, 555–1212, is quite free, and you preface it with the area code—913 for Topeka—for the city concerned. One second, the operator comes on the line and tells you more about Alf Landon's telephone arrangements than you could possibly want to know. If the information operator had been sitting in Washington, or Ames, Iowa, it is more than conceivable she would never have heard of Topeka, let alone Mr. Landon. And so the process of finding his number would have taken twice as long.)

But, back on the tracks. He had two numbers—one, his secretary, the other, his home. I called his secretary. 'From an English paper, eh?' replied the girl. 'He won't want you to go through me. Call him at home—he'll take care of you himself.' And so I called the great man: his voice was a little shaky, perhaps, but he seemed keen and enthusiastic that I should come over. 'No need to identify yourself further when you come. Just give me a call when you get into town—I'll leave the day free.' It was John Gunther revisited, I thought. And, like Mr. Gunther, what followed, when I finally got to the dusty, wheat-rich town of Topeka, was 'one of the best bouts of talk I have ever had in America'.

Alfred Mossman Landon was born in Pennsylvania in 1887. His father, an oil tycoon of sorts, moved west to Independence, Missouri, (Truman's home, and the town where he eventually moved back to, and where he died) seventeen years later—a move which Irving Stone, in his book on Presidential campaign failures, *They Also Ran*, says was considerably more than an accident for the teenage oil heir. 'It was a gift of benevolent fate, for he became the apotheosis of Kansas: he changed his name to Alf, began to talk through his nose with a Midwest twang, later took to wearing his clothes with a farmer's disregard of elegance.' Alf Landon, like Al Smith before him, was a plain man's man, or a Plainsman's plain man, and it was not too long after he became Governor of Kansas that someone nominated him to fight the 1936 Presidential election for the Republican Party. As Stone says: 'They called him the poor man's Coolidge. This was less than justice: he had a warm and lovable personality, and could name nearly every Kansan his friend.'

One factor dogged him throughout his futile campaign for the White House—a factor that was confined to a wheelchair, had poor eyesight and was currently the incumbent at the White House and a man who was destined to stay in that same executive mansion for another nine years—Franklin Delano Roosevelt. 'Running against him', Landon says now, 'was like trying to get on a moving express train and stop it. There was no chance for me—but it was a good fight, and a fair one, and we both respected each other.' Landon, who campaigned hard, beset by an inappropriately cornball campaign song played to the tune of 'Oh, Susanna!', and who was hamstrung by bad weather and bad health and, in the end, by a bad choice of issues, lost by a huge margin. Roosevelt collected

27,476,673 votes, and Alfred Mossman Landon limped home with 16,679,583—he had won only eight votes from the electoral college, and was thus to enter the record books as having suffered the second worst defeat int he college of any Also Ran in history.

On the morning of the day in 1936 when his loss became common knowledge, Alf Landon put on his overalls and a hat, stuck an old pipe in his mouth and went duck-shooting. He was not sulking, he said—'just getting away from it all, like I should have done in the beginning'. He went back home to Topeka, and started work on a house—Alf's Kansas White House, the locals called it, a little unkindly—in which he would live out the rest of his years. He was then not yet fifty—a tall, ascetic-looking man with rimless glasses and a pink severity of appearance that betokens a Scots presbyterian attitude and a fit and healthy physique.

Alf Landon's White House is just that—a huge, multi-pillared mansion just by the zoo in Topeka, and two hundred yards from that most remarkable of psychological institutions, the Menninger Clinic, which gives Topeka as much fame in the world of the mind as Rochester, Minnesota, has in the world of treating the body. The folksiness of the man is apparent the moment the house appears: all mail is put into a box out in the entrance to the drive, and the letters have dropped off the box, so the nameplate reads A-F L-NDO-, Box 52—, Top-ka. No Richard Nixon could ever have tolerated such contrariness from his mail box.

He shuffled to the door when I rang. He was a slight figure, a little bowed, with big age-blotches mottling the backs of his shaky hands and his balding forehead. He was wearing a dark blue polo-neck shirt, jodhpurs and tall, brilliantly shiny black riding boots. He had them specially made in England, he said—the best you could get anywhere. He invited me in.

Outside, even though it was March and early morning at that, the sun was already high and the day was turning hot. Inside was cool and quiet: the room smelt of tobacco smoke and last night's wood fire, which was still glowing faintly in the great inglenook in the study. There was a long flight of stairs, with a leather-covered teakwood electric elevator chair on rails on one side, that would allow Alf Landon to ascend to his bedroom with the minimum of effort. Mrs. Landon rarely used it: she was younger ('I outlived my first') and a great deal more spry.

In the drawing room there were twenty-one chairs and three

sofas, a harp and a piano, and all manner of exquisite bric-à-brac of coloured glass and silver and leather and polished brass. There were family portraits—one in pride of place of the great man's three great-grandchildren sitting around him and his grandson, who was a lawyer in Hutchinson, Kansas, fifty miles away. The piano sported a pile of sheet music—the latest to be played ('Mrs. Landon played it to me last night') was called 'A Deserted Farm', was written by one Edward MacDowell in 1896, and was to be played 'with deep feeling'. On the wall was the famous portrait of candidate Landon by John Doctoroff—a picture of a small town Chamber of Commerce Manager, perhaps, or of the eldest son of the family before he set off for the seminary and a life of cloistered decency.

'Stay just as long as you like,' Alf Landon said. 'Shut me up when I've talked enough. We'll go down to a restaurant I know and have some good plain American rations, and then come up and talk until you can't talk any more.'

For the first hour or so he ranged over every conceivable country on the globe, wanting to know what I knew, asking what the British newspapers were saying about Portugal and the Keflavik base in Iceland, and the situation in Berlin and Brazil and goodness knows where else.

He read the *New York Times* and the *National Observer* and pounds upon pounds of weekly and monthly journals of fact, opinion and speculation, and was, in consequence, every bit as well informed, or as badly informed, as anyone out in Washington. He was an inveterate, and excellent, public speaker: only the night before he had been out on the campus at Manhattan, nearby, speaking in the place of William Simon, the Treasury Secretary, whose plane had been fogbound: he had received, he said, a very good round of applause, and he was having to speak again that night.

Over lunch—down at a country food place, very much the local greasy spoon, where he had a hamburger and I a cheeseburger, and he kept cadging cigarettes ('Only don't tell Mrs. Landon'), and where the waitresses called him 'Governor'—he talked at length about the growth of Presidential power and the destructive tendency that it would be bound to have, he believed, on American democracy and its institutions. 'There was an argument for it back when Roosevelt was President, I guess—but things have gotten just that way again, and there's no need at all. There are these powers now they're talking about in Washington to allow the President to fix tariffs—the Trade Reform Act, it was. The fact is, the power to tax is the power to rule, and if future Presidents can fix taxes with no reference to the Congress, then that's another step on the way to a dictatorship. They're talking about nationalising offshore oil drilling—and give the President the power to control it. That's another example—the President, whoever he is, should never be allowed power like that.'

Richard Nixon, old Mr. Landon said, was the most complex man he had ever met. 'Books will be written about the mysterious make-up of that feller until the end of the century at least. Putting him in the White House, with all that power around him, and all those strange complexes inside him, was asking for trouble.' Yes, he had voted for Richard Nixon in 1968, but not four years later. He had suspected something was in the wind.

It was, he said, 'inevitable' that Gerald Ford would run for his party in 1976. 'I can't understand the political reporting we get these days from Washington, questioning whether Ford will run— of course he will. And not only will he run, but he'll win.' Ford had great crowd-appeal, he said: it was not the same sort of paternalistic radiance that pulled the people out for that other great Kansan, Dwight Eisenhower, maybe, but it was an asset which few of the other candidates seemed to possess. And no President before or since could hold a candle, Landon said, to Harry Truman—the greatest President America has ever had, and one of the best contributions Middle America had ever made to the nation.

Landon, as conservative and frugal a man now as he was in 1936, when he was preaching conservatism and practising frugality, is suspicious—but in an informed manner—of the Communist intentions behind détente. 'There are great contradictions in détente— the moderates in Russia are all being eliminated, and moderate countries all over the world are being slowly rubbed out while America sits back and plays friendly with the Soviets. By the time this interview gets into print, we'll know how things are shaping up. Frankly, I'm worried quite a bit.'

Did he see, through his slightly Calvinistic spectacles, the imminent decline of America as a world power, or any signs of domestic decadence. There were severe problems ahead, he said. The *Imperial Presidency*—the phrase was Arthur Schlesinger's, but he borrowed it with acknowledgement, he said, pointing to the signed book he had received—was one severe problem. The tendency towards greater and greater deficit spending was another. The Congress was confused, the Democratic Party was floating at sea without a captain or a rudder, and in fact, he said a little bitterly, 'I just cannot recall a time when there was such a dearth of political leadership.' A lot would depend on whether President Ford did manage to be re-elected and then 'by applying the anti-trust laws and managing the economy and beating back the Congress, does manage to turn back the tide of Presidential power-grabbing. If he manages all that, he will go down as a good and worthy President, and this country could get back on course.'

And did he have confidence in his country? 'A few more years and you might find us turning towards isolation again—perhaps with West Germany and Japan doing the same thing. There is a great danger that America might find herself isolated politically as well as economically: an awful lot depends on how well Ford manages these coming years. They are very crucial for us all.'

And of Watergate? 'I can't say that there will ever be a real change in the kind of morality that came out after that scandal. We had it when I was running—we have learned that FDR had Eleanor's phone tapped, and we only learned that because of the great tide of self-exposure that came after Watergate. In fact, so many things have come out that Richard Nixon doesn't look as bad as he once did. Humphrey seems to have been mixed up in some very funny business with the dairy industry and that $200,000—you can bet that kind of thing would never have come out at all if Watergate hadn't happened. So in that respect, while I honestly don't think the affair will ever change men, and the way this political system attracts men who are not wholly honest, I do think it has raised public awareness of the kind of things that go on, and so they may stop for a while. If that happens, and we have cleaner elections we'll have a lot to thank Watergate for.'

'But if LBJ got by, I don't see why the rest of them shouldn't have done so too.

It was difficult to leave. I had spent six hours or more with this delightful old man—an individual who, with Justice William O. Douglas, must still rank as one of the finest, most likeable elders on the American political scene. Landon is cautious and prudent and a little cantankerous and testy at times—though he didn't display these latter features at all when I was there—but he is also imaginative and well informed and kind and immensely warm. One feels, coming away from a day in his company, not only a profound wish that politicians of today could aspire to similar stature, but that the great in America should occasionally step down from their pedestals and come to find out what real Americans think about and believe in and dream of and hope for. Landon did—and Landon lost. Were he, or a man like him, plain speaking, honest as the day is long and imbued with the unique power of being able to reach out to the little man and turn the big man to one side, to run today, he would sweep the boards.

And yet not only was Alf Landon an obviously good and worthy man. He was also the kind of fellow one finds great pleasure in spending a few hours with—shooting the breeze, looking back and forward and outwards from the middle lands. It had been a privilege to meet Alf Landon; a gratifying experience it would be difficult to forget.

Back up in Minnesota I had been caught for speeding by the local highway patrol. The fact that I was not to be caught again was, I am slightly ashamed to say, little to do with my having cut my speed to the federally imposed limit of 55 m.p.h. It was, instead, just the excellent working of a little trick I had been told about in a truck-stop in northern Iowa.

Trucks—the huge, red-light festooned monsters that are so much a part of the scenery between towns like Des Moines and Oklahoma City—only very rarely get speeding tickets these days, and yet they tear along the highways at 65 and 70 and even 85 miles an hour. Truckers claim that 55 m.p.h. gives them poor and thus costly mileage-per-gallon rates, and that there are sound economic reasons for ignoring the speed limits. In the days when they were given tickets, a few months after the imposition of the 55 m.p.h. speed limit, they were able to write the costs of the citations off against the money they had saved in taking less time. But then the local state police, especially in places like Arkansas and Oklahoma and Kansas, began to tighten up, and the costs for the truckers began to rise to inordinately high levels. Something they said, had to be done.

What was done in the end was to make use of citizens-band radio and the sturdy co-operation of the thousands of long-distance truckers who use it, to outwit the waiting policemen at their own game. Sit in a truck these days as it runs down the Kansas Turnpike from Topeka to Salinas, and listen to the 'c-b' radio set which the driver has bought for a hundred dollars or so and wired up beside him, and the conversations will go approximately thus:

This is Arkansas Red here, out on I-70 at the 435 marker, westbound for Salinas and Denver. Anyone listening who can tell me if there are any Smokies around please?'

Back comes one reply. 'Hi there Arkansas Red. This is Ryder P. Smith in a silver P.I.E. eastbound on I-70 at the 400 marker, bound for Kansas City and St. Louis. There is a bear convention under the overpass by the Manhattan turnoff, Route 177, but no others from there. Texas Jim, ten miles ahead of you westbound reports nothing so far, so let the road roll. Over.'

'Many thanks Ryder P., this is Arkansas Red here again. We'll keep talking. Over and out for now.'

'Smokies' or 'Smoky Bears' or just plain 'Bears' are, in the vernacular of the highwaymen, policemen—so called, naturally enough, because of their park-ranger-shaped hats which give them some resemblance to the singed fire-prevention-symbol bear, known to every American child for the last half-century. It is grossly illegal to use radios to warn of the presence of any policemen on the road ahead: but to issue warnings about 'Smokies' and 'Bear Conventions', while intensely irritating to the police, gives their position away and allows the truckers to avoid costly brushes with the law. Arkansas Red, once hearing of the total absence of 'Bears' for several miles ahead of him, would have pushed his foot hard to the floor. Gobbets of flame would have roared up and out of his two side-mounted, silver-plated exhausts, and his rig would have lurched forward, out into the fast lane, and switched into a steady eighty rumbling miles an hour, passing cars and lesser, radio-unequipped truckers until the warning came over the 'c-b' to 'cool it', because of 'bears ahead'.

The trick, then, is to spot a truck with the distinctive twin aerials of the 'c-b', and fall in behind him. He may speed, but he will have the invisible eyes and ears of his colleagues for miles around to protect him, and thus protect you. Providing you are polite and make no trouble for the big trucker as you fall in behind him late at night for a 90 m.p.h. ride down the 'pike, he won't complain: he calls it 'taking someone through with me', and, if he can pick up a healthy train of attendant speeders, he will have something about which to brag when he gets to the next Union Oil

Truckstop, with which the plains are littered.

I was at a Hojo—a Howard Johnson's Restaurant—forty-seven miles east of Wichita, back on the Interstate. It was about six at night, and I had been hightailing it down the road behind a massive Peterbilt rig—the best made, they say—that was going back to Montana, according to its proud 'I'm from Montana' stickers on his mudflaps. He signalled he was turning into the Hojo, and so did I. We parked together, and as I got out of the car he climbed down the chromium ladder from his tractor and waved. 'Glad to have taken you through back there,' he said. 'Come and have a cup of coffee.'

He was a burly man with very short hair and almost no neck at all. He wore a pink shirt, open-necked and revealing a crucifix on a chain. He had tattoos on his upper arms, and grimy fingernails. He ordered a cup of coffee and a slab of coconut cream pie. He was indeed bound for Bozeman, Montana, with twelve tons of soda bottles back from a factory outside Chicago. 'By god, I've seen enough snow and ice these last few hours to last a man a lifetime. But Kansas—you're great. It's windy and cold, and the rig gets swept around a bit—but that sun is great and warm inside the cab, and it's good to see it again.'

He had been happy, he said, to bring me through the Kansas Highway Patrol—he had never had a great deal of time for them: they were a force that had always stopped truckers for the most picayune of reasons, and they were pretty unpopular all across the states. But there were times, he said, when the Highway Patrol and the truckers did work together—and, moreover, made use of the 'c-b' radios to accomplish that co-operation.

'It was in Arkansas it happened last,' he said. 'I was gunning on down I-40 from Memphis to Little Rock, when this drunk pulls ahead of me. Soon as he was in front, he steps on his brakes, and I have to slow the rig and go down through maybe ten gears—and then he speeds up again, and I get going once more—and there he is waiting on the shoulder, and when I pass him he rushes up ahead of me, slams on his brakes and we have the same old thing again. Boy, was I mad at that guy.

'So I got on the old "c-b" and asked if there were any bears out there, because I wanted to talk to one. An eastbound truck said yes, there was a Papa Bear and two Baby Bears under a bridge at the 128 marker, about five miles ahead, so I called them up, and said "Papa Bear, you-all under the bridge at 128, I want to speak to you—you copy me?", and the bear comes on, says "Where are you, what do you want?" So I tell him about this drunk hassling me like he is, and the bear says "Right old man, you bring him through here at 90—we'll deal with him."

'So I speed up to 90, and sure enough the drunk gets his old Chevy going and roars along beside me, trying to pass me out, weaving here and there. And then we pass the 128 marker and the bridge, and sure enough the bears are there, and the instant we go through they all turn on their blue flashers and come roaring out to get the car. He stops dead about a hundred yards up the road, surrounded by the bears. I slow back down to 60 for a while, and then git goin'.

'I heard they got that sonofabitch on three counts—doing 35 m.p.h. over the limit, driving while intoxicated and for a violation of the broken seal laws by having an open liquor bottle in the back seat of his car. He was in gaol for a week, his license was taken away and he had to pay a thousand bucks in fines. The police down there say this feller could not understand how he was picked up when he was following a truck with a citizens-band radio—he thought that was the safest way to speed. Sure it may be, but you gotta be nice to the trucker, too!'

And with that he paid his 70 cents for the coffee and pie, eased himself off the stool, and waddled over to his magnificent Peterbilt, now glowing ruddy gold in the evening sunshine. A powerful blast of blue smoke shot up from the exhausts for a couple of seconds: the truck shuddered, moved slowly backwards, then forwards and out of the park into the freeway ramp. A minute later he had built up through his twenty-six forward gears, and was steaming west again, reaching for 55 and then calling out: 'Hey fellers, anyone out there—tell me the location of the Smokies in your area please . . .?'

For truckers and travelling salesmen, the state of Kansas is, because of its location at dead centre of America, a busy cross-roads through which people hurry, but rarely stop. Oklahoma is the same: for that reason the two states have turned their major east and west bound routes into toll roads, with specific provisions to exact unpleasantly large sums from motorists who are impolite enough to want to drive from one end of the state to the other without pausing for business between its boundaries. For drivers taking

the Kansas Turnpike and I-35 from Kansas City across and down
to Wichita, the state will take very nearly six dollars—no small sum,
when you remember that with petrol at 50 cents a gallon in 1975,
the cost of actually performing the driving from border to border
was almost exactly the same.

The state is a crossroads for more than motorists and the ever-
rolling freight trains that criss-cross the wheatfields and the long
stands of high grass. (The Atchison, Topeka & Santa Fé is the most
celebrated railway line to pass through Kansas: the *Official Guide to
the Railways* lists, however, four other rails that use Topeka's
Union Station, including the Rock Island, the Union Pacific, the
Missouri Pacific, and Amtrak, the Government-financed passenger
railway company. Kansas City sports these and others: the Chicago
& Northwestern, the Frisco Line, the Kansas & Missouri Railway,
the Missouri-Kansas-Texas Railway, the Burlington Northern, the
Chicago, Milwaukee, St. Paul & Pacific, the Gulf Mobile & Ohio
Railroad, the Kansas City Connecting Railway, and the Norfolk &
Western. Kansas is truly a mecca for those who love to see the
great four-headed freight expresses lumbering along, lights blazing,
bells clanging, horns keening mournfully across the prairies. The
Santa Fé engines are long and yellow and black, and look magnificent, especially when they are rolling west into the evening sun,
and the rails take on the appearance of liquid gold, along which this
vastly extended snake of freight wagons will press ever upwards—
1,000 feet every 200 miles—all the way from the Missouri River to
the Rockies.)

The state, in addition to all this, is a crucially important cross-
roads for America's internal and external communications: it is
one vital fulcrum for the transcontinental telephone system—a
network that marks America out as having the most progressive and
advanced telephone system anywhere in the world.

For better or for worse, the bulk of America's 132 million telephone instruments belong to that most gigantic of corporate super-
stars, AT & T—or, as it is best known, the Bell System. There are
other phone companies—2,300, in fact—ranging from large concerns like General Telephone, in California, which numbers its
subscribers in millions, to tiny one-horse companies like the JBN
Telephone Company in Nebraska, which has less than a hundred
people to interconnect. But the bulk—well over 80 per cent—of the

telephones belong to Bell, are made by Bell (by Western Electric, its wholly owned subsidiary), researched by Bell (at Bell Labs., in New Jersey) and connected together by Bell (the AT & T Long Lines Division, wholly owned, and operators of most of the major telephone and cable and radio long-distance commercial links in the country).

Kansas figures prominently on the maps drawn up by the men at Long Lines headquarters in New York. Many radio channels run north and south, east and west, through Kansas. At least one of the principal defence communications lines runs north and south through Kansas. Several small cables, snaking between the big Midwestern cities and used almost exclusively by Southwestern Bell, the local AT & T subsidiary in the area, run underground across Kansas. And perhaps the single most important communications link between the east and west coasts, the L-3 cable from Boston to San Luis Obispo, runs without ceremony, four feet under the rich dark Kansas earth, from Kansas City in the east to Concordia and St. Francis in the west, and from there on to Denver and over the mountains.

The L-3 is not the biggest or the best cable the Bell System operates—it is about as thick as a man's wrist, and has twelve copper tubes around a central core, ten of the tubes carrying 9,300 conversations each, and the remaining two waiting as 'protection' in case a fault elsewhere in the system requires that L-3 be called in to work as a supplementary route. A woman living in New York who dials the area code and number of her friend in Los Angeles may well find—especially if it is day-time, and the circuits are busy with business calls—that her voice will bound from microwave aerial to microwave aerial across mountains, rivers, deserts and prairies from one coast to the other: if, however, her call is routed, by one of the Bell System's extraordinarily sophisticated switching systems—in her case, most probably the centre at White Plains, New York—via cable, then her chatter, and that of her friend, will carry swiftly through the subsoil of Kansas, on the big L-3 trunk line four feet under. Every four miles or so, buried deep and unattended in the soil, the L-3 cable is nurtured by small automatic relay stations —each a collection of powerful amplifiers, connected to the local mains electricity system, that will boost the level of the telephone signal and prevent it from deteriorating into the kind of whistling-crackling-screeching sound more commonly associated with telephony in Europe and the Soviet Union. These amplifiers are checked regularly by teams sent out from one of the most extraordinary subterranean worlds imaginable, six miles south of the little Kansas village of Fairview.

Six miles south of Fairview is flat, tediously unremarkable grassland, with nothing save for the occasional windpump and even more occasional grain elevator to serve as scale or anti-soporific. There is, however, the traveller will note, another of those tall, spidery steel structures topped with strange metallic horn-shaped sculptures that one gets so used to seeing in the flat-lands. The tower is a microwave relay station: there are thousands of them dotting America, each one within line-of-sight of the other so that the radio signals transmitted by each pair of horns can be 'seen', and thus received by the horns on the next tower. In hilly country, line-of-sight can be as much as a hundred miles: here in Kansas, where curvature of the earth becomes a more important factor than intervening slopes, the aerials have to be at most thirty-two miles apart: since I had passed a microwave tower twenty-six miles further south, the structure at Fairview appeared to be very little different. But there was, I noticed as I got closer, a small white hut beneath it, about the size of a suburban one-car garage: it was a little surprising, then, to see that about ten cars were parked outside the hut: if the ten drivers were inside, they would be sitting on each other's laps, it was so small. The place must have more to it than that.

And sure enough, it did. Up at the door of the small white hut was a button to press and a television camera that pointed down from the ceiling in the direction of any visitor. There was also a telephone, which had a notice suggesting anyone on official business should pick it up, and press the button. I did so, a voice came on, tinnily, and asked me to hold my press card up to the TV camera: then there was a hideous buzzing, and the doorlock snapped open, and I went in. Ahead was an orange staircase made of steel, which zigzagged downwards steeply about thirty feet. It was contained in a concrete shaft about the size of the hut—which I could see now was really only a roof above the staircase, and had no other noticeable function—on the walls of which were a series of ten circular steel plates that stood out from the walls like horizontally sprouting mushrooms. At the bottom of the steps was a door, which even as I walked towards it, was opening very, very slowly.

Jim Watkins, a cheerful, brightly dressed New Yorker who came into view once the door had swung fully back explained that the paraphernalia behind me—the locked door, the steel mushrooms and the ten-ton steel vault door he stood behind—were to ensure the nuclear security of the building. This complex was, he explained, a vitally important communications centre, from which were served telephone and radio links that not only kept friends on the opposite coasts in touch, but also generals at Strategic Air Command in touch with the President of the United States: it was important, then, he explained, by way of an apology for the inconvenience of the impersonal entry, that both radiation and Russians were kept out. No person could get into the hut above ground: and once the radiation and blast detectors up in the nearby fields smelled trouble, the mushrooms—which were in effect blast protectors—would bang shut, the heavy blast door would swing to and lock, and the Fairview Communications Center could hunker down and keep going for weeks, and even months, without contact —except for the telephone—with the rest of America.

Two ends of the L-3 cable burrow down into the Fairview Center, their thousands of component wires snaking here and there across massively complicated grids that continually monitor both the quality and the volume of conversations passing through the state. The specially hardened cable from SAC HQ in Omaha, Nebraska, comes through Fairview—though the switching and routing of calls on this Government network, known as the Autovon network is performed by another underground centre sited fifty yards away from this one. The neighbour is not operated by the Government though; by fine irony it is run by a private company that has civilian business in Nebraska amounting to a hundred private phones and no more.

From Fairview there radiates a major radio net: the tower above the garage-hut is one of seven that have to be maintained by men based underground at Fairview: if ever one tower is felled by a tornado—and Fairview is in the very heart of the tornado belt— then Jim Watkins will dispatch men and machinery within five minutes and communications can be fully restored in a few hours only. The Bell system has few such accidents to deal with; when they occur the Company responds magnificently. One case involving a radio tower collapse, and which the Bell System likes to talk about, occured at 4.07 p.m., one June 1st.

By 4.07.20 the disaster triggered alarms. At 4.09 checks began to find out what had happened, and the Defense Communications Agency in Washington was told of a potential threat to communications. At 4.10 the local Restoration Control Center—there are eight such centres, one of them in Kansas City—arranged for the rapid re-routing of calls that had been passing along the affected radio link; message traffic monitors began issuing automatic controls such as the switching on of recordings saying 'Lines through Kansas are busy, please try later' and other similar consumer-irritants—to prevent the circuits over-loading dangerously and causing multiple failures. Also at 4.10 the Bell control offices that supervise private networks—like those of the Associated Press, for instance—undertook measures to re-route those circuits. By 4.11 the location, within four miles, of the disaster became apparent to the underground communication centre. At 4.20 a crew of men was sent off to the spot. By 4.45 re-routing had been accomplished by the engineers at the Restoration Center, and all failed circuits were up once again—though this is not a comfortable situation for the company, since re-routing uses up all of the 'protection' circuits contained in cables like the L-3, and there is no further way of protecting that part of the country if any other, more routine mishap takes place (and farmers dig through cables, and manhole workers accidentally join the wrong wires, at the rate of several dozen incidents every day).

By 5.30 the men sent out from the underground centre had radioed back to base the news that the mast was down. At 5.40 the underground manager decided he would have to send out a crew with a temporary new mast. By six o'clock the huge truck, white, with the blue and yellow stripes, the symbolic Bell and the words 'AT&T Long Lines' trundled out of the yard and sped to the wrecked aerial. Crews worked throughout the night, and by 8 p.m. next day completed the first of the three antennae and hooked it in with the waveguides. By 4.30 on the afternoon of the second day all work was complete, and the Restoration Center switched its calls back through the affected area: it took three more weeks for the wrecked aerial to be cleared, the new permanent aerial to be built and the temporary structure crated up once again and loaded into the trailer.

But users of the systems would have noticed an interruption of their service for only about nine minutes; and controllers would only have had two sleepless nights, worrying about their 'unprotected' circuits. The process of such technological marvels is directed from strange subterranean villages like that under the garage-hut at Fairview, and by sleek, slightly mechanical men like Jim Watkins and their slickly programmed teams who work in the dayless, nightless, isolated limbo of the underground.

The building itself is huge—nearly as big as the hamlet of Fairview itself, and totally encased in walls a foot and a half thick, made of steel and concrete. There are millions of dollars' worth of emergency gear stored inside, not so much directed to repairing fallen masts and blown fuses above ground as to keeping the underground centre going and the staff happy if ever an atomic war were to break out above. There are generators and water-distilling machines and batteries—long serried ranks of Exide lead and acid batteries that fill an entire room—and oxygen-making systems and waste-disposing machines and dormitories and cafeterias and gigantic caches of food that are changed every six months or so to prevent anything going stale or mouldy. In the event of an atomic war all the Long Lines men and women from Kansas City are supposed to repair to Fairview—'In four minutes, I suppose,' one girl there said sardonically, pointing out it was a hundred miles distant. Once inside they will be able to sit out the blast in rooms set upon thick steel springs weighing half a ton apiece; they will have almost limitless supplies of candles and Campbell's soup and their own company, and an enormous amount of work to do in the bizarre special emergency restoration room that presently sits, quite empty and deserted, but ready to go at one minute's notice, in the furthest recess of the underground centre.

In this room, which is the size of a small aircraft hangar, are perhaps twenty desks, all facing the same way, all with telephones, yellow legal pads of paper and with sharpened pencils and new erasers on top. The desks are arranged in groups of four, each group facing a Regional Restoration Desk, behind each of which is a great white map of the region—it may be the Midwest, or the Pacific, or the North-east. By the map is a bank of coloured chinagraph pencils on which the Regional Emergency Restoration Manager—who has a desk, with that very description chiselled on a plastic tag stuck on it—can outline the kind of damage done to communications circuits in his region, and set about his plan for re-routing, or repairing the trouble.

There is even a National Emergency Re-routing Desk—which

has a relation to the rest of the desks as High Table to the Junior Members' tables in an Oxbridge dining hall. It is entirely possible, Jim Watkins told me, that a nationwide disaster that knocked out Bell head offices in New York and San Francisco, and almost everywhere else in the nation could be managed from here in the Kansas wheat countryside. There was both the equipment and the knowhow to repair all the country's communications there—and to judge by the scrupulously sharpened pencils and the total absence of dust in the emergency room one gathers that there is nothing the twenty-four permanent Bell System moles who work in the structure would like more than to have to show the Bell managers at head office on Broadway, New York, they can accomplish what they boast.

The only trouble, of course, is that when the time came for the Fairview crews to show off their prowess, there quite probably would be a singular absence of audience. Only the President in his War Room, the SAC Generals in the Underground Command Center in Nebraska, the NORAD Generals under Cheyenne Mountain, and Air Force Lieutenants and Majors in Minuteman Flight capsules in Missouri and North Dakota and Wyoming, and Titan Commanders in Arizona would be grateful for the work done at Fairview: and they, as workers down below are ready to acknowledge, do not make up the most human, or humane, of audiences.

Fairview itself presents a considerable contrast to the whirring, clicking and humming of the underground electronics. It is a dusty little village of a couple of hundred souls; there is a main street with a once-weekly cinema, a drug store and the Fairview Café, which proudly says on the outside window: 'Welcome to a House Well-Kept and Serviced Regularly by the Hickle Pest Company'. The café is run by two elderly ladies, one of whom, Mrs. Leainne Fanning, has also single-handedly run the village weekly newspaper since 1939. Only once—for six months back in the late 1960s—was she forced to halt publication: otherwise this doughty seventy-year-old, craggy and grey and given to printing-ink stained cardigans, newsgathers, writes, edits and editorialises and hand sets four, or six or even eight pages of tiny type, rolls her press and distributes her 2,500 copies of the *Fairview Enterprise* every single week.

It is a remarkable little paper, full of the flavour of the Midwest, straight out of Sinclair Lewis. The front-page stories, if they can be called stories, are of locals returning home after visiting their parents in hospital in Kansas City or of the village petrol station being given an award by the Goodyear Tyre Company. The advertisements are for Baking Hens for Sale, Round Bale Feeders Just Arrived, and 'I will give $500 reward to the person who can give information for the arrest and conviction of the person or persons who turned on the valve at my fertiliser plant in Fairview and caused the loss of several thousands of dollars of fertiliser—Leslie Wikle, Fairview.' Inside there are any number of reports of those most famous and durable of Middle American rural institutions, the Dorcas Societies—much hated by Lewis's Carol Kennicott, but devoted entirely to the self-improvement of the minds of country housewives who otherwise—before television came along—would have become narrow-minded isolationist fossils of the fields before they entered their fourth decade. The local Dorcas Club whose meeting was reported in the edition of the *Enterprise* Mrs. Fanning gave to me had a Mrs. Skinner across to talk about 'Vitamin Use and Abuse', and neighbour societies talked of 'Eyes for the Needy', the 'Wathena School of Instruction' and the 'World Day of Prayer'. One can see why Mrs. Kennicott, newly out of the fleshpots of Minneapolis, would have wanted for more on Main Street than the Dorcas ladies could offer.

From Fairview, through Topeka and Wichita to the Kansas border is some 300 miles. Drivers pass by the wheat capital of Emporia, and the town where one of America's most distinguished newspaper editors, William Allen White, grew up in the closing days of the last century. White was one of the marvels of American journalism, much respected during his lifetime, much remembered and revered in death. His daughter, Mary White, died tragically in 1921 when she was only seventeen: her father's editorial written for the *Emporia Gazette*, established him throughout the country which, thanks to syndication and reprinting, was able to read his writings within days of the funeral—as one of the finest and most sensitive newspaper writers of his time. He wrote:

For her pallbearers only her friends were chosen: her Latin teacher, W. L. Holtz; her High School Principal, Rice Brown; her doctor, Frank Foncannon; her friend, W. W. Finney; her pal at the *Gazette* office, Walter Hughes; and her brother Bill. It would have made her happy to know that her friend, Charley

O'Brien, the traffic cop, had been transferred from Sixth and Commercial to the corner near the church to direct her friends who came to bid her goodbye.

A rift in the clouds in a grey day threw a shaft of sunlight upon her coffin, as her nervous and energetic little body sank to its last sleep. But the soul of her, the glowing, gorgeous, fervent soul of her, surely was flaming in eager joy upon some other dawn.

If it sounds a trifle overdone today, recall that this was the time of the Yellow Press, and Kansas was the place ill-regarded as a fount of literary talent: William Allen White went on from there to join Mencken and Greeley and Pulitzer as one of the grandees of the American newspaper industry.

The southern border of Kansas marks no end to the topographical continuity of the Great Plains; it does, however, mark a sudden termination of the American Midwest. South of Kansas is Oklahoma; and Oklahoma, while plainslike and prairie-peopled, is very much the South. The coming of the sudden change is nowhere more apparent than outside the little town of Eldorado, Kansas— twenty miles north-east of Wichita, and sixty miles from the state line.

At Eldorado there is wheat and there are cattle and there are Republican Congressmen: but there are also, for the first time during this southbound odyssey, a collection of curious black machines set up in the flat fields—machines that have twenty-foot-long arms, one end sporting a pear-shaped pulley head, that swing up and down, up and down, ceaselessly and soundlessly. These are the 'nodding donkeys' of the southern plains—semi-eternally pumping devices that, until the earth 10,000 feet below runs dry, extract every last bottle-full of that thick, black oozing substance on which a thousand southern fortunes were made, and on which a hundred glittering cities base their success—'Texas Tea' they called it for a while. The Arab nations and the rest of the world call it simply after the Greek word for the olive—oil.

6

Oklahoma!
Of Territory Folk

It is difficult to think of the word Oklahoma without the exclamation mark immediately following it. The musical did that, of course —but the exclamatory notation is deft and appropriate to the energies of the people that built this young, pan-shaped state on the northern fringes of the Great South-west. There is a sense of exuberance and hearty, back-slapping, wealth-gathering about Oklahoma—a sense that is a long way removed from the Indians after whom the territory was named (the word is Choctaw, meaning Red [okla] People [homma]) in 1866, and some way removed from the 'Boomers' and the 'Sooners' who populated the territory on that most mystical of Middle American occasions, the famous federally organised distribution to the white man of what were at the turn of the century known as the Unassigned Lands.

The first of the land runs began on April 22, 1889, when massive camps of white men and women—the 'Boomers'—gathered expectantly on the fringes of the Unassigned Lands of Oklahoma Territory waiting for the Government to announce the land was theirs to claim. A fence was built by federal troops to keep early settlers out—they were called 'Sooners', because they had entered Oklahoma Territory too soon—and it was around this picket that the Boomers massed. At noon on the appointed day, a cannon roared and the fences came down: thousands of prospective settlers raced by horse and buggy, by bicycle or by surrey, by train or by foot, to the plot of land they fancied. By evening of the same day 20,000 whites had flooded into, and staked claims on, the hitherto Unassigned Indian Lands. Some parcels of the countryside had already been spoken for by the unscrupulous, but generally envied 'Sooners'. The pushiness of the 'Sooner' spirit led to and flowered into the loud and expansive neo-Texan race that runs the state today—the kind of men and women for whom an exclamation mark appended permanently to their homeland seems appropriate, both as applause as a measure for their achievements and a measure of mild distaste for their methods.

Oklahomans are rich and conservative—at least, those who live in Tulsa and Oklahoma City and Bartlesville are. The money and the power comes from oil, though the slow decline of the state as the giant of oil production (it is now fourth, behind Texas, Louisiana and California) is taking its toll. The boom is sounding less vibrant in Oklahoma today, and there are problems in the cities and the countryside. Combined with the rigorous—one might almost say 'red-necked'—conservatism of the average Oklahoman, there are reasons why the state may have trouble rekindling the self-confidence of its earlier years. In many ways Oklahoma gives the impression of a place having come too far too fast: neither its people nor its institutions are the best equipped for the kind of long-term stability enjoyed by a state like Minnesota, say, or even Texas.

Much of what outsiders dislike about Oklahoma and Oklahomans—'dumb Okies' is how the people in New York have often described them, especially after Steinbeck immortalised the breed in *The Grapes of Wrath*—is summed up by the country-and-western song Merle Haggard wrote into the hit parade of 1970, 'Okie from Muskogee'. The town, in the east of the state, was not known at the time for much tendency to waver, say, from the Vietnam war policies of Richard Nixon, and the idea of growing one's hair and dodging the draft was, to the quintessential Muskogean, worse 'n hell.

> *And I'm proud to be an Okie from Muskogee*
> *A place where even squares can have a ball.*
> *We still wave Ol' Glory down at the Court House*
> *White lightnin's still the biggest thrill of all*
> *In Muskogee, Oklahoma, USA.*

Even the car number plates reflect the smug self-satisfaction of the place. 'Oklahoma is OK' they say, in red on white. I first saw one of those on the back of a southbound Ford Thunderbird, 1975 model, in white and silver, as we were heading south from Wichita, through the toll plaza and out to the village of Braman, in the far north of the 'Sooner State'. There was a man in the car, he was about sixty, his hair was thick and white and sculptured with grease; he wore a sports jacket made of doubleknit polyester in red and white checks; he was smoking a small cigar.

He looked very rich, very smug and self-satisfied, and he had a

bumper sticker that read 'America—if you don't love it, leave it!'
He seemed the best person to sport an 'Oklahoma is OK' license
plate—and it seemed appropriate to my cynicism and irrational
dislike of this man, his car and his symbols that as he accelerated
my radio suddenly interrupted with a Bulletin from Oklahoma City
which told how the last governor of the state, Mr. David Hall, had
just been found guilty of bribery and extortion and other un-
pleasantnesses during his term in office. Hall was later to appeal;
when I saw him on television later that evening he looked essentially the same as the man in the Thunderbird. The two gave me an
uneasy feeling about Oklahoma, unlike any feelings I had had in the
four states to the north.

The north, incidentally, was by now a long way away: down here,
even though only a little further south than Kansas City, where the
streets were still piled with mounds of greyly melting snow, it was
hot and sticky. The clock on the bank in Braman was equipped with
a digital thermometer that indicated eighty degrees: this was the
southwest all right—the car heater could go off now, and stay off.

The last time I had been in Ponca City—named after the Ponca,
one of the region's most populous Indian 'nations'—was in the
mid-summer of 1974, when Richard Nixon had come down from
Washington to talk to people in the one state that could be guaran-
teed to give him a good time. He was to speak at Commencement at
Oklahoma State University, which is in the town of Stillwater (a
place, incidentally which, like Chattanooga, Tennessee, appears to
be crawling with Welshmen, for some reason that is not entirely
clear). At the time I wrote of Nixon's desperation at having to
come down to the political wastelands of Oklahoma for one last
shot of ego-soothing cheering. I rated his standing in the nation as
dismally poor, after seeing that, even at the harshly conservative
old 'cow college' of OSU, there were protesters, and large numbers
of protesters at that. I suggested that the Stillwater trip might well
be Richard Nixon's last political appearance—and, give or take the
odd rampage on television from the White House, it was. When a
man like Richard Nixon is given a rebuff in a place like Oklahoma,
he knows it is time to throw in the towel.

Ponca City then was a dreary slum of motels and truckstops, the
entire city dominated, it had seemed, by the flickering flame,
twenty feet tall, that blazed on top of a steel venting pipe on the

Continental Oil Company's huge refinery. Oil rules Ponca City's economy: it brings in men whose sole aim is to make money fast, and in consequence the Ponca City I saw exudes the same insubstantial impermanence of an oil camp in some jungle wilderness. There is no good reason, one feels, for a place like Ponca City to stay where it is once the oil has run out.

But the impression gleaned from that two-day stay when Richard Nixon was near by was probably coloured by the bustle and the late arrivals and long night maunderings that so characterise reporting of Presidential visits anywhere. One thing I do recall vividly was the astonishing application of that particular locality's liquor laws. We arrived late, sometime after 11 p.m., after a long flight from Washington and a longer drive from Tulsa. Late at night, the bars stay open, but no drink is to be had unless you are lucky enough to have brought your own bottle with you beforehand. The barmaid, a pretty girl from Oklahoma City, proudly revealed the neat rows of bottles, each, as prescribed by law, in a brown bag and each bag with the owner's initials written in pencil. If a man wanted a drink, he had only to ask for his bottle and one would be poured. For those ignorant city folk like us who had no notion such goings on were commonplace, the barmaid had a kind suggestion. Why didn't we each have a glass of the liquor she kept in her own personal bottle? And why didn't we slip her a couple of dollars' tip, under the table? Then we wouldn't be buying it, would we, and the law— 'which is pretty darn tough round these parts—your durn' tootin' ' she explained—would have nothing about which to complain. We were happy to fall in with her friendly gesture, and were each poured a large—a very large—glass full of a syrupy red liquid. We asked what it might be, and then promptly wished we hadn't.

The liquid, which courtesy and the donation of the large tip forced us to imbibe, was nothing so innocent as Red Rose Wine, the tipple of the local tramps. It was Cherry Brandy and Coca-Cola, mixed, and with sugar added. The kind of drink that would kill most normal mortals, but which is apparently tolerated by the Ponca City Holiday Inn's pretty barmaid, and by the tool-pushers and roughnecks and salesmen who came in to swig from their brown-bagged bottles during the night hours. Ponca City, on half a pint of Cherry Brandy and Coke, can appear a pretty town.

But Ponca City on a Wichita rancher's breakfast, and with fair skies, a soft breeze and eighty degrees, and spring green fields on all sides, is altogether another story. The centre of the town sports very few motels: there is a long, broad main street, with white stucco-walled buildings, some of vaguely Spanish appearance, marching down it for quarter of a mile. The shops are much the same kind of shops in any Middle American town, except that there seem to be a large number of shoe shops, most of them doing a brisk sale in cowboy boots, spurs, saddlesoap and horse brushes. The boots are made by a variety of celebrated cowboy suppliers: strangely, the best known 'western boot', which is made by Frye Boots of Massachusetts, doesn't sell at all out here in the real cowboy country. In this part of the world the men who work on the ranches buy Acme or Tony Lama boots; they can neither afford the money or the fancy upkeep needed to own a pair of Frye boots. Frye makes western boots for eastern feet, and a nice profit in the process.

I had come to Ponca City to see the local police force. Originally I had planned to stay a day with the Oklahoma Highway Patrol; but that organisation had taken so much bad publicity over a peculiar case involving a laboratory technician, a car crash, and a mass of plutonium found in a bologna sandwich—more of all which later— that the public information office was distinctly unhelpful. The Ponca City police chief, Mr. Forrest Walker, whom I spoke to by phone from Minneapolis, said he would be glad to see me, though, and looked forward to meeting an Englishman—the first one in Ponca City for quite a long time, he said.

Mr. Walker, who is sixty and tubby and overall-grey coloured, from his trouser turn-ups to his hair, had been in 'the law enforcement business' as he calls it, since he left school at the age of eighteen. Since the Second World War he had been, in turn, Undersheriff and then Sheriff of Kay County, Oklahoma, then chief of police in the town of Tonkawa, and now chief of police for Ponca City, a post he had held for nearly a decade. His office is a small, cluttered, bathroom-sized den just to the right of the front door of the Police Department Office, where, were the building some business corporation, the receptionist would sit or would have her waiting room. He liked being the first person a visitor to the station saw: it gave him a bit more authority in his job, he thought. His office is covered with photographs of colleague officers, with pictures of the mayor of the town and of other dignitaries, and of his family. There is a small Ronson electric shoe-shine machine near the door, and from time to time patrolmen hold their legs through his open doorway and buff their toe-caps before walking out on to the street. 'I believe in a smart force,' Chief Walker says.

His force consists of fifty-one men and women, of whom forty-two are in uniform; Ponca City sports a population of about 30,000, so the ratio of police to civilians is about one to 600, which is a good deal better than the big cities of the east, where one policeman can be responsible for the safety of as many as 5,000 men, women and children. The rank structure in the force is as required by the Department of Justice: a Captain of Police, an Assistant Chief, seven sergeants, ten corporals and twenty-two regular officers. There are a number of secretaries and a gaoler named Wesley Vannote who is responsible for looking after the prisoners who live on the upper floor of the two-storey building.

The town makes a fair bit of money from taxing the big oil men who live near by, and the taxes pay for a reasonably smart and well-equipped little force. There are eleven 'vehicular units'—American police jargon is as cumbrous as the 'vehicular units' themselves—of which five are 'beat cars', one is a detective car, another the captain's car, another a juveniles' car, two sergeants' cars and one 'pick-up unit' into which the drunks and the burglars and the very occasional rapist will be herded to be brought round and booked.

The beat cars, which cruise the city streets incessantly, are all-white Fords, with two red lights and a siren than can play three quite different nerve-jarring versions of the emergency wail. Each car is marked by a shield, two feet tall, painted on the doors: it has a spread-winged eagle above a motif of the five-pointed Oklahoma star and the words 'POLICE patrol, Ponca City, Okla.' written around it. A movable spotlight in front of the driver's side window completes the picture; the wireless aerial, with which the patrolman will communicate with the duty sergeant back at base, is no different from a car radio aerial. But for the red lights and the shield, Chief Walker's cruise cars are virtually unmarked—a way removed from the blue-and-white patrol cars in New York and Washington, or the big yellow and black and white highway patrol cars financed by the state of Oklahoma itself.

The Chief was in a reflective mood, and a sombre one. He had to attend the funeral later in the day of one of his men, who had been on the force for eight years. The officer had died of an ulcer. 'I'm not rightly sure,' he said, when I asked him if he would be a policeman all over again. 'There have been so many changes it's not so swell a job as it was when I first joined up. The courts and the lawmakers—both of them—are giving us cops a bad time, and we have more and more trouble doing our job well. In many ways it's a dog's life today.'

His particular gripe that day—perhaps he had just cursed one of his colleagues, but he didn't say—was that it is quite impossible for him to fire anyone on the force, no matter how bad he is. 'Time was when any cop who rubbed his chief up the wrong way would be out on his ear. These days a guy can sass you and be lazy and good-for-nothing, and you've got to give him a year's suspension, and keep on paying him, and pay him compensation if he is said to have been wrongly dismissed. The judges, too—they're just as bad. You can't seem to be able to get warrants any more: in the old days you could just pick a guy up and throw his ass in gaol and he'd know not to do it again. Now it's darned difficult to get him in gaol for more than a single night, and he'll most likely be let off with a slapped wrist. That's not the way to keep a city like this in order.'

He said he was very much in favour of bringing back the death penalty—in Oklahoma, that meant killing by an electric chair down at McAlester State Penitentiary—which was outlawed, along with the capital punishment provisions in the other states, by a Supreme Court ruling of 1972. 'Nowadays you find totally uncalled-for killings don't get any stiffer sentences than robbery does. So many guys used to say to me, after they had dropped their guns, 'The only reason I didn't kill you was that I didn't want to fry'', and that's a pretty darn good reason, don't you think?' He was appalled by the even lighter sentences being imposed on users and sellers of drugs —that 'filthy stuff'—and said 'There was a time when we had a good law, with possession of the stuff being a felony, with good, heavy sentences. Now there's all this crap about decriminalising the stuff—why, have you ever seen a really spaced-out addict, have you ever seen the kind of things drugs make people do? I'd have it off the streets darn quick, I can tell you—none of this tickle-on-the-wrist-and-don't-do-it-next-time stuff, I can tell you!'

Chief Walker, in common with most other white and middle-aged Oklahomans, calls black people 'coloured folk', just as they did in the Deep South before Selma and Martin Luther King and

Lyndon Johnson came along and directed the mood of white America along more tolerant and kindly channels. 'Coloured folk', though not as offensive as 'groids', which is what blacks are called in some other parts of red-necked Midwest, is patronisingly insulting, as it is probably meant to be. The word 'uppity' sounds all right next to 'coloured folk'; but Chief Walker claims the 400 or so 'coloureds' who live in Ponca City give him little enough trouble. 'There's more robbery and so on reported down there, but it's mainly against themselves, and it doesn't cause the rest of the city that much bother.' There are a few hundred Indians—Poncas, naturally enough—whom Forrest Walker likes even less. They drink too much—especially the young ones, he said, and he has to watch out all the time in case, after affairs like Wounded Knee and the Wisconsin Monastery Siege, the local Indians get ideas of staging some kind of dramatic protest. Chief Walker would not care for the world's press to drop in on a dispute between his men and the Ponca militants.

There is not a great amount of custom in the local gaol, but Wesley Vannote, who is twenty-six, and weighs at least twenty stone, manages visitors with courtesy, tact and a dose of new-fangled religion whenever they cross the threshold. Mr. Vannote, who joined the force as Ponca City's official gaoler in 1973 ('It was against my religion to carry a gun, but I wanted to join the police, and this was the only job I could get that didn't require a gun') is a Jehovah's Witness, and any unfortunate who happens to be put into his charge is, he readily admits, 'given a few minutes of preaching'. Wesley Vannote is a very pleasant sort of gaoler. He is compassionate—he will tell you that he never condemns a man—or a woman; there are six cells for women, though they are rarely used—for being in prison. 'I just feel sorry that they've gone off the tracks, and I try to do what I can for them. When the guys bring them in off the hoot-owl shift [the late shift, eleven o'clock at night until seven the next morning] most of them are drunk and they can't abide my talking to them. But the next morning they often feel like a message from God, and so I do my best to give it.'

There had been an unhappy incident the day before I arrived. 'We had a young guy in here,' Wesley explained, 'who we had arrested because he had gone AWOL and the army wanted him back. He had come from down Fort Sill, I think. Boy, when we put that guy in the federal cells [in a block of cells, separate from the rest, where all men arrested for federal offences are segregated] he hollered and kicked and yelled for all he was worth. We stripped him down so he couldn't harm hisself, and then I went off to get some chow. When I got back—it can't have been more than an hour at most—blow me, if the feller hadn't strung hisself up. He had ripped his pants into long strips, tied them together and hung himself from the bars of the cell. He hadn't broken his neck—he had choked to death under his own weight. It must have been a terrible way to die.' Did he know why this wretched man had killed himself so suddenly and so horribly? 'No, I never have figured out what was behind it. No one here heard a sound, and the sergeant was downstairs all the while. I can't have given him too hard a time with the religion, can I, d'you think?'

The prisoners who were normally in his cells—small cupboard-sized spaces, each with a washbasin and a low-level bowl and a hard and hairy mattress on a sheet-iron bed, and with inch-thick bars and sliding barred doors preventing escape—fared pretty well, Wesley said. They had three good meals a day, prepared under contract by Jean's Café up the street. Only that morning the two prisoners in the cells had each eaten an egg, hash-brown potatoes, toast and coffee; and that evening, as every evening, they would get the Night Special from Jean's 'and that can be very good'.

Outside, Uncle Walt was brushing the gaol corridor, along which all prisoners came after the ride up in a bizarre Victorian-style cast-iron lift, which has a swinging iron partition inside to guard the gaoler and the lift controls from the possibly violent intents of the potential inmate. Uncle Walt was one of the regular town winos, Wesley said. Each evening he would go down to the ABC store, buy two bottles of Gallo White Port, which would set him back 85 cents a pint, and drink it in some alley-way. By eleven he would be out cold, and an officer would drag him into the back of the cruiser and lug him into the gaol. 'He's been coming in here every single evening for the last ten years,' Wesley said. 'We dry him out in the cell, give him a good breakfast and set him to work sweeping and polishing. Then we let him go, and he panhandles a few pennies from the townsfolk, and goes down to the ABC store and gets another two pints of White Port and there we go again. Sometimes I ask him if he wouldn't rather have a regular job here, but he says he has no one to go home to and no home anyway. So we let him stay. It's a pretty fair arrangement.' Uncle Walt is an old man, perhaps seventy. He is black, with white stubble poking through his dusty chin. His eyes are small red slits behind two puffy folds of dark watery flesh, and his hair is receding and grey. He wears a ragged brown coat and a sweat-soaked brown shirt. He manages a wave when I see him, and he lifts his sweeping brush in mock salute. He smiles a little, though it is as ardonic smile at best. One wonders how he might have fared in Oklahoma had he not been 'coloured folk'.

I was pleased to note, when I went back to my car, that I had not made the usual mistake of leaving town with a pink parking ticket stuffed into my windscreen wiper. In towns around the Midwest parking meters have small boxes into which an offending motorist can slip the fine—usually half a dollar at most—before he leaves. But in Ponca City, even though I had spent half a day and had only deposited a quarter in the meter that morning, neither the 'offence' flag was up, nor was there a ticket on the windscreen. Ponca City, it turned out, is one of those few remaining bastions of the penny parking meters. The meter has slots that will take one cent pieces, and will deliver twenty-four minutes of parking in return. There have been moves in the city council to have the fee increased, but tax revenues from the rich men in town keep the council happy, and so, for now anyway, penny parking is in Ponca City to stay.

The funeral of the ulcer-stricken officer was beginning as I drove away: a long line of ten of the 'vehicular units' was driving over to the cemetery, half a mile down US Route 60. I had to press on down I-35, however: and so I turned west, under the ragged flame of the Conoco refinery, and ten miles or so to the freeway. Our road dipped under it, and from a distance the highway, slightly higher than the flat north Oklahoma grassfields, displayed long lines of fast-speeding trucks heading north and south between Wichita and Oklahoma City. I eased left off the access road once I had passed under the freeway, and joined the upward ramp. A few seconds later, and I eased between a big rig carrying aircraft parts down from the Cessna plant at Wichita and another towing a drilling tower to a new exploration site, which to judge from the truck licence plate, was near the city of Enid, off to the west. It was a warm day, brilliantly sunny; and though the corn was far from being as high as an elephant's eye, this being March, the ground looked rich and fertile. It was eighty miles to Oklahoma City, and to Indian country.

Fifty miles south of Ponca City the Interstate crosses a muddy stream, fifty feet wide, called the Cimarron River. It is the third most important waterway in the state; the Canadian River which passes through Oklahoma City is the second; and the first is the Arkansas River, which, thanks to the US Army Corps of Engineers is now navigable all the way up through Little Rock to Tulsa. This makes Tulsa the North American seaport that, with the single exception of Duluth, is the most distant from the sea.

The Cimarron River, like the others, flows eventually into the Mississippi; it rises in the Sangre de Cristo Mountains in New Mexico, appropriately close to the site where, on July 16, 1945, the world's first atom bomb was dropped. It is appropriate because half-way between New Mexico and the Mississippi, and in a town called Crescent, some eight miles west of where I-35 crosses the stream, a factory has been built where the ingredients for future nuclear weapons can, in theory, be made. The plant is known as the Cimarron Facility of the Kerr-McGee Corporation; one of its functions is to manufacture fuel rods and pellets made of plutonium, for use in an atomic reactor being built in the state of Washington. It was at the plant, in the autumn of 1974, that one of the more unsettling mysteries of the recent nuclear age took place.

Karen Silkwood was twenty-eight years old. She was driving, quite alone, southwards down highway 74 on the evening of November 13, 1974. In her white Honda Civic, when she had left the Hub Café in Crescent, there was a manila file folder. She left the cafe at 7.15 p.m. At 7.30 p.m., when she was seven miles away, the Honda left the road and crashed full pelt into the wing-wall of a concrete culvert over a small stream. A truck-driver found the car at 8.05 p.m. Karen Silkwood was taken to the Guthrie Hospital nearby but was pronounced dead on arrival, from multiple, compound fractures and internal injuries. The manila folder has never since been found.

Karen Silkwood was a Kerr-McGee employee. For the months before her death she had been agitating inside the company—and outside, with her union bosses in Washington (she was a fully paid-up member of the Oil & Chemical Workers' Union Local 5-283, and was, in fact, a member of the Local's council), about what she claimed were serious violations of the plutonium safety rules, and the generally slipshod practices inside the chainlink fences and under the searchlight glare of Kerr-McGee. When she died she had been travelling to Oklahoma City to see another union man from Washington, together with a reporter from New York. Her allegations were about to become national news: instead, her death, and its bizarre surrounding circumstances, leaped to the front pages, and stayed in the news for months.

The first 'problem' was that, in spite of the Oklahoma Highway Patrol's 'finding' that the white Honda had left the road of its own volition, a respected private investigator found marks on the Honda bumper that suggested—incontrovertibly, he said—that her car had been forced off the road by another vehicle. The second 'problem' was the missing folder—a folder that was said to contain horrendous new allegations about impropriety within the company. The third was the extraordinary extent to which Miss Silkwood, who was employed as a laboratory technician, had become contaminated with plutonium since she had started making complaints against her firm. The flat she shared with another girl in Oklahoma was hot with pollution—especially, according to a later report from the Atomic Energy Commission, inside the refrigerator, where a bologna sandwich reeked of plutonium dust and buzzed with a fearsome amount of particles of potential lethality.

Suspicion has hovered ever since that Kerr-McGee—or some other champion of the nuclear cause—had some as yet unexplained role in the strange fate of Miss Silkwood. Was she, as some critics have said, a 'troublemaker' who was 'against big business' and who was 'on drugs' and 'could well have contaminated herself' to dramatise her complaints about company practice. Or was she, as her champions will claim, a sincerely motivated girl who was harassed, intimidated—and finally killed—by men who didn't want the secrets of the plutonium industry revealed to the outside world? The Atomic Energy Commission sided with the dead girl when its investigators toured the Kerr-McGee plant—Government investigators found numerous cases of sloppy and, in some cases, downright deceitful practices, and ordered the company to tighten up its procedures. The general public—egged on by a spate of unrelated, but coincident documentary television films about the hazards of this most poisonous of nuclear-age materials—began to sit up and take notice of the danger, and the power, of the atomic lobby and the atomic industry. Karen Silkwood became a posthumous folk-hero of sorts, who achieved far more for her cause in death than one suspects she ever would have done while living.

The case says a number of things about Oklahoma in particular, and Middle America in general. For Oklahoma, the story points up the gigantic concentration of wealth and industrial power in the hands of a few big men—Robert Kerr, a multi-millionaire oilman who became the state's first native-born governor, and Dean McGee, who joined him in business to become a multi-millionaire as well, and a formidable political force in the state, are two such. It also points up the sternly uncompromising nature of the authorities —the stubborn, mulish behaviour of the Highway Patrol, in this case. And it points up the general resentment of Oklahomans—and other Middle Americans too—directed towards any 'slick Easterners' who travel to their country to examine its foibles, its power structure, and its faults. The local press in Oklahoma never gave much space or time to the Silkwood story, believing, probably, that the greater good was achieved by keeping the Kerr-McGee plant just where it was, and making sure young hussies like Miss Silkwood were not allowed in to make 'trouble'.

What the Kerr-McGee saga says about the American midlands is how over the years they have become repositories for much of what in this country is noisy, dirty, smelly or dangerous. Plutonium in Oklahoma; bombs in New Mexico; atom tests in Nevada; atomic plants in Idaho; nerve gases in Utah; an artillery school in Oklahoma; tank training grounds in Texas; missile ranges in New Mexico. The further from Washington, it seems, the greater the ability of the civil servants to direct the unpleasantries of twentieth-century industry there. One imagines that had the Kerr-McGee plant been outside New Rochelle, or suburban Montgomery County, Maryland, it would have either been closed down or the contract been handed elsewhere, had there been a Karen Silkwood in operation. As it is, Kerr-McGee goes happily on producing rods and phials of one of the most dangerous substances known, and only the Easterners and the Far Westerners read enough to suggest that what is going on there should be stopped, before it is too late.

Just south of Oklahoma City—one of the dreariest big cities in the country, although the oil rigs in the grounds of the State Capitol, and the National Cowboy Hall of Fame, provide some temporary relief—is the city of Norman. It is very modern, and very rich-looking, and it houses the glittering new buildings and the amazing football stadium of the University of Oklahoma. There is, however, a poor side of town—a place that, while still officially on the campus, is filled with decaying old wooden barrack-block buildings that house the less glamorous sides of the university. In one of the barracks is an office that, since 1965, has tried hard, and with a good measure of success, to cope with the tremendous problems of the Indians of Oklahoma: the story of Oklahomans for Indian Opportunity, as the organisation that inhabits the office is known, is one of the most encouraging in a field littered with sad sagas of failure and despair.

The story provides a distinguished counterpoint to the more violent, and more highly publicised activities of those other Indians who have lost all patience with the white man's system, and now want to change it by policies of confrontation and High Plains drama. A serious split has been evident in the ranks of the American Indians since 1972, when militant red men first occupied the Bureau of Indian Affairs offices in Washington: while not the precise antithesis of Indian militancy by any means, OIO has come to represent the constructive approach to Indian problems, and as such is applauded and denigrated by turn.

According to the Bureau of the Census, there are more Indians in Oklahoma—some 99,000 in 1972—than in any other state. Some unofficial estimates say that as many as 200,000 Oklahomans are in fact full- or half-blooded Indians, and one survey has suggested that as many as half a million people in the 'Sooner state' have red man's blood in their veins. Certainly, to look at a crowd in Oklahoma City or Tulsa or Anadarko or Lawton, one thinks one spies an inordinate number of people who look very different from the Scandinavian or Yankee pale-faces one saw in Minneapolis or Kansas City. In Oklahoma the *gestalt* is very significantly different, and that difference is almost certainly due to the Indian influence.

The reason Oklahoma is so liberally filled with Indians has a great deal to do with one of the most callously inhuman episodes of white American history—an episode that has made the state of Oklahoma, to a great extent, a living symbol of the injustices meted out to this proud and noble people.

Until the beginning of the eighteenth century the lands that are now called Oklahoma were sporadically occupied by wandering bands of Plains Indians; after 1803, when the fledgling American

Government took over the vast tracts of Deep Southern lands from French authority—the so-called Louisiana purchase—the land began to fill up with wretched masses of refugees, displaced by Government fiat and ordered from the Deep South and out west along what has appropriately been termed 'The Trail of Tears'.

The trail took the so-called Five Civilised Tribes—the Cherokee, the Seminole, the Choctaw, the Creek and the Chickasaw—away from the southern homelands that the white man so greedily coveted, and turned him westwards, under the watchful eye of stern army sergeants, up to designated Indian Territory in the Plains Indians country. The episode is rightfully judged by modern Indians to have been one of the more shameful in post-revolutionary history, and the 'Tears' for which the Trail is named flowed freely, and with reason. Starvation, tuberculosis and a variety of other diseases of the enforced wanderer took a terrible toll. Of the Cherokees, less than a third survived the thousand-mile trek across the Purchase lands.

The Government had assigned the eastern part of the Territory to the Five Civilised Tribes; the western regions were for the Plains Indians. For a very short while there was some development of a new, though uprooted red man's culture in the new home. But then came the stage lines and the railways, and the battles and bloodshed of a sort one sees romanticised and distorted on the late night television shows. The local buffalo herds were decimated by white traders and railway bosses, in a deliberate attempt to steal the Indians' livelihood away, so they would steal away themselves and stop worrying the silk-clad gentlemen and the brave pioneer ladies who had the temerity to take those first westward journeys on the Union Pacific and the Santa Fé. Trouble brought the Union Army into Oklahoma Territory in mid-century, and a violent Phoenix-style pacification programme was unleashed, which few Indians, spurred on by the legends and folk-songs handed down through the years, are able or willing to forget.

The land runs ordered by President Harrison effectively ended what suzerainty the Indians claimed; and although there was a brief attempt—defeated by a fearful Congress—to establish an official state of Sequoyah, exclusively for the Indians, in the eastern part of the territory, Indian power and authority effectively crumbled to nothing. Oklahoma became a fully fledged state in 1907, and since then the Indian people have essentially been the under-represented, poverty-stricken and disenfranchised minority they are in most other states. Oklahoma's experience is more dramatic than the experiences of other Indian strongholds, like the Dakotas, or Wisconsin, or Florida: and it serves as the best illustration of what is wrong with white attitudes towards the red nations, and can explain just why the American Indian is a bitter, angry man today.

In 1965, when rebellion and disaffection were starting to become a dominant feature of the contemporary American order, there was a sudden realisation among Oklahoma Indians that they, by virtue of their numbers, their native wit and their ready accessibility to the growing tide of public sympathy, could organise and take charge of their own destiny. A group of young, intelligent and articulate Indians—the prime movers of whom, LaDonna Harris and Iola Hayden, were married to white men of stature and authority in the state—formed OIO; and, while surviving internal power struggles and clashes over policy, their organisation has given the Oklahoma Indian a sense of identity he never had, and a new sense of capability that is leading him to explore unthought-of regions of opportunity, denied to him before by reason of bigotry, poverty and the lack of what Americans call 'clout'. OIO gave the Indians clout, and the organisation now is a formidable force locally and, given its legacy in Washington and elsewhere on the Great Plains, over the nation.

Iola Hayden is a Comanche, and she now oversees from her post as Executive Director an organisation that has grown from being able to disburse a total of $11,000 in grants to assist Oklahoma Indians, to a giant entrepreneurial warehouse that had a 1974 budget of well over half a million dollars. All of this money, skilfully applied by Mrs. Hayden and a dedicated staff of co-directors working from the barrack block in Norman, goes for the sole purpose of helping local Indians pull themselves up by their bootstraps from their posture of total subjection to a position of total equality with the white man, and total equality of opportunity within the white power structure.

As an example, Mrs. Hayden—a handsome, dark-haired woman of enormous energy and apparent severe determination—tells of one Kiowa Indian family who opened a drive-in restaurant in the suburbs of Oklahoma City. 'We helped him with a grant to buy the place, but then the owner just decided he would "forget" to pay his taxes. He had never really thought about it—until one day the

Internal Revenue Service came along and told him if he didn't pay up, they'd close him down. He came to us and asked what he should do—and we paid the bill on the strict understanding he joined the Oklahoma Restaurant Association and learned how to do things the right way—O.K., the Establishment way, if you will. Our mission here is to help the Indians drag themselves up; while I've enormous sympathy for those militants like Dennis Banks and Russell Means [the Wounded Knee Leaders and chief officials of AIM, the militant American Indian Movement], my personal intuition is to continue to work within the system.'

Mrs. Hayden said that one problem, particularly with the plains Indians who were still concentrated in the western dry regions of the Panhandle, was their signal reluctance to stay in any one place for more than a very short time. 'We helped a young couple of Araphoes [who, like the Cheyennes and Apaches, are Plains Indians] to buy a radio and television franchise store out in Lawton. One day they just upped and left. They shut up shop and just decided they had had enough, and it was time for them to move. It is sometimes very difficult to persuade them they have to stay around if they want to succeed in this kind of a job. It didn't appeal to them, I'm sorry to say.'

She, like the leaders of AIM—which drew its strength from her organisation's early successes, but then drifted away in the early 1970s into more spectacular fields—feels contemptuous of the patronising attitudes of the Bureau of Indian Affairs, with which Washington has successfully subdued Indian passions for the last century and a half. (The first twenty-five years of the BIA's life, incidentally, was as a part of the War Department, a conception that critics charge has coloured the Bureau's attitudes ever since.) She is happy that AIM is having some success, but resents the way some young Indians, who feel she and the OIO could be more radical and more extreme, assail her with invective. More than once she has been called an 'apple' by ill-tempered militants—the term suggesting she is, like the fruit, red on the outside, but *white on the inside*. (The term is only one of a range of culinary insults: the first was to call a black man an 'Oreo', after the cream-filled chocolate biscuit of the same name: it means black on the outside, but white on the inside. The newest, which one hears on the fringes of San Francisco's straining Chinatown, is 'banana'.) But Iola Hayden shrugs off the obloquy, which she considers misdirected and ill founded. 'We have something like sixty tribes here in Oklahoma now. The Indian population here has risen by a quarter in the last ten years. Indians are coming to realise that there is opportunity—a future—for them in Oklahoma. I consider the fact that the opportunities exist now—and they did not really exist before we started our self-help programmes and managed to get the money from the Government and the Ford Foundation and all the others—is directly to do with OIO. The tribal councils are flourishing. The Indian people are happier and more peaceful and more prosperous than in most other states. We have had something to do with that I'm sure.'

Curiously, Mrs. Hayden has little time for either her former colleague and co-founder LaDonna Harris, or for Fred Harris, her husband, and the former Senator for Oklahoma who tried to run for the Presidency on a Populist ticket in 1972. Fred and LaDonna Harris, who one sees at half-smart dinner parties in Washington more than a few times, are faded darlings of the Old New Left who have ambitions of great power still: Fred Harris, a burly man who looks more like a docker than a former Senator, is an announced candidate for the 1976 election. He moved too far to the left for Oklahomans in the 1970s, and too far to the left for the Democratic Party to take him seriously in 1972. His candidacy, when it was announced in the winter of 1974, drew cheers and heavy publicity from the more chic of popular political journals: the fact that his financing in 1974 amounted to rather less than $2,000—compared with the $1,700,000 collected during the same period by George Wallace of Alabama—suggested to many that his hopes of entering the White House in any capacity other than visitor or guest, were slim indeed.

Iola Hayden finds his populist theories 'half-baked, not well thought out and extremely naïve'. Other observers find him hugely likeable, and hope he will manage to assail the system sufficiently harshly so that he will be a power to be reckoned with in the 1976 struggle. The majority, though, tend to agree with Iola Hayden; Fred Harris, sad to say, was written off almost as soon as he had thrown his hat into the ring.

Between Norman and my next stop, the small town of Ardmore, are the only mountains over which Interstate-35 is forced to cross. One might almost say they are the only mountains on the Great

Plains—a small gathering of Ordovician and Silurian limestone wrinkles that momentarily interrupt the steady east-to-west upslope that inclines gently between the Mississippi cliffs and the huge folds of the Rocky Mountains.

The hills in Oklahoma are known as the Arbuckle Mountains: they rise to the grand altitude of 1,438 feet—lower than the lowliest of the Appalachian ridges. Yet they are variously described locally as 'breathtaking' and 'craggy' and 'spectacular'; and indeed they are. For after 1,200 miles of almost total flatness to the north, and with half that distance again of virtual flatness to the south, the sight of rocky mountains, though only pimples in reality, is a comforting brush with the reality of the outside world. The only better sight would be the sea. Since that, even for American technology, is impossible, one has to make do with the Honey Creek, a river that rises in the Arbuckles and, for five turbulent miles, has all the appearance of a Colorado freshet—ice-cold, rushing, bubbling and noisy. By the time it splashes down on to the grassy Plains and makes its way up to the Red River and the Prairies, it is as mud-thick and turgid as any other Oklahoma stream—a joyless transition, made all the more upsetting by the contrast.

Ardmore is another oil town, booming these days thanks to the shortages and the new stimulus to production and exploration being afforded by the vastly higher prices for crude. Generally the days of Oklahoma oil are on the decline—Tulsa, though it still calls itself the 'Oil Capital of the World', has had to watch helplessly while giants of the industry have moved out to Houston, and has to accept that the largest employer in the state's second city is now American Airlines, a consumer of oil, and not a producer. But in a town like Ardmore, where one can see the rigs humming and clanging under their neon strip-lights every hour of every day, and where one can see the new offices of the drilling and well-logging firms like Halliburton and Schlumberger and Reading & Bates, and the Hughes Tool Company, the power of crude oil is still very apparent indeed. If Ponca City is a town that owes its fortunes to the refining of oil, then Ardmore, nearly two hundred miles further south, and on the fringes of the real oil kingdom of Texas, owes its prosperity to the exploration for and production of the thick, dark liquid.

But I had come to Ardmore for quite a different reason. A girl I know in Kansas City had been brought up in Ardmore, and had explained to me one night how her old home personified the glittery, foot-loose, brash world of the greasy-haired American teenager of the 1960s to perfection. The film, *American Graffiti*, which took a hugely successful multicoloured look at the world of a small town's Main Drag was set, the cognoscenti say, in some community in California's San Joaquin Valley; the girl in Kansas City said that Ardmore, Oklahoma, was much the same when she was a high school girl—and from what she had heard, not much had changed.

But it had changed, of course. For one thing, the waitresses at the Sonic Drive-In no longer wear roller skates to speed their orders, although the place has a slogan quite appropriate to its name—'Service with the Speed of Sound'. The speed is accomplished now with the aid of small microphones on stalks that rear beside every car-parking stall. Customers—and they are mainly teenage, though with a large complement of housewives, their hair in curlers and only half-hidden under ill-fitting scarves—drive up to the microphones and press the call button. Ned Albert, who runs the place and stands by the order console from nine in the morning until eleven at night, with only a two-hour break for supper, answers. 'Your order please,' he says, and the motorist responds. 'One hamburger, educated, and a large Dr. Pepper please!' Ned Albert writes it down, in ballpen squiggles as indecipherable as a doctor's prescription, and sticks the order paper on to a revolving steel carousel above the young and extremely pretty girl who is slaving over the huge hotplate. Three minutes later an educated hamburger (meaning one with lettuce, tomatoes and mayonnaise, as opposed to a *fixed* hamburger, which has mustard, pickle and onion) and a ten-inch-tall wax-paper cup of crushed ice and brownish red Dr. Pepper are being carried out to the car by a two-dollars-an-hour waiter, most of whom seem to be Indians. The money changes hands, and the driver turns up the car radio and sits back for half an hour to enjoy the vehicular repast, before it is time to drive off, and carry on with the shopping, or whatever. There are thirty-two spaces for cars at the Sonic, and since most customers come two or four to a car, there is little time for Ned Albert and his wife, Wilma (who comes in to help most days) to take time off.

Ned Albert is so typically a part of the American Dream, it is hard to imagine he is not some creation of the Gallup Poll. He came over here with his father from the Lebanon, forty years ago; his family lived in Texas and Kansas, and then, when he was old enough and his drifting jobs had brought him enough cash to put down on a franchise stake, he bought a restaurant. Not this one at first, but a small place further upstate that went reasonably well. Now he runs the Sonic, he works so hard he has hardly any time to think, and yet he feels he is doing all that his life demands of him. 'My father was poor, very poor. I have done better. The money I make out of this place is all going on educating my four sons.' One of them—the last he has to educate—is now at a pediatricians' training school in San Francisco. 'When he graduates I'll be free to lay all this down'—he gestures at the hamburger wrappers and the soft order pencil and the cartons of cooking oil—'and retire with a good conscience. My sons are all well educated, and they've all got good jobs. The one in San Francisco will go on to be a doctor, and he'll make a hundred thousand a year if he's lucky. So from now on the Alberts will be O.K.—my father saw that I was O.K., and I've seen that my sons are too.'

In England, where education is nominally free at point of delivery, the need to work hard for the sole purpose of pushing children through university and giving them tickets to a better world than you experienced, is alien to modern ways. But America is filled with powerful incentives for hard work like this, and the incentive tends to breed the kind of man embodied in Ned Albert. He and his wife are, without a doubt, kindly, warm, generous and well intentioned. One comes away from seeing them at their work full of respect for the way they will slave and save, and full of admiration for their utter dedication to improving the lot of their offspring. And yet one wonders—should life really be like this? To be sure, their hard work, and the equivalent work of their colleagues in the motor factories and the steel mills and the coal mines, all similarly motivated and boosted by similarly powerful incentives, maintains productivity and output at phenomenally high rates: perhaps the constant holding of carrots like college fees in front of the American working class has been one reason for the huge success of the country's industrial might. But should the Alberts have devoted their lives to the soulless repetition of frying a million hamburgers and pouring ten million Dr. Peppers: could not the Government have helped them, and lifted the burden a little from their shoulders? They would say not: they would point to Great Britain, where just that has happened, and bemoan the 'flabbiness' and the 'laziness' that has overcome the country as a consequence. The constant, but not entirely necessary, provision of incentives to work seems to be a part and parcel of the American way of life that is not just about to change.

I might say that a Sonic Drive-In hamburger (especially one ordered with the bark: 'Fry one, hold the tears, on wheels!' which, literally translated, means 'without onions, to take out') is an extremely pleasant half-dollar's worth. And for anyone passing through Ardmore I would recommend in addition a visit to the Cooper's Farm Dairy and Ice Cream Store and Soda Fountain, where, for as little as a quarter, or for as much as a dollar-and-a-half, you can have scoops of the following flavours of ice cream:

Rum Raisin, Tutti Frutti, Butter Crunch, Irish Coffee, Black Walnut, Toasted Almond, Cherry Vanilla, Cherry Jubilee, Peppermint Swirl, Chocolate Marshmallow Nut, Butter Pecan, Banana Nut, Chocolate Ribbon, Black Cherry, Strawberry Cream, Lemon-Orange Sherbet, Peppermint, Coffee, Vanilla Nut Fudge, Chocolate Chip, Fresh Peach, Vanilla, Chocolate and Strawberry. Or you can have sherbets in pineapple, raspberry and lime. Or mixtures such as Banana Split, Malts, Sodas, Parfaits and Floats, with nuts a nickel extra, and a choice of plain or sugar cones. It is hardly possible or decorous, to try them all, but Fresh Peach was splendid, and a Vanilla Coke Float will remain a superb memory of the drifting life on the Main Drag of a dusty little south Oklahoma town.

From Ardmore the Interstate rushed south for another thirty uneventful miles, past sleeping cattle and brown streams and ever-rocking oil wells and ever-rumbling drilling rigs. A survey completed by the State Department of Highways told how the road, which ran parallel to, but essentially superseded the old black-top of US Route 77, had spoiled the livelihood of half a dozen small villages that once drew their trade from the journeymen who passed by. Now the big trucks and the private cars stop for petrol and food only at big junctions, where they will find cafés and car washes and telephones from which to call in their next orders or call back to their homes. The small towns of this part of southern Oklahoma have been badly hurt by the highway; but you don't notice them as you hurtle by. For the last thirty miles of the state is essentially a no-stopping zone for most motorists: like any people on the verge of crossing into a new land, they hurtle on and up the great concrete bridge that crosses the wide, sludgy, *eau-de-nil* slake of the Red River.

In the mid-point of the bridge is a simple sign which says 'Welcome to Texas', the last state of this southbound progress. The cold of the Canadian border was well over 1,000 miles behind: here it was hot and sticky and lush, and by all first impressions—a sign pointing out it was 500 miles to San Antonio, for example—it was appropriately big.

7

Texas:
The Giant Changed

On January 3, 1959, Alaska, all 586,412 square miles of her (as large as France, Germany, Spain, Ireland and the United Kingdom combined) joined the United States as a fully fledged state, Number 49 on the roll. The date is one that many Texans feared would live in infamy: it denied to their proud, haughty home, the one of only two (the other was Vermont) that had been an independent nation that had joined the United States of its own goodwill, its pre-eminent position as the largest, grandest, wildest member of the Union. From that bleak January day Texas, which has a constitutional right to divide itself, at will, into five separate states, became a runner-up. Texas is now an also-ran in the ridiculous gigantomachy of 'girth, bulk and heft' that led the American mega-states to jostle and push amongst each other for some kind of statistical supremacy.

Alaska's entry to the Union meant that stories like the following, culled from an old copy of the *Texas Almanac*, no longer had any real meaning. This purported 'speech' by a visitor to Texas, satirises the vast, loudly nationalistic plains monster as it used to be, before January 3, 1959.

Texas occupies all the continent of North America except the small part set aside for the United States, Mexico and Canada . . . and is bounded on the north by 25 or 30 states, on the east by all the oceans in the world except the Pacific . . . and on the west by the Pacific Ocean, the Milky Way and the Sidereal Universe.

Texas is so big that the people in Brownsville call the Dallas people Yankees, and the citizens of El Paso sneer at the citizens of Texarkana as being snobs of the effete east.

It is 150 miles farther from El Paso to Texarkana than it is from Chicago to New York. Fort Worth is nearer St. Paul,

Minnesota, than to Brownsville . . . the United States with Texas off would look like a three-legged Boston terrier.

The chief occupation of the people of Texas is trying to keep from making all the money in the world . . . Texans are so proud of Texas that they cannot sleep at night. . . .

Unless your front gate is 18 miles from your front door you do not belong to society as constituted in Texas . . . one Texan has 40 miles of navigable river on his farm. If the proportion of cultivated land in Texas were the same as in Illinois, the value of Texas crops would equal those of all 47 other states. . . . Texas has enough land to supply every man, woman and child in the world with a tract five feet by twenty.

If all the hogs in Texas were one big hog, he would be able to dig the Panama Canal in three roots. If all the steers in Texas were one big steer, he could stand with his front feet in the Gulf of Mexico, one hind foot in Hudson Bay and the other in the Arctic Ocean, and with a sweep of his tail brush the mist from the Aurora Borealis. Some state!

It is still true that Texas could, if it cared to, wear Rhode Island as its watch-fob. Pecos County is very nearly as large as Connecticut. The *Guinness Book of Records* might well be able to list Texas as the locality sporting the most world records. A perfunctory glance at the *Book* indicates the Lone Star state has within its borders a Houston man who was several times over a great-great-great-grandfather; a Mr. William Fuqua of Fort Worth who can stand perfectly still for over four hours; the costliest hotel suite in the world, on the ninth floor of the Celestial Hotel in Houston, that would set you back in 1974, $2,500 for a single night; the world's tallest monument; and the largest public dance, which attracted 16,500 participants, together with 4,000 who had to be shown the door. The vulgar opulence of department stores like Nieman-Marcus in Dallas is legendary; the vastness of the King Ranch, in the south of the state, is worthy of the best Hollywood epic films; the size of its cowboys, who are all believed to look like John Wayne and ride horses the size of small tanks, has imprinted a lasting vision of Texas in the mind of every schoolboy of today and for the past five decades gone.

But now the older order has changed. Possibly it has something to do with an inexplicable shift in public sensibilities that has made the big and the brassy and the braggish no longer amusing, interesting, admirable, or even tolerable. Perhaps, too, it had something to do with the Kennedys, and the aura, however history reveals it had been contrived, of low-key fashion, classical music and the best of European chic that surrounded them. The election of John Kennedy transformed a social attitude in which the Texan of old could cheerfully and grotesquely flourish: after Alaska, and after the seating of the young first family from Massachusetts, Texas would never be the same.

The final blow rang out soon after noon on Friday, November 22, 1963—that immensely sad day when Texas, and Texans, became instantly identified with the savage murder of that once-loved young man. Controversy and contention still rages over the assassination: for Texas, however, the facts of the case are less relevant than the undisputed location of the crime. The killing of Kennedy, and the murder of his alleged assassin, and the all-but forgotten killing of Police Officer J. D. Tippit left the entire nation, and most of the world, groggy with horror and shame. And Texas took the brunt of the anger: it was almost as if the braggart had gone too far, and Americans and all the millions of residents of the 'global village' were condemning him, using him as the scapegoat for one of the saddest triple killings America was ever to experience. Texas have never entirely recovered from that wretched November weekend: even now, tell someone you're from Dallas and they'll think, instantly, 'That's the place where Kennedy was killed!' Dallas has a world-wide reputation now little better than Treblinka, or Sharpville, or the Jalianwallah Bagh.

The three episodes—Alaska, the assumption of power by John Kennedy and his killing three years later—proved a 'triple whammy' from which the state still suffers. To those seminal events must be added one other, which set the seal of disapproval on Texas-style. Lyndon Johnson himself, picked by the Democrats in 1960 as the ideal ticket-balancer to keep the Southerners happy with Kennedy, and the man who was to succeed the fallen leader and follow him into office by the single farcical election of 1964, remains one of the more tragic of American Presidents: a man whose reputation for having fashioned the Great Society was tarnished by the Vietnam War, whose personal foibles and incipient paranoia were never happily balanced by his native charm and wit and warmth, and whose abrupt departure from the political scene in 1968 was a response to a tidal wave of cynicism and despising that, by a massive irony, led Americans to vote by the millions for a successor who would prove one of the most despicable Presidents America has ever had the misfortune to endure.

As the run-up to the 1976 Presidential campaign began, one Texan was being singled out as the proud new son of the re-shaped new state. By 1975 it was being said that Texas had come to live with its new role. It had come to accept that size and riches and noise were not the sole paths towards influence and respect and goodwill. The riches of the state were still there, it was true; but they were second-generation riches now, and the loud *nouveau riche* folk who once characterised Dallas and Fort Worth and Houston so vividly were giving way to cool, Brooks Brothers-dressed figures with dash and style and sober appeal—men who could wield the power that their position had given them without the tendency to ape the Grand Panjandrums they so well resembled. Lloyd Bentsen was the man Texas chose to send forward as its candidate for 1976: and if he failed to win the nomination of his Democratic Party it would not be because he was too brash, or possessed of too little taste or manners. Rather it would be because, unlike every single Texas politician before him, Lloyd Bentsen was adjudged as being too *dull*.

'On one Sunday afternoon . . . the day Gerald Ford pardoned Richard Nixon, a lean, distinguished man in his early fifties waited to check in on Flight 11,' read one of the first appraisals of Lloyd Bentsen, in the *Atlantic Monthly*. 'From the cut of his brown plaid suit and the detached, slightly impatient look on his face, he might have been a banker from Connecticut on his way to discuss investment possibilities in the computer industry, or an executive of the Rockefeller Foundation preparing for a conference at the University of Texas. He received no more attention than any of the several hundred other passengers in the terminal, which was unusual only because he, unlike anyone else in the building, was at work trying to become the next President of the United States.'

Bentsen is a prime example of second-generation Texas money, and his father, Lloyd Senior, a prime example of the old wheeler-dealer style of first-generation Texas money-grubber. Lloyd Senior made his fortune from what is politely known as 'the immigrant land business'—and what cruder men would call 'ripping people off'. Lloyd Senior and brother Elmer Bentsen would advertise south Texas land for sale to people who lived in the cold and wet of Iowa and Minnesota and Wisconsin, and fly any potential buyers down for a weekend of luxury amidst the citrus groves and beside the clear streams that coursed down from the Balcones Escarpment. The poor Midwesterners would sign up, and pay up—to find they had bought land, at $500 an acre, that had everything except water rights. That had, in other words, nothing but a few tons of rubble, mesquite and greasewood bushes. The Bentsens made a fortune out of the business: Lloyd Junior inherited the money—there has never been an allegation that he was involved in his father's questionable business activities—and used it to further his own career as lawyer, politician, insurance man and, after eighteen years spent self-exiled from Washington making respectable money back in Texas again, politician once more in the United States Senate.

In the senior chamber—where he was the Junior Senator from Texas, ranking below the drawling conservative figure of John Tower—he quickly moved to divest himself of the image of rigid Texas-Toryism he had devised to beat his primary race opponent, Ralph Yarborough, and moved just as rapidly to persuade observers to see him as anything but a reincarnation of Lyndon Johnson. He was, he persuaded observers, no beagle ear-puller, no scar-displayer, no fellow likely to urinate against the leg of his Secret Service guard, and retort, as Johnson did when the guard mentioned it apologetically, 'That, suh, is mah pre-rogative!' Rather Bentsen is a man of grey suits, narrow-striped shirts and diagonally striped ties in blues, whites and greens. He has a screen-star smile, an accountant's appeal, a great deal of energy and, in the field of economics, an excellent mind. He is certainly an example of the new breed of Texan; but, when I saw him in Missouri at a Sunday political lunch, he has an unsettling ability to put a lot of people to sleep at the same time—and that, for a future candidate for the Oval Office, is not the finest or most useful of attributes.

It was with this view of a drastically changed Texas that I pointed my car over the Red River bridge and entered the mighty state for the drive down to the Mexican crossing gates. Since this was now by no means the middle of America, I planned to stop only a few times: the people to whom I spoke, and the places that I saw served to reinforce the thesis that the state is changed for the better, and is no longer charged with the chrome-plated, oily-handed vulgarity of ten years before.

The first visit, though, was to a new Texas venture that, in many ways, marks the durability of Texas kitsch all over again.

In the winter of 1973 the largest airport in America was formally opened on a site almost exactly half-way between the twin cities of Dallas and Fort Worth. Publicists for the venture pointed out that the airfield was larger than the entire island of Manhattan, that it could handle more flights than the world's busiest airport, Chicago, and yet would be so deftly constructed as to allow motorists to park less than a minute's walk away from the ticket desks, the loading bays, and the luggage ramps. And changing airlines (which in Chicago and Atlanta—the two principal 'hub' airports in the nation—means walking distances of as much as a mile) would be simple and speedy at the DFW Regional Airport: small noiseless trains would swish on rubber wheels from terminal to terminal, connecting the most distant airline gates in no more than a couple of minutes.

It all sounded fine, and, when I saw the field first from a specially chartered Braniff 747 on opening day, it was difficult to deny that it was a remarkable achievement of engineering—'Only in Texas', people kept saying. One of the first aircraft to land there was the French-British Concorde, on a sales mission which, to all intents and purposes, failed. But the size of the new field did make for one great advantage: it allowed Concorde to creep on to the land so far from the listening devices mounted by the control tower that everyone in Texas that day thought it was about the quietest airliner they had ever heard. New Yorkers would have a different opinion two years later.

But grand and impressive as it all appeared on the opening day, troubles soon seeded themselves, and multiplied rapidly. Firstly, a lot of Dallas businessmen who had hitherto used Love Field, which is ten minutes from their central city, began to complain that it took as long to slog through the freeway traffic to get to the new airfield as it did to fly to Austin, or to Oklahoma City. Then there was the mandatory fee of a quarter, imposed on everyone whose car passed through the airport toll gates—so even if you were just driving in to meet an inbound passenger, it cost 25 cents for the privilege. The baggage-handling devices, while looking immensely handsome, had the nasty habit of chewing pieces of luggage into very small pieces, and snapping golf clubs—of which there are as many in Texas as trees in Siberia—into matchstick-sized shards of aluminium. Perhaps the worst blow, from a public relations viewpoint, was the money-changing machinery installed in the airport lounges; you inserted your dollar bill, portrait side uppermost, whereupon it was seized by a pair of rubber rollers and dragged out of your hand, and after much clanking and clicking, a fistful of change was delivered into the pouch underneath. Only the machine did not spew out a dollar in dimes, nickels and quarters: it gave forth only 95 cents, and Dallas cowpunchers and New York businessmen alike found that, to put it mildly, a rotten swindle.

Nearly all the major airlines, though, had agreed to change their schedules to bring their Clippers and Astrojets and Whisper-jets and Ambassador Service flights into the new airport: by 1974 the new field was welcoming flights from every corner of the continent, and from a host of international capitals as well. One company, Southwest Airlines, however, balked at what it saw as a conspiracy amongst the other major carriers: it refused to use the DFW airport, it held on grimly to its hangars and ticket counters at Love Field, and it hunkered down for a long and bloody battle with the big warhorses of the US airline industry. It had two weapons in its locker with which to beat off the challenges of big business: it had the sympathy of a disgruntled Dallas travelling public, and it had sex.

For Southwest Airlines is America's first to sell itself entirely and unashamedly on the well-rounded pulchritude of its specially selected female staff. The man who founded the tiny Texas company—even today it has only five aeroplanes and fewer than 350 employees—is a tanned, middle-aged playboy figure called Lamar Muse: and it was he who saw the double entendre in the phrase Love Field, and who realised the money that could be made flying from it, with love and sex as his selling theme. So he gave his airline a new symbol—a small orange heart—and he took on fifty of the best-looking girls it was possible to recruit from the fleshpots of Dallas. He dressed them in the shortest and tightest of orange shorts, knee-high tan leather boots and tight polka-dotted red and white shirts, and let them loose on a delighted Texas public. The advertisements that dominate the freeway skylines for miles around Dallas show pneumatic young women, arms outstretched like wings, zooming in over the flatlands of Dallas with their breasts heavy and pendulous, like some new type of landing gear. The airline, Lamar Muse promised his passengers, would take the very best care possible of them, and the stewardesses would just *love* to have them aboard.

The ploy worked. Southwest Airlines, as its 1975 Company Report says, 'took off in 1974'. From a stumbling small-city airline that chuntered across the grass strips of central Texas with little obvious success and no apparently star-studded future, the doughty struggle against the big guys of the industry, the resultant court fights, and the thighs and breasts and ever-fluttering eyelashes of fifty nubile Texan women have catapulted Mr. Muse's business into an overnight sensation. In 1971, Southwest did $2 millions' worth of business; in 1974, the first full year of fighting and flying from Love Field, it did $15 millions' worth. In 1973 it made a net profit of $175,000; in 1974, a profit of $2 million. 'It was the year', Lamar Muse says, 'that we turned the corner.' For him, the opening of the Manhattan-sized airfield twenty miles west of his base was the best thing ever to have happened.

But Love Field now is a terribly sad place. The multi-storey car-parks that surround it are being sold or torn down—'Would make ideal Convention Center', a sign on one pleads. The terminal buildings are echoing and empty, except when a massive man in cowboy boots and a ten-gallon Stetson struts through on his way to his private Cessna parked on the glaring-white concrete ramp outside. Only in one small section of the building is there any more than this desultory activity: around the Southwest counters there is a perpetual throng of people, all lining up for the very distinct privilege of buying a round-trip ticket to Houston, or San Antonio, or Harlingen Airport down by the Rio Grande, and buying it from a lissom blonde with brown thighs and a deep cleavage, who rolls over the counter licking her shiny lips with well-practised anticipation. It is all very much old-style Texas cornball, but for Mr. Muse and his 323 colleagues, it appears to be working very satisfactorily indeed.

Dallas in the early 1960s had an ugly reputation for vicious conservatism and old-fashioned religious intolerance that culminated in the murders of November 1963: Johnson, it might still be remembered, was showered with spittle when he passed through the town, and Adlai Stevenson was pelted with coins and abuse when he visited the city the month before John Kennedy. In more than one respect the city then had more in common with Montgomery, Little Rock or Mobile, than with the old cow-towns like Fort Worth, or Austin, or Wichita Falls. It was a Deep South city: its religion was ultra-Protestant, and the First Baptist Church still is the most massive and most wealthy southern Baptist church in the country. The newspapers of the early 1960s—led by the indefatigable Dallas *Morning News*, was only exceeded in rampant extremism by the Manchester (New Hampshire) *Union Leader* (whose editor keeps a revolver in his office all day long). The *Morning News* ran a savagely anti-Kennedy advertisement in its columns of November 22, 1963—an act of intemperate incivility which has not been forgotten yet.

But Dallas today, like Texas today, is all changed. There are almost as many young men with long hair to be seen there as in any principal city in the east; the newspapers are more moderate in their tone, less determinedly anti-Communist, anti-drug and anti-gambling than—although in the most hypocritical of senses—they used to be. The massage parlour industry flourishes in Dallas these days, and advertisements for 'fun centres of the south-west' are as common in the morning press as are those for cruise season fashions just shipped in to Nieman-Marcus. The Congressional District is now overwhelmingly Republican, as one might expect from a centre whose fortune is constructed on a solid foundation of insurance, banking and computer hardware. The old, rigidly doctrinaire southern conservatives who were once spawned by the barrel-load in the north Dallas suburbs—where the millionaire oil man, H. L. Hunt, built his replica of Mount Vernon—have been replaced by more moderate, less brash, more 'respectable' figures: Jim Collins, the sixty-year-old Congressman who has represented the Sixth District of Texas since 1968, is a Baptist, a soldier, a businessman and an extremely wealthy Harvard graduate—a fine example of the breed Dallasites are now looking to for leadership. That Mr. Collins has come under grave suspicion of being involved in a sordid kick-back scandal—although no indictments, like those that sent his chief assistant to federal prison, were ever issued against him—does not seem to have any deleterious effect on his political fortunes. He was re-elected handsomely in 1974.

Dallas has one other interesting feature that would have been unheard of in 1963: it comes second in the nation, after Boston, in dollar support for its local public television station. Public television is totally non-commercial and is supported only by grants from the Government, with the largesse of private industry, and by contributions from viewers. This rickety financing has produced very few stations of any excellence, and the nationally produced programmes are still, by comparison with the BBC, both dull and poor. But in Boston, station WGBH is both wealthy and very good. San Francisco residents are proud to have station KQED. And in Dallas, where culture was once subservient to the counting of money, and the only opinions expressed were to do with the prices of oil, and where it was often adjudged better to kill a man (it was legal if he was having intercourse with your wife at the time, under Texas law) than to wear your hair below the shoulder and smoke dope, the viewers have turned in large numbers to KERA, a public station of great energy, initiative and imagination, that serves the greater Dallas and Fort Worth area. Public television is still thought of in the Midwest as being a slightly insidious form of socialised television, and fit only for the pinkos of the north-east and in northern California. That public television is now so well established in the city where John Kennedy was shot says a great deal for the metamorphosis of this once harshly unpleasant plains metropolis.

There are many grand and stylish hotels left in America, in spite of the steady erosion of the phenomenon by the motel, that road-side assemblage of standardised boxes where travellers can sleep, eat and watch television in carefully controlled comfort, and without the least hint of what might be called 'atmosphere'. New York City has the Plaza, Washington the Hay-Adams, Boston the Ritz-Carlton; there is the old Muehlebach in Kansas City and the Brown Palace in Denver; the vast and imposing Broadmoor in Colorado Springs and the Mark Hopkins and the Fairmont in San Francisco. A report in a 1972 newspaper noted, with scarcely concealed regret, however, that 'every 30 hours, somewhere in downtown America, an old hotel closes. Every 30 hours, somewhere in suburban America, a new motel opens.'

The collection of brass-brick-and-timber structures which

housed the men and women who journeyed through this country a century ago is becoming depressingly small—so small that even the presence of an indifferent example of the old style can trigger waves of nostalgic nonsense in the travel journals. A legion of plywood-and-plastic-and-styrofoam nonentities, where people are known as 'persons', and rooms are known as 'units', have been springing up for the past twenty years at every intersection and at every suburban sprawling entrance to the major cities: the Holiday Inns and the Best Westerns and the Travel-Lodges may be convenient—they are a continual blessing to the weary motorist, there is no doubt—but they are just one further factor that, unwittingly perhaps, is stripping the individuality from the States, and replacing regional traits with a preordained, boardroom-designated practice of efficiency that is much the same in Nebraska as it is in Alaska.

All of which is by way of introducing one Texas motel—and not a hotel—that has taken the care to step out of the pre-programmed line, and present itself as a stopover for the Texas journeyman, and not just for the 'person' who happens past on the Interstate that night. It is called the Stagecoach Inn, and it lies beside a pretty and endearingly tranquil stream in the little village of Salado, a few miles south of Temple—which is itself two hours' drive south of Dallas and Fort Worth. The village itself, which is not too far from LBJ country and has an appealing air of big-ranch richness, is being restored: the old houses that were once built beside the old Chisholm Trail—the north-south route by which nineteenth-century cattlemen took their herds up to the Kansas railheads—are being repainted and their nails buffed up; antique shops are springing up in every other house, it seems. The Stagecoach Inn itself, which is probably the biggest building in town, has all the proper attributes—a swimming pool, a small golf course, and colour televisions in every room—but it also happens to have one of those very rare restaurants that specialises, without making any particular fuss about it, in regional American food. And so, instead of the standard steak-and-salad, cherry-pie-and-coffee, on which every other motel seems to rely, one can find delights like hush puppies and strawberry kisses and legs of ranch lamb, all the offerings being recited by middle-aged waitresses who will not hear of writing their wares on a menu—a frugal practice that seems oddly at variance with the normal profligacy of the average Texan.

I had come to Salado to drive past the greatest assemblage of military might it is possible to see on the surface of the United States: the biggest Army base on the continent, known as Fort Hood.

There are, of course, dozens upon dozens of military bases in America—distributed among the states as part of the 'pork barrel' of Government spending that is handed out each year by the Pentagon—though rubber-stamped by the Congress—to the district represented by the most helpful Congressmen of the day. Since the Army became an all-volunteer force in 1972, and with the onset of Congressional hostility to excessive military spending, there have been plans to condense and refine the once unwieldy structure of the modern US Army: one plan calls for the establishment of just four truly massive bases inside CONUS—the Army's word for the Continental United States. These bases, which would be huge expansions of existing facilities, would be expected to become established in North Carolina (at Fort Bragg), in Georgia (at Fort Benning), in Oklahoma (at Fort Sill), and here in Texas, at Fort Hood. Fort Benning would be established for infantry, Fort Bragg for airmobile divisions; Fort Sill for artillery; and Fort Hood for armour. Appropriately it is at the Texas base, hundreds of square miles of it that stretches across the low hills and scrubby plains to the north-west of Salado, that the real muscle—the tanks, the armoured cars and the self-propelled guns—is destined to be kept.

The base is officially the home of the Second Armoured Division —whose motto is 'Hell on Wheels'—and the First Cavalry. Some 60,000 men live and work on the base and in the town of Killeen nearby—a terrible little permanent shanty town of trailer homes and strip joints and beer cellars and run-down supermarkets that has one of the highest rates of crime of any place in Texas. Army bases in America manage to attract the very worst of society's flotsam around their gates: the little town next door to Fort Benning, for instance, is said to sport the greatest concentration of massage parlours anywhere in America. Georgians are none too proud of that fact; and Texans—particularly the more genteel folk of Salado and Temple—are embarrassed by the proximity of such scar-tissue as Killeen by Fort Hood.

But the base, while not beautiful, is mightily impressive. It is easy to slip inside. A duty sentry with a white bandana around his neck and an M-16 rifle around his shoulders will salute crisply as you drive by—no need to stop and show an identification here, remarkably. Once past him there is a mile or so of yellow-washed wooden buildings, with the base commissary and the beauty shop and the cinema and all the other devices that try to make Army life in some vague way equivalent to civilian life, but which so palpably fail to do so. After that mile is over, the single most impressive sight I can recall seeing in Texas, if not in the entire journey from Canada, swings into view. It is a great big car park—the greatest it is possible to imagine, and containing, not cars, but tanks—thousands upon thousands upon thousands of tanks.

At first you turn right: this way will take you past the Second Armoured's 'motor pool' as it is called. For six solid miles the motor pool goes on—dozens of field-sized enclosures, patrolled constantly by bored-looking sentries and surrounded by barbed wire and searchlights, and each holding line after line of gigantic tanks. All are painted in camouflage colours—some light and sandy, and ready to use in a Middle Eastern war, others dark and sludge-brown, and destined, without doubt, for the defence of the central European plain. There are ordinary M-60 tanks, their huge 120 mm. guns trained slightly over the horizon in unending ranks, their turrets swathed in enveloping tarpaulins to keep out dust and the occasional rains; there are self-propelled large-calibre guns; there are signals vans and three-ton support trucks and 10,000 jeeps and patrol boats on the back of special launchers and bridge-building tanks and mine-clearing tanks and still more M-60 tanks, wireless trucks and ready-made cranes and notices saying '402nd Engineer Battalion' and '594th Administrative Support Group' and '1st Battalion Mechanised 41st Infantry', and petrol tankers and howitzers and all manner of machinegun-laden special vehicles for performing the most arcane of belligerent tasks.

Or if you turn left, you drive for six miles in the other direction through a motor pool of the First Cavalry Division; here there are no tanks, but a bewildering assortment of armoured cars and half-tracks and special fleet trucks and stripped-down jeeps and self-propelled guns of lesser calibre and higher speed. In all, the motor pool is a dozen miles long and half a mile wide: it must contain well nigh 100,000 vehicles—perhaps a million tons of armour, all told, together with—and you can see the distant humps of protective earth away on the horizon—hundreds of thousands of tons of ammunition. All are greased and fuelled and crated ready to go from the great airstrip to the west of the base, to any destination on the globe, at a moment's notice and on the orders, friendly or angry, of the Commander-in-Chief in Washington.

Every so often a squadron of tanks would churn out of one of the enclosures and grind and clank and squall off to the north for a day's training on the hills—hills that look for all the world like the lower slopes of the Golan Heights. There would be a bark of orders, a sentry would open double gates in the compound fence, the diesel smoke would belch in black clouds, and a dozen or more gigantic metal monsters, headed by a flying wedge of jeeps and a three-tonner full of wooden shell boxes, would swing out of the compound, on to the dirt road, and slowly rumble away to the hills. An hour later and there would be a flashing and a crackling from the distant black creatures parked up on the horizon: five seconds later the crump of explosions and the rattle of heavy machinegun fire would echo across the barrack squares. No one would pay the slightest heed: at Fort Hood, gunfire is more common than the beating of raindrops on the barrack roofs.

Austin is the capital of Texas; but for all that, its notoriety is probably greater than its fame, for it was at Austin, in 1966, that a young man named Charles Whitman took a rifle up to the top of the twenty-one-storey tower at the centre of the University of Texas campus there and coolly shot fourteen people dead. More people will recall Charles Whitman's act than almost any Act that has been passed down through the cumbersome pomp and circumstance of the Texas state legislature—somehow mass killing fits in more with the admittedly unfair perception of the state, than does the making of debate and the positing of law.

In 1975 the legislators in Austin were debating once again whether to de-ratify the proposed amendment to the US Constitution that gave theoretically equal rights to women. The state had approved the Equal Rights Amendment back in 1972, but three years later had developed a case of excessively cold feet. They were not debating the issue in the same philosophical terms as they had three winters before: rather they were inveighing at great length— and Texans can inveigh at very great length—on whether or not the ERA would mean that men and women have to share the same public lavatories and same college dormitories (the dormitories may be entirely co-educational at a place like Carleton College, in the liberal wilds of Minnesota: in Texas, though, where hell-fire and damnation are still preached in abundance, sleeping next to each other is tantamount to sleeping with each other, and that, as any middle-aged Texan will tell you, is a Bad Thing) and the same barracks blocks and the same prison cells. There was much similar concern over whether women could be drafted into the army, or accused of raping a man—unless, as their subsidiary fear, rape ceased to be a crime altogether—or forced to support their husbands and children during, or even after, the marriage.

In Fort Worth a strong lobby group was started with the name Women Who Want to be Women: its members would come down to Austin to weigh in on the ERA sympathisers with such rhetorical offerings as: '[The ERA supporters are] pushing to tear down the home. Lesbianism and homosexuality are their goals for the next year, to get that legalised so that these gay people can adopt children . . . it's the most damnable thing that has ever hit our nation, some of the things they stand for . . . I think we've got to speak out against this evil. God has destroyed whole nations because of this.' The WWWW group is believed to have strong ties with the Church of Christ, one of the more flamboyant of fundamentalist groups that spreads its influence the length and breadth of the most primitively receptive parts of the Bible Belt.

Perhaps the most interesting resident of Austin is a small, rather ill-printed newspaper that appears every fortnight under the banner the *Texas Observer*. It calls itself 'A Journal of Free Voices' and 'A Window to the South', and it has a readership and influence far more widespread than its humble appearance, its minuscule staff and its shabby offices would suggest. The journal celebrated its twentieth anniversary just after Christmas 1974, and printed, for the only time in its history, an all-colour cover (showing, on the front, a large single eye embedded in the cactus plains, sniffed at by an armadillo and surrounded by a score of candles). On the back was one of the nicer left-inclined advertisements one would see in the Texas of the mid-1970s. 'Long Live the Longnecks' the slogan read—a plea from environmentally concerned locals to the breweries to keep up production of returnable, long-necked beer bottles, rather than, as the breweries had wanted, divert all their production to the stubby-necked, disposable 'one-way' bottles. The 'Longnecks' campaign is the Texas equivalent of the more voguish 'Be kind to animals—Kiss a Beaver' campaign (actually a double entendre of extreme offensiveness) that flourished for a while in the east.

The *Texas Observer* was created by a small band of Texas liberals in the mid 1950s, and was then sold by its wealthy Houston owner, a Mrs. Randolph, to an impoverished University of Texas student named Ronnie Dugger. Dugger bought the paper, lock stock and galleys for the next edition, for a dollar: it now has three rooms on the top floor of an old lawyers' house, an editorial staff of three and a circulation of about 12,000 copies. Its editor is a bespectacled, faintly academic-looking writer named Kaye Northcott, who believes that, if nothing else, her little muckraking journal has 'improved the other Texas newspapers quite a bit', and has brought to light 'one or two little stories down here that the national television people and the east coast papers have gotten pretty interested in.' Her claim is modest, to say the least: the *Texas Observer* is, without a doubt, the journal that Eastern reporters will always telephone first—or nearly first—when they are thinking of coming down to the Lone Star state to do some writing. 'We don't display the slavish loyalty to the Texas establishment the rest of the press here do—or did; and so we get trusted more by the papers in the East who aren't used to being loyal.'

Texas, Miss Northcott says, 'is a bad state for poor people. And there are a lot of poor people. It's a bad state for Chicanos. And there are a lot of Chicanos. The whole political structure here is designed to foster what they call 'a good business climate', rather than a good social climate. The whole tax structure is designed for the big man. The education system—especially for the migrant workers—is in bad shape. There are all sorts of scandals surrounding the water issue down in the far south. There are all sorts of stories the press here should do, but it doesn't. We have had some success in digging them out, and that's why we have a name down here.'

Kaye Northcott is thirty-one and she earns a salary of $8,400 a year: she probably realises she could be earning five times that in New York, but doesn't want to leave. For the time being she was planning to fight an immense lawsuit—$5 million was being claimed from the little paper by a fundamentalist preacher from Georgia named Lester Roloff (the *Texas Observer* called him the Reverend Ripoff). He was asking for a total of $45 million from a variety of other newspapers who had disbelieved the good he claimed he was doing by whipping sixteen-year-old girls within an inch of their life in his highly profitable 'homes' spread across the

Deep South. The *Texas Observer* had conducted a campaign to ask for money to fight the case—it would cost well into six figures, Miss Northcott thought—and every fashionable journalist in the country, from I. F. Stone downwards, seemed happy to contribute to stop the 'Journal of Free Voices' from going under.

While I was driving down I-35 from Austin one story floated in over the car radio that the *Texas Observer* would later write about at great length and with a characteristic lack of the fear that seemed to characterise most other reporting of the event. The story, as I first heard it and read it, in the *San Antonio Express* (a newspaper owned, incidentally, by Rupert Murdoch: it looks in many ways like a superannuated version of the old *Daily Express*, and sells well and, according to writers on the *Texas Observer*, is unusually fair when dealing with the radicals that occasionally pop up on the plains) began as follows:

San Diego, Tex.—Duval County Judge Archer Parr was temporarily suspended from office Monday (March 24, 1975) by state district judge O. P. Carrillo. And the Parr family suffered another blow later Monday when the 5th U.S. Circuit Court of Appeals at New Orleans upheld the conviction of George B. Parr on federal income tax evasion and perjury. He faces five years in prison for the offences. Carrillo's ousting of Judge Parr here was viewed in some quarters as the latest punch in a power struggle between the Carrillo family and the long-dominant Duval County political forces of the Parr family.

At the time the story struck me as rather more unusual than the run-of-the-mill corruption stories one hears every day in America, if only because this time it involved a judge, two brothers and an evidently grave and long-standing power struggle. But I would have thought little more of it if, just a few days later as I was driving through the fringes of Duval County, the radio interrupted itself to say that George Parr, the one whose conviction had been upheld in New Orleans, had gone up to a lonely spot on his sister Hilda's near-by ranch and put a bullet through his head. As the *Texas Observer* said 'It was a suitably violent ending for one of the most infamous public figures of the century. . . .'

Duval County, all oil, mesquite and cattle, with a few orange groves, a great deal of cactus and many, many Chicanos, is one of several regions of south Texas that was by reasons of history and big business and corruption, a virtual fiefdom. It, like many others nearby was ruled unshakably by a '*patron*', who was always a white man; the men and women of Duval who were held in perpetual thrall were invariably Mexican. For Duval County, and all points south, east and west, is Mexican Texas—or Mextex, as Neal Peirce somewhat inelegantly terms it. It is country where every other *hombre*, has a name that ends in the letters 'z', 's' or 'o', in which poverty and exploitation—and revolutionary politics—flourish abundantly.

Bill Moyers, whose book *Listening to America* provided a brief narrative account of a similar situation in San Patricio County, down near Corpus Christi, gives a lexicon of suitable, and unsuitable addresses for south Texans and non-Texans alike. Language is very important in this part of the world, and Mr. Moyers's hand-book kept me on the right side of a host of quick brown and white fists for my stay there. The words are thus:

Chicano—corresponds to the use elsewhere of the term 'black' or Afro-American; i.e. it's the word most Chicanos would like used.

Latin or Latino—corresponds to current use of the word 'Negro' —in other words, while not insulting, it is rather dated and not quite the correct version of the modish patois.

Mexican-American—corresponds to current usage of the word 'coloured'—is patronisingly offensive, in the way that Chief Walker was in his references to the blacks of Ponca City.

Mexican—(If used by whites) corresponds to 'nigra' or 'nigger' or 'groid'. Highly insulting.

Anglo—a non-Chicano Caucasian. George Parr was an Anglo.

White—(If used by Anglos to describe Anglos) apparently if you are talking to Chicanos at the time, deeply insulting, since it suggests they are non-white.

White—(If used by Chicanos) means not black.

Gringo—(If used by Chicanos) corresponds to black use of the words 'whitey' or 'The Man'; hardly polite, but used more to convey a feeling of oppression rather than to convey individual dislike.

Gringo—(If used by Anglos) means a hardliner, rather as an Anglo might describe a 'redneck'.

The Parrs of Duval County, Anglos all—and gringos in many

ways—has been *patrons* in Duval County for most of this century. Archie, the original, came to Duval County as a cowhand, and, like the other ranchers who were cowhands first, built his economic power and prestige slowly and steadily. He died a wealthy man; and when his two sons took over, their rule, like their financial base, was sturdy and almost unassailable. George Parr kept a small private army of some 200 *pistoleros* to keep him in power and the country electorate in line. Any candidate for high office who received the say-so of the Parrs usually came away with the entire county vote—Lyndon Johnson, who was blessed thus, was an early beneficiary. When he first ran for Senator in Texas in 1948, it seemed as though he might lose by the slim margin of 112 votes, out of more than one million votes cast throughout the state. But then a Parr stronghold—Jim Wells county, next door to Duval—declared, and gave LBJ 203 extra votes by virtue of an amended return. It looked mighty suspicious—it earned LBJ the moniker 'Landslide Lyndon'—but it put him on the road to success, and it was all dismissed as a great joke back in Washington and put down to typically Texan wheeling and dealing.

But, after half a century, another Duval family, the Carrillo brothers, decided that the Parr family had outstayed its welcome. Early in the 1970s a mighty feud erupted. Men whom Parr had chosen to sit on the County School Board, for example, were summarily dismissed by the one Carrillo who then had a position of authority as a state district judge; Archer Parr was ordered to stand down from his judicial office because of his conviction for graft—he refused, and for a while Duval County had two county judges, and a posse of Texas Rangers had to be sent downstate to make sure the two didn't shoot each other. A strange and extremely wealthy recluse businessman was called in by the Carrillos to further ruin the Parrs—and, early in 1975 George Parr gave what was to be both his first, and his last, press conference in Duval to denounce the strange businessman, whose name was Clinton Manges, of trying to take over the county on behalf of the Carrillo brothers. It was a messy, and yet somehow vaguely romantic power struggle.

Finally old George Parr was summoned to appear in court to explain why, at one stage during the feud, he had threatened Judge Carrillo with a pistol. He never turned up to answer the writ. A warrant was issued for his arrest as a fugitive from justice. The old man had already been found guilty elsewhere of tax evasion: he must have known he would probably be going to prison. The pistoleering charge was, it now seems, the straw that broke the old curmudgeon's back.

On March 31, 1975, a week after his conviction was upheld in New Orleans and his prison sentence there was set, provisionally, at up to five years, he got into his great Chrysler car, drove to a pleasant spot on the family's Los Horcones Ranch nearby, pointed his .45 revolver at his head, and fired. It was truly the end of an era.

He had, for all his faults, been the county *patron*, and the local Chicanos did, they felt, owe him something. As the *Texas Observer* noted 'Duval County was stunned by George Parr's death. An estimated 2,000 persons attended the Rosary that was held in the courtyard of Parr's expensive villa. No one had a mean word to say about the Parrs that day. The Carrillos stayed out of sight and the rest of Duval County went into mourning. . . .' And as the *Texas Observer* found, there were more than a few who would miss him. 'He was a wonderful man,' said Mrs. Eugenio Hinojosa. 'We went to him many times for money for the hospital. He would help with all his heart and he would never say to pay him back.'

Something, it seemed to me, was very familiar about all that. It was almost a relic of Empire, a faint and scratchy recording of the practices of some deep Dorsetshire village of a century ago, and a recollection of how the villagers had looked upon the Squire at the moment of his passing. The Parrs were a good deal more corrupt than most knights of the shires, but as benevolent, when it suited them to be, and as occasionally mindful of the needs of the serfs as political necessity demanded. 'George was quite a guy,' young Archer Parr would later say. 'He wrote his own skit. He led and decided the play. He called the shots until the end.' Quite literally.

Thralldom has been the unhappy lot of south Texas Chicanos for more decades than they care to remember. The tradition— forced by economic necessity rather than by romance, or by whim— that the Chicano is a migratory worker has meant that very few have had the time or the stable base needed to create a political movement of any strength in the region. Every year the hundred and thousands of Chicano workers who live in the area roughly bounded by Corpus Christi, San Antonio and Del Rio in the north, and by the Rio Grande in the south, fan out in a vast wave of humanity to gather in the millions of tons of America's summer crops. Some stay inside Texas, to pick the cotton on the High Plains; others progress further north, east and west, fanning out like the branches of some great live oak: they go in droves (by rickety bus, or by even more rickety cars, jammed solid with sweaty working men, hungry and thirsty beyond imagination) through the deserts to California, to pick strawberries and lettuce and grapes; they go up to Washington state to pick apples, and to Oregon to gather in the hop harvest. They drive through to Idaho to help dig and clamp the potatoes; they reach into Wyoming and Montana for the sugarbeet. They go to the Great Lakes for the nuts, tomatoes, apples and peaches; to Delaware for the asparagus; and they roam all across the Great Plains, up to the Dakotas and to the very edges of their country, to win some money from helping the combines bring in the corn, the wheat, and the soy beans. The Chicano has never been able to stay where his home has been made: his political strength, therefore, has been minimal, and his dependence upon cantankerous old bully-boys like the Parrs has been both understandable and, from his limited point of view, an almost worthwhile expedient.

Now, though, militancy among the younger Chicanos has broken through and, like their Indian colleagues to the north—though many would think, rather more successfully—they are nurturing a small, but fast-growing new political party, La Raza Unida. The centre of that power now is a small farm town off to the east of I–35, known to Anglos as Crystal City, and to Chicanos as *Cristal*. The town had little enough distinction before the powers of La Raza were established there, save as the Spinach Capital of the World—a status that was marked with a life-size statue of Popeye standing outside the town's plaza.

La Raza, which is rightly described as radical and militant and nearly all Chicano, has been running *Cristal* since 1970: the *Texas Observer*, which might have been thought to favour any development that gave a voice to this most dispossessed of peoples, noted in 1974 that the results of La Raza's takeover were, at best 'mixed'. Molly Ivins, the paper's star writer said somewhat bitterly of the place that 'Plus ça change, ol' amigos, plus c'est le same damn thing.'

The field in which La Raza has made definite progress in the town, Miss Ivins noted, was education. The Texas school system has long discriminated, though perhaps neither knowingly nor deliberately, against Chicanos, in much the same way the white-dominated public school systems of cities like Boston gear their classes and their teaching procedures to white children rather than to black children. Discrimination of some kind inevitably results. Since its victory at the polls La Raza now calls the shots in *Cristal*'s schools: and it has taken one crucial step that is the basal plank of all current American Populist platforms—it has dropped the teaching of English. Why, the teachers say, should we bother if the Chicano children don't bother with English at first? Learning takes priority over language. La Raza has pumped more money into the school system; it has managed to inveigle more federal money for the public schools by virtue of a great deal of highly effective special pleading.

The ambitions of La Raza go a good deal further than one city, of course; and it is now thought probable that Zavala County, of which *Cristal* is the seat, will fall to the party within the coming few years. The drift of Anglos from *Cristal* which started quite dramatically and is getting faster and faster, will probably spread to the county; economic deterioration, already firmly established in the city, will spread to the county; and allegations that La Raza bosses are dictators, and racist dictators at that, will spread. There is no doubt that the creation of La Raza is a successful and perfectly proper reaction to dozens of years of exploitation of the Chicano by his Anglo bosses—by the Parrs and their *patron* colleagues; but there is a very real fear now that before another decade or so is gone, Mextex will have the character and aspirations of another state: the senate's rejection fifty years ago of the foundation of the Indian state of Sequoyah may be tested again if La Raza decide that the southern bulge of Texas, from Del Rio to Brownsville, should detach itself and run itself, and cease participation in a constitutional operation that results in Senators like Tower and Bentsen, neither of whom is a fluent Spanish speaker and one of whom has ambitions beyond the needs of the Chicanos, being appointed to represent them.

When I was in south Texas the *Cristal* council had decided it was not going to pay its gas bill to the suppliers, a company called the Lo-Vaca Gathering Company. Lo-Vaca promptly ended its contract to supply the city with natural gas, and threatened to cut off all supplies, and leave the entire community without fuel. It was the kind of ugly confrontation that would become more and more common in Mextex as the strength and hostility of La Raza's militancy grew.

And finally, Laredo—where, confounding those who would denigrate Middle America as having no interests in the world outside, the local newspaper, the *Times*, headed its edition with 'KING FAISAL ASSASSINATED' as must have the papers in New York and Washington that particular day. There was, of course, a subsidiary reason for local interest in the Saudi King and his demise: Laredo now is one of the most active centres of the oil and gas drilling industry anywhere in America: for mile upon mile on every approach road south and east of Laredo, there are drilling rigs and new wells working away like the legendary Spindletop must have been half a century before. A huge new gas field has been found close to the city; and Laredo's economy, which had depended before on a factory that made jeans and on the shops and garages and hotels that supplied the border-crossing traffic, was booming like few other cities anywhere in the north.

The town has very nearly 70,000 inhabitants, of whom 52,000 have Spanish surnames. It is a town of small shops and slow-moving trucks with bizarre and unfamiliar license plates. It is a town of market places and shouts and dust and three-legged dogs and a newspaper that is written in English on one side and Spanish on the other. There are McDonalds and Holiday Inns and Dairy Queens there; but all the restaurants serve *tortillas* and *frijoles* and the bars will serve one after another of that most drinkable of drinks, the salt-rimmed tequila-and-lime-juice *margarita*. Laredo is a Mexican town, and its ambience, while delightful, is still a long way removed from any resemblance to the Laredo of the famous old 'Cowboy's Lament':

> *As I was a-walking the streets of Laredo*
> *As I was a-walking, quite early one morn,*
> *I spied a young cowboy, all dressed in his buckskins,*
> *All dressed in his buckskins, all fit for his grave.*

Walking the streets of Laredo now, one would more likely find a sweaty trucker from Monterrey, having a quick cup of coffee before hauling his load of lettuce up to the market in San Antonio or a border patrol officer cursing the night operation, in which a dozen more 'wetbacks', as the illegal Mexican immigrants are known, had slipped under his nose. If there are any cowboys in Laredo, they must be in disguise.

Interstate 35 ends its mighty stretch about a mile north of the border with Mexico: the four-lane highway merely slopes downwards over 500 yards, a sign says 'End of Highway', and another, later, says 'Signal Ahead'; and then there is a red traffic light, and the steady southward progress one could enjoy all the way from Duluth, nearly 1,600 miles away to the north, comes to an abrupt end.

From the red light you execute the most contorted of dog-legs until the ground suddenly drops away and there before you, is the river. The Rio Grande—wide, brown, surprisingly fast-flowing, and bordered on each side by a hundred yards of lush grass that is oaviously covered six feet deep every time the river floods. The Rio Grande is way, way down the bottom of a deep valley; spanning it are two bridges, the one for the railway line, the other, choked and seething, like the Howrah Bridge across the Hooghly in Bengal, being the International Bridge, upon which the United States of America, and the United States of Mexico meet.

Never believe all that public relations guff about the borders of the United States being free and open and unbarred: here, as in Tijuana and Mexicali and Ciudad Juarez and Matamoros, there are seven-foot-tall chain-link fences; there are observation towers, almost, and there is barbed wire around the supports of any bridges. Armed officers of the border patrol drive constantly between posts on the American side, and at night the no-man's-land between the neighbour nations is bright with searchlights and buzzing with radio messages. The border with Canada, like that between Northern Ireland and the Irish Republic, is open for all to pass across at will; that with Mexico is more akin to the crossing between Italy and Yugoslavia—and, thanks to the Treasury computers and the sophisticated equipment carried around by the border patrols, probably a good deal more efficient a barrier.

But for Anglos like us, crossing was no problem, whichever way we chose to go. So we set out to match experiences with Canada, and strolled across the half-mile bridge—at a toll fee of 5 cents each passing southwards and one penny each coming back into America. Coming north, the first item you see on the bridge is a red letter box, with a stern notice saying 'If You Have any Drugs, Drop Them in Here. If You don't, and We Find Them, You will go to Prison.' It is signed 'US Customs', and is not the most friendly of greetings one country can bestow upon visitors from another. Though the fact that the notice is in English suggests it may be a greeting for returning Americans more than for any others.

The immigration shed here, compared with the shack up at International Falls, is quite vast. Dozens of men sit and ask questions where only one had sat and asked up north. The fact that this is the American terminus of the Pan American Highway, Fairbanks to Buenos Aires, was almost evident. We were asked how long we planned to stay, what the purpose of our visit was, and did we have any liquor, because if so we would have to pay tax. The TEC computer checked us silently, and we were free to go. It was all a little unreal—all the more so when we saw people being turned away behind us, and told to get back to the crowded middens of Nuevo Laredo across the Rio Grande again.

We got into the car, which had been parked on a bluff overlooking the river, and was thus baking hot inside.

It was coming up to ten in the morning, and we switched on the radio for the local news and the weather. It would be getting cooler here, the forecaster said—it would probably dip down from ninety-nine degrees of yesterday to the mid-eighties. The drop, he went on, was in part a ripple effect from a vast snow and ice storm that was sweeping through the Great Plains and the northern states. Up there, though it was difficult to believe, the farmers were having fifteen inches of unseasonably late snow. And up there, it was very cold.

It might have been ninety degrees on this border, but as the forecaster said, 'The coldest spot in the nation last night was, once again, International Falls, Minnesota, with ten degrees below zero.' Nothing much had changed.

8

The Promise of the Heartland

For the first time in more than a month, the car was heading eastwards again. No longer would the noon-time or evening sun glare relentlessly through the windscreen each day, forcing southbound or westbound drivers to squint and frown with rosy-coloured faces. No longer would I be driving into the spring and out of the winter. I was off the Interstate for the first time in weeks of driving and hundreds of miles of uninterrupted progress; from now on, such Interstates as I would take would have even numbers, like 10 and 20 and 44 and 66, until, ten days and 1,500 miles later, after a slow passage through the Texas Gulf oil fields, through the bayous and the teche country of Louisiana, through the endless swampy forests of Mississippi, the steel mill towns and speed traps of Alabama, the rolling mountains of Tennessee and the lush green Virginia countryside, with its white fences and its finely cropped meadows, I would be back in Washington, D.C., and see the white dome of the Capitol and the mighty houses clustered on the banks of Rock Creek Park from where all the people with whom I had spent the last weeks were governed.

The journey home provided time for some reflection on the American heartland, at a time when a sound heart and a strong constitution were sorely needed by this most remarkable of countries.

America has recently suffered three of the most debilitating tragedies. It has seen uncovered an orgy of high-level wrongdoing, lying and cheating and gross immorality, and the timid burgeonings of police state oligarchy that would shake the most devoutly patriotic from his previously sound trust in his elected leaders. It has seen one of those leaders, Richard Nixon, thrust from office by the combined efforts of the constitution, public opinion and a hardhearted press—the first time ever that an American President has had to leave his post in utter disgrace. In the eyes of the world, America herself was in disgrace—a blundering, myopic giant of a nation that seemed to pollute every institution she touched and ruin everything good that she befriended. Her leaders seemed worthless men, quite lacking in moral courage or intellectual achievement: at lower levels too, politics and the law seemed to attract the moral and intellectual dropouts of the country, while those with any real talent seemed either to stay in the universities or the ivory towers of big business, or else leave for some comfortable exile elsewhere.

And then there was the collapse of Cambodia and Vietnam—a sudden, tragic loss to America's standing and reputation across the world, that some historians would claim was a direct product of the evil genius of Henry Kissinger, the only man the American public seemed to admire through all the domestic traumas of earlier months. By the middle of 1975 there were no heroes and no leaders, no legends and no illusions. Everything was tarnished: the stumbling giant had fallen on its face, and the rest of the world that had felt the sharpness of her tongue or the blows of her knotty stick were laughing, and it was not the best time to be an American, even if it did happen to be the two hundredth anniversary of the country's birth. Two hundred years—the oldest continuing Republic on the face of the earth; and yet the people were not really very impressed with themselves; they were only dejected at their failings, and alarmed with the prospects for the future.

It was important then that the mighty engine that is America, that was spinning so fast and so furiously within, and that was straining with the internal tensions brought about by intolerance and crime and over-crowding and poverty, and that was wobbling dangerously with the depression and bewilderment engendered by the sad events that followed Watergate, the Paris peace accords and the collapse of the Indo-Chinese puppet theatre, had a governor at the centre to check and slow its progress. Middle America has traditionally provided that governor: a comfortingly large body of solid, hard-working, reliable men and women to whom the eccentricities of the west and effeteness of the east were mere foibles, to be tolerated but not emulated, endured but not affected. My journey made clear to me, I think, that at the time of this great loss of nerve in America, the middle land was holding as firm as it dared, and the country was not about to fly into small pieces, fragmented and disarrayed.

The Midwesterners would not forget that it was they who had expressed faith in Richard Nixon, that it was they who had turned blind eyes to the early tales of wrong-doings in the distant capital, that it was they who had condoned the Vietnam expeditions as necessary and right and proper conduct for the American giant. By the time Nixon was ready to go, they had, however, deserted him; by the time Cambodia and Vietnam were throwing in the towels, many had seemed to have come at last, albeit painfully, to a collective condemnation of that war.

'That stupid war,' a farmer from Storm Lake, Iowa, commented to a *Washington Post* reporter in the spring of 1975. 'That wrong war,' said another. Try as he might, the reporter could not find a soul to talk in any supportive way about the country Americans had died by the thousands to defend: the farmers were too wrapped up in grain prices and the imminent collapse of the Rock Island Railroad to argue the merits or otherwise of a conflict 10,000 miles away to the west. It was not that they lacked interest or awareness —few small Iowa villages of the 1970s lacked a cross or a monument to a son fallen in the Asian mud, and occasionally a legless man could be seen wheeling his chair down some dusty main-street in the depths of the Corn Belt, as permanent witness to the familiarity an Iowan has for U Taphao, or the intimate knowledge a Kansas man has for Khe Sanh. Easterners who scorn Midwestern farmers for their isolationism should beware: out in the heartland they *know* what happened, they *trusted* their leaders to do right by them, they were failed time and time and time again by those leaders, and they want to know more.

Sometimes, the reporter from the *Post* heard, there were flashes of brief eloquence. 'A lot of mistakes have been made,' a farmer said in Bedell, Iowa. 'And some of the people who made the mistakes are still in there [in Washington], and they're making noises like they're going to make the same mistakes again.' Another farmer wondered out loud what could be done about the State Department—'It just seems crazy, selling arms here and there and so forth' and then, the reporter noted, discussion wandered off into a denunciation of diplomats being chauffeured around in long black limousines. There probably isn't a long black limousine anywhere in Iowa, and certainly the drivers, if there were chauffeurs, would be white, not black, and the slave-boy attitudes with which ambassadors and the other flunkeys of Washington's slavish diplomacy are endowed, would never get a hearing out in the farmlands.

It was obvious to the men and women out in the midlands that no matter how many long black limousines you had in Washington, and no matter how many of the smartest people you invited to your dinner parties, you still went right out and made the silliest decisions in the world and you still did things that left thousands dead in a country that never knew what a black limousine was until you came along. The only bitterness out in the heartland was that the people who drive around in the limousines would still be there in a decade's time, living the same style of life and engaging in the same rounds of cocktail-parties and dinners, long after the errors of their ways had been uncovered and the people they had killed across the world were safely buried. For a Middle American it is terribly easy to grow cynical about Washington—and even more so in the aftermath of the tragedies and traumas of the first half of the 1970s.

One national magazine surveyed the middle country a few days after Phnom Penh had fallen, and a few days before the Communists set up government in Saigon. A Texas housewife complained bitterly that 'We can't keep fighting other people's battles for them.' A black newspaperman in north Texas noted: 'I served in Vietnam for thirteen months. I can't see why we poured lives and money down a rat-hole and then copped out. Now we are trying to make ourselves feel good by adopting children. . . .' An Oklahoma lawyer wanted some revitalisation of the American spirit, so badly dented in recent years. 'The Bicentennial celebrations', he thought out loud, 'might bring back a little patriotism—something that's been missing in this country.' And from Perryville, Missouri, a young woman admitted that 'I had thought about going into politics once, but now I've changed my mind. I don't know who or what to believe about the country any more.' A teacher in northern Indiana was more philosophical about it all. 'It isn't the people in power who are ruining things. It's all the people who don't hold politicians responsible. We either worship people in power and follow them blindly, or we turn against them completely and hate them.' Only one note of jingoistic confidence sounded, and this, perhaps oddly, from the state of Minnesota. A civil engineer in the town of Hopkins said that, in all honesty, 'I'm confident about the future of America and the world. The good guys are going to wear down the bad guys.'

Well, would they? After the succession of 'bad guys' with which

America has had to grapple for the last decade, the possibility that the 'good guys' will ever win seems, to say the least, remote. Even now the two men whom the Midwest had thrown up as possible contenders for the Presidency—Harris and Bentsen—were far from being individuals of totally sturdy moral fibre and intellectual bent. There were good men in the middle lands—Governor Anderson of Minnesota, Senators like Mondale and Humphrey, Congressmen like Iowa's Mezvinsky and Barbara Jordan from Texas and old stooges like dear Mr. Landon from Topeka. The ordinary people were good, too—the farmers and the Iron Range workers and the men and women who worked for AT&T in Kansas City and the policemen and judges and teachers. But would they be enough? Would they not, like the girl from Perryville, decide against any possible political adventure and turn back in on themselves, saying blindly and hopelessly: 'I don't know who or what to believe about the country any more.'

The Middle Americans should not lose their faith. It is up to them, the true governors of the spinning engine, to hold fast at this time of danger, and do all they can to help this great, diverse and difficult country stay together in its moment of peril. And, far from shying back from the political limelight, they should tear a leaf from the textbooks of Midwestern men like Alf Landon, and steel themselves to take the country by the scruff of its neck and shake it hard until it settles on a more orderly course, directed by men of common sense and integrity, who are lacking in greed and single-minded ambition for self-aggrandisement and glory.

And these good people, this sturdy breed of men and women who still have the sparkle of promise in their eyes, should not despair and say they have no one in whom to believe. They above all Americans do have someone in whom they can place their trust and confidence and hope: they can believe in themselves, and perhaps if they do, the rest of this mighty land's uncountable millions will believe in them too.

Index

Note: Two-letter abbreviations of State names are those recommended by US Postal Service. Boldface references are to subjects of entire chapters.